M E T R O N O M I C S

METRONOMICS

ONE UNITED SYSTEM TO GROW UP YOUR TEAM, COMPANY, AND LIFE

SHANNON BYRNE SUSKO

LIONCREST
PUBLISHING

METRONOMICS

One United System to Grow Up Your Team, Company, and Life

ISBN   978-1-5445-2130-5   *Hardcover*
      978-1-5445-2129-9   *Paperback*
      978-1-5445-2128-2   *Ebook*
      978-1-5445-2131-2   *Audiobook*

*"When you start something, you finish it,
and you finish strong!"*

*In memory of my Mom, Helen Sylvia Byrne, known to many
as "Dander", who was a great example of commitment, discipline,
determination, dedication, consistent, practical, efficient, and
systematic. Metronomics is founded on all of these behaviors
for business and life! Thank you, Mom, for showing me the
way. My mother was a force. A force I miss every day!*

CONTENTS

INTRODUCTION

Think back to every single business book you've ever read in an effort to become a better leader. Count them up.

I'm talking about *everything*—the big to the small. From *Good to Great* and *The Five Temptations of a CEO* to the lesser-known titles you often see recommended in your mastermind groups and business networks.

I'd be willing to bet that the final count of books you've read is in the dozens. Perhaps it even breaks into 3 figures. You've read them *all*. As any good business leader does, you've committed yourself to learning, to the constant pursuit of knowledge that you can use to strengthen your company—and your own professional game as a CEO or member of a leadership team.

You've put in the work.

So why does your business *still* feel like a struggle?

It's not a problem with the books, that's for sure. The books you read are fantastic. Each time you learn a new concept, system, or framework, you're fired up and ready to go implement it in your organization. You even give the book to your fellow business leaders so that they can align to the new "thing" you're all going to put into action to scale, grow, and reach success faster.

You have all the information you could ever need. So why does it feel like it never truly gets a foothold in your business? Why is making all these incredible ideas a reality so *hard*?

The answer does not lie in the "what" but in the "how." As a CEO or leader of your first startup early-stage, or a seasoned 20-year Fortune 500 CEO, you have learned "what" to do but have little step-by-step guidance on the "how" to implement the "what" with your team.

Nothing ever seems to connect.

You have a team and a plan. But they do not connect.

The same is true of thought leadership. You've read every great book the business world has to offer, and the ideas are great but separated. They're not connected.

How do you pull them all together into one connected system that will work for you, your team, and your business? How do you unify every tried-and-true business framework, glue them together, and create and align a repeatable, structured, strategic execution process for your whole business?

The answer is this book. The answer is Metronomics.

I WAS A DESPERATE CEO

Even though you're experiencing these struggles, you probably don't think of yourself as *desperate*. I know I didn't. It was only after I developed Metronomics to pull myself out of burnout and overwork, and saw how much freedom I could truly have in my life as a CEO, that I realized how desperate things had been. I coined the term *Desperate CEO* to describe the place business leaders find themselves when they've read every book, tried every method, and still can't get any momentum going in their business.

When I started my first company, Paradata, things didn't start in the Desperate CEO zone. My co-founders and I were in our late twenties. We had tons of energy, optimism, and drive. We had discovered a problem in the world for which we had a unique solution, and we were venture-funded from day two of starting up our business. We had a great global growth opportunity. I was a super-young CEO, and I had gone from begging for money to the phone ringing off the hook for customers who wanted to buy from us.

But while we had all that energy and excitement in spades and were thrilled with our chance for growth, we had no idea *how* to grow the business up. We started putting in extremely long hours, grinding it out, working harder, like it was a badge of honor. Cool! With all that extra effort, all the time away from our families and friends, the endless hours spent working and not living the play-hard life we had all envisioned, we were killing ourselves.

And as a result, the only real "grind" was our growth as it damn near came to a halt.

Like you've probably done from the moment you became a CEO or leader, I started reading obsessively. I read the books of all the most respected and renowned business thought leaders. I attended their workshops and conferences like a rock-band groupie, trying to find them wherever they were and showing up whenever possible. I read four books a week for 24 months straight at one point—taking in a ridiculous amount of data and information—hoping to find some kind of repeatable system, a silver bullet, that we could implement to start taking full advantage of our opportunity and achieve the goals our investors expected.

And I couldn't find it. There was no one system.

It was unbelievable. With all the successful businesses in the world, no one had taken the time to write down the system they used.

As human beings, we crave repeatable, structured systems. We seek them out. You can see this in sports—which I lived and breathed for decades, growing up as an athlete. When you play a sport, the most successful teams always have a system and a cohesive culture that determine how that team operates and behaves. You always know who is in what role, what is expected, and what part every role plays in the team's success. Every individual is committed to the common team goal.

I thought the same thing should be true of business, and I wanted— needed—to find that blueprint. It had to be out there, right?

Well, I've already told you. It wasn't. Or at least I could not find it.

Instead, there were great pieces, but they were disparate, taught as siloed frameworks or tools on specific areas of a business: culture, cohesive teams, hiring, strategy, planning, execution, finance, cash. The problem was that, if they were implemented one by one, they weren't working together. In my business, it felt like I was constantly saying, "Look over here and fix this. Now look over there and fix that." They were one-and-done tools that only gave us one perspective at a time, not a connected, sustainable system. It was here, then there, then there—like a game of Whack-A-Mole.

That was not going to get me and my co-founders the growth we so badly needed for the company and what we committed to our investors.

I went to work with my leadership team and coach to create a system that pulled everything together. It wasn't easy, and it wasn't quick. There was a lot of guesswork, a lot of failures, and the pain of only seeing slow incremental evolution when what I wanted, as a Desperate CEO, was to wake up one morning and have my business run effortlessly.

But, over time, we started to see the results of the connected system we were building, and step by step, things got easier. We had less stress, more free time. The team understood the Core Purpose and actually had a connected system to drive measurable team results. We could see business outcomes grow up, quarter after quarter. Eventually, it was clear that we were on to something. This is the system I eventually named Metronomics.

Later, after we sold our second company less than six years after the first, for an exponential valuation, it was recognized as one of the top 3 midmarket deals on Wall Street that year by ACG New York. I was contacted by a CEO colleague who had observed our success. He congratulated me for selling two companies so quickly while complaining that he was still slogging it out for over a decade on his first. It was taking much longer and was much harder than he had thought it would be. He asked if I would consider being his coach, and I asked him what he meant. He explained that he wanted a coach for himself and his leadership team, and I asked why he was calling me. He said, "I watched you grow up and sell two companies at an unheard-of valuation. I saw that the second was even more valuable than the first. You must have a system, and I want to implement that system with my team to achieve the same success."

I thought about what he said about having a system. How intuitive. Yes! Yes, we did have a system. And I let him know that although I had never coached another CEO+Leadership team, other than being a CEO and an executive, I would absolutely share our system to allow them to achieve their goals.

That's how I went from Desperate CEO to Repeatable System CEO to CEO+Leadership team coach. I had a repeatable, structured system that I could coach in any kind of business, of any size, and that clients could put into practice immediately to create forward growth momentum, step by step, quarter by quarter. Metronomics meets a team where they are and grows with them.

Since then, I've not only coached hundreds of businesses, I've also trained Metronomics coaches from around the world who have coached this system into thousands of businesses.

THE SPORT OF BUSINESS

Business is a team sport. Just like soccer, baseball, hockey, or any other sport you played once upon a time and now wistfully watch on TV, any successful business involves a highly cohesive, culturally strong team of results-focused individuals committed to working together for the team win. They're driven by a score—the measure of how they're doing—and what they need to do to reach the ultimate goal. They have a clear process and a game plan. They regularly reflect on their games and how well they ran plays. And most importantly of all, they're guided by a coach and the coach's repeatable, structured process for the whole team to win.

That's a topic we'll come back to throughout this book. I'm going to put it right up front in simple terms: you need a business team coach. No sports team goes to the Olympics without a coach. And no business team should go to their "business Olympics" without a coach. You can't afford to risk not achieving your most important goals in the time frame you want.

I had coaches when I was creating Metronomics. They were CEO coaches only. They had good experience—they just didn't know this system. Believe me, when I interviewed coaches, I asked about their system. They were experienced and successful CEOs, but over time that wasn't enough. I wanted to find the system for myself and the whole team. I wanted a business team coach.

That said, the system you'll learn in this book doesn't require anything more than your willingness and desire to evolve your behavior. To follow the steps and the system. It's very human and organic!

With this book, you'll have what you need to create and sustain real forward momentum and growth in your business, right now. Right from the start.

In all those hours I spent reading books that taught independent strategies, tactics, and tools, I discovered the answer I was looking for wasn't in one of them—but in *all* of them. I've taken the best of *what* I learned in all that time reading the theories, strategies, methods, and tools, coupled with the lessons I've learned from the abundance of mistakes we made in my first business, and developed the highly needed and sought-after repeatable, sustainable growth system: Metronomics.

Metronomics will allow you to spend less time, less effort, and fewer dollars invested in order to grow your business. To stop grinding. To stop working ridiculous hours.

To get your life back and build the one you always envisioned.

If you're coming to this book having read my two other books, *3HAG WAY* and *The Metronome Effect*, you might be saying to yourself, "Shannon, this sounds like the same thing you've been saying for years. Why is this book any different? What makes this system unique compared to what you've taught in the past?"

It's a fair question. *The Metronome Effect* mainly provided a prescription to implement an execution system and touched very lightly on the other systems. *3HAG WAY* went a step further and shared one of the other key systems that I naively thought most people already knew—the Strategy System, how to implement a strategy system and how it connects to the execution system—and again very lightly touched on the other systems.

The concepts and strategies I shared in those books were only half of the system. And I realized that, without explaining the other half of Metronomics, it would not have the same impact as we realized in my own companies and with my clients. The system is so clear now that it has been refined for over 10 years. I've coached many companies who have implemented Metronomics and gotten the same fantastic results we did. I've also trained the top business coaches from around the globe who now coach the system, and I've learned a lot more about what works and what doesn't. I've incorporated all those lessons to develop and fine-tune the system.

Compared with my previous books:

- I didn't think then that I needed to explain the whole system—and I wasn't sure I could.
- Back then, I only really explained 3 of the seven systems that make up Metronomics.
- I could always see the whole system and coach it out—and this time I've been able to get it all on to paper so anyone can follow it and benefit.
- I've learned from our coaches that, frankly, there were parts of the system that I just never explained all that well.

It became increasingly clear that while the concepts and strategies were crystal clear in my own mind, I hadn't taught them in a way that made them easily reproducible for others to implement.

The coaches who worked with me told me I was holding out on them—and they were right.

I'm now able to do a *much* better job than I did in my other books of explaining how all the pieces fit together in one connected system. And with this book, that's what I'll do. With this book, any business—from a large global Fortune 500 to a small startup—has the one system they can implement to create enduring, repeatable growth with ease, speed, and confidence.

ALIGNED EXECUTION

As I just said, this book is for all sizes of business. So many business books are focused on startups. They're often focused on helping brand-new CEOs take small companies from zero to ten. This book is for all CEOs and leaders of any size of business as Metronomics works for any business, no matter what size.

Bigger companies have the same challenges as startups. Why? Because there are people involved, and a team of any size requires coaching. In fact, I predominantly coach businesses that are over the $100 million level and far larger. Whatever the size of your business team, you will benefit.

Pulling together all the pieces of business-thought leadership isn't just about the systems. You definitely need a system. But just as important is the team. A team with a clear plan connected to "widgets" is the backbone that makes Metronomics work. Every time!

(You'll hear a lot more about widgets. They're nonfiscal things that flow through your business that a team member owns.)

Metronomics is founded upon vision, connected to strategy, connected to tactics, as Jim Collins eloquently describes in *Beyond Entrepreneurship 2.0*.

Metronomics connects the team and their behavior to the seven systems that exist in every business: Cohesive, Culture, Strategy, Execution, Cash, Human, and Coach Cascade.

Metronomics keeps these systems in balance so you can grow your team, company, and life.

You can think of Metronomics as a waterfall fountain that constantly renews. It begins with you, the leader, and flows out through the company. It's a Compound Growth System that doesn't just allow you to think about strategy but *demands* that you do. It creates a single active, collaborative, strategic brain that connects the CEO, leadership team, and every single person in a company. It gives your team a shared language and focused team results. It's the glue that connects all the best business thought-leadership principles together and unites them with the mortal side of your business.

And it works.

It so works.

Damn, it works!

I want you to spend less time and money building the company you want. I want you to have more fun as a CEO. I want you to be happy when you come to work, and happy when you leave work. I want you to "grow up" your company. You don't have to sacrifice the life you want in order to get the company of your dreams—you can have both.

I know this works because I lived this system. I've had clients who lived the system and achieved the same benefits I did. The clients of Metronomics coaches around the world have done the same.

You can too.

CHAPTER 1

GOALS, PLANS...REALITY!

A lex drove into the office that Monday morning with a heaviness in his gut, dreading the day ahead of him. He hadn't slept much over the weekend. He also hadn't spent much time with his wife, Lisa, and their two daughters. No, he'd been at the office. As usual.

It wasn't that his SaaS company, OpenDoor, wasn't doing well. Quite the opposite, in fact. In the 10 years since 48-year-old Alex had founded OpenDoor, he and his small leadership team had grown from a bootstrapped bank balance to $10 million in annual revenue and $1 million in monthly recurring revenue. This past year, they'd landed a huge Fortune 500 client, and the resulting attention had required hiring a dedicated sales team for the first time. Now, with a 5-member leadership team and steady growth, the company finally started to feel less like a 10-year-old startup, and more like the big time.

The only problem? Alex and his leadership team were exhausted.

In the first 3 years of the business, Alex had been full of energy, goals, and endless ideas. Now, he felt ground down into dust. He was tired. He was burned out. He still had big goals, but he could not see a path forward to achieve them.

Worse, he felt like his leadership team wasn't on board with his vision. They didn't seem to be aligned around a clear plan or direction forward. They were constantly coming up with great ideas, but those ideas would fizzle. Execution just wasn't happening. There was zero momentum. It felt like they were just continuously driving around the block.

A friend at a mastermind group had recently asked him about his company's strategy for the year. "Strategy?" Alex had laughed. "We can barely see two feet in front of us. I *wish* we had time to think about strategy. We're just trying to keep our heads above water."

Pulling into the parking lot, Alex looked around; there were no other cars there. He was the first one in—and he'd been the last one out the previous night.

This isn't what I dreamed about when I started a company, and now we are 10 years old.

At his desk in his office, he flipped on his laptop. His inbox immediately dinged. The red badge seemed to laugh at him—he'd *just* hit inbox zero less than 12 hours ago, and yet he was already back up to double digits! He sighed and got to work.

It was only about 20 minutes before his CMO, Chris, popped his head through the office door with a light knock. "Hey, you're here early!"

"Yeah. And I was here until six last night—on a Sunday, no less," Alex grumbled.

Chris came into the office and sat in front of Alex's desk. "I feel the same way—I was here past 8 p.m. most nights last week. It's like there just aren't enough hours in the day."

Alex paused his inbox grooming and sat back in his chair, looking thoughtfully at Chris. "Answer me this. If you could identify our biggest problem as a company, what would it be?"

Chris frowned, thinking. After a moment, he replied. "Honestly, our biggest obstacle is that we don't have time to plan into the future. We can't see where we're going. We have no strategy. We are all just reacting, putting out fires every day."

Alex nodded. "Agreed."

"I'm in marketing. I see what our competitors are doing. I hate to admit it, but they're beating us to market with new features, sometimes at double speed."

This wasn't news to Alex. In fact, it was the deepest fear nagging at his gut: they were falling behind in the market. They couldn't keep up—because they couldn't seem to get anything *done*.

At noon, Alex and his leadership team held their weekly sync meeting. It was the first one in a couple of weeks, actually; they skipped these meetings about half the time because everyone was so busy.

Usually, Alex led the agenda. But today, he asked his COO, Jen, to lead the team through the discussion topics. He watched.

Watched in growing disappointment as his leadership team reinforced his fears about the company's direction.

Three of them—Chris, the CMO, Jen, the COO, and Andrew, the VP of Sales—had all the traits he knew would keep moving the company forward. They were results-focused. Even if they didn't always work well as a team, they were optimistic, highly intelligent, and low-ego.

But the other two members of the leadership team—Daniel, the CTO, and Alison, the CFO—were the opposite. They shot down ideas pessimistically and interrupted the others. They never seemed to bring new ideas to the table. Now that he was thinking about it, Alex realized that when the leadership team skipped their weekly sync, it was usually because either Daniel or Alison had requested it. They constantly claimed to be "underwater." Aren't we all? Alex thought.

A nagging feeling was starting to take up residence in his gut. Daniel and Alison had been with OpenDoor from the beginning, and he felt a tremendous amount of loyalty to them. But he was seeing now that they didn't belong on the leadership team anymore. They weren't going to be able to take the company past $10 million. Worse, they were holding everyone else back. He could feel the frustration in the room as though it was hot, stuffy air.

After the meeting, which concluded with a weak rundown of that week's "action plan"—which Alex knew would only come about halfway to fruition or be forgotten by their next meeting—he excused himself and took a walk outside in the sunshine.

He thought back to that past Saturday night at home. He'd dragged himself home from the office just in time to shovel down some dinner before what was supposed to be their family movie night, something his kids looked forward to more than anything. He'd fallen asleep 15 minutes into the flick.

After his wife, Lisa, had put the kids to bed, she'd jostled him awake on the couch. "Come up to bed."

"Sorry," he'd told her. "I'm sorry I fell asleep. I'm so tired."

"Honey, I know work is busy, but this isn't sustainable. We hardly ever see you. At least when you worked for someone else instead of yourself, we got to have time with you."

Now, as he strolled around the busy street block, his stomach starting to rumble for lunch, Alex knew Lisa was right. In becoming a CEO, he'd been trying to build the life he'd always dreamed of. But despite his demonstrated success, that life was still out of reach.

Something big was missing in his company. And he had no more hours to give to figure out *what*.

As much as he hated to admit it, he was starting to wonder if all this was worth it. He was starting to think about giving up.

That afternoon, he went along to his YPO monthly forum. The forums always energized him and gave him great new ideas. He was feeling particularly desperate, and in a shift in pace—he was traditionally a listener, not a sharer—he opened up to his forum mates about his struggles with OpenDoor.

"I just feel like I can't get any traction, no matter what I do," he said. He noticed a dozen faces in the room nodding. "I'm so frustrated. The company is making money. We've got a huge client list. I should be working on scaling our success. But I can't get out from under the daily grind. I'm exhausted."

The amount of commiseration that immediately surrounded him took him aback. Apparently, many—no, *most*—of his cohort had been feeling the same pain in their own companies.

"Have you read *Scale Smooth*?" another CEO recommended. "They have a great system for scaling execution in that book."

"Yeah, and also *The Ego-Free Team*. That's a great one."

"I loved that one. *Lost Leaders* is amazing too. It really shifted things for me."

Alex resisted the impulse to take a huge, dejected sigh.

He'd read all those books. And then some. In fact, there didn't seem to be a book out there he *hadn't* read. He listened to audiobooks obsessively while driving, sneaking in his daily run (okay, maybe he only squeezed it in 3 mornings a week), walking the family dog, and any other spare moment he could find. His nightstand was stacked five books high.

It wasn't that the books didn't give him good ideas. They were all great. But for some reason, as many times as he'd tried to bring those ideas into the business, they'd never caught on. He couldn't seem to make anything stick.

The last thing he needed was another book recommendation.

At home that evening, his inbox dinged. He clicked into it; it was an email from a YPO forum mate, Mark, who had been at the afternoon's meeting.

Hey, Alex! I figure you've already read all those books people spoke about. I was right where you are about 6 months ago. I got introduced to a business team coach who knows this great system. Ever since things are moving in the right direction. I finally feel like I have my head above water. I wish I'd gotten a business team coach 5 years ago, honestly—would have wasted a lot less time!

My coach's name is Lee, and she coaches this system called "Metronomics." Do you know it? Do you want to meet her? I can't recommend her highly enough.

Alex read over the email two more times. Then he clicked Reply.

Hey, Mark! You know what? Yes. Please. Introduce me. I've tried everything else. I'm willing to try anything at this point.

Two days later, Alex had an appointment on the calendar with Lee. It was time to go in a new direction.

METRONOMICS

Every great company is founded upon a CEO+Leadership team that wants to achieve their goals with the least amount of effort, time, and investment. This is not to say that CEOs and their leadership teams are lazy or don't want to put the effort in. Quite the contrary. They are gritty, committed, ready, and willing to achieve their goals, and they're eager to gain the greatest efficiency, ease, speed, and confidence to do it.

So many business leaders, including myself, start out this way, excited by the vision of figuring out how to do it. And so many—again, including me—slowly but surely get disillusioned and conclude the opposite: that there just isn't an easy way.

What I was looking for was a structured process that would be successful in growing up our company with ease, speed, and confidence, with great returns to shareholders.

At the time, I thought this would be easy to find. There had been so many great CEOs and leaders who built such incredible companies with huge success. Surely they had written their systems down for others to learn and leverage?

No was the answer. Hence Metronomics.

Metronomics is the system we have repeatedly utilized with great success, providing exponential returns to shareholders and team members alike. It's the system I spent years searching for when I became a CEO.

I'm sharing it so you can stop looking and leverage a system that will meet you where you are today, activate the growth you are in search of—and make sure it lasts.

Metronomics is for the whole company. The whole team. It's a systematized approach that combines the Compound Growth System—the repeatable, structured system that your whole team yearns for—with a known, transparent, accountable, and aligned way for the team to play on the "field" together under the guidance of a CEO+Leadership team coach, an expert at the system who ensures that the company and team grow with the momentum to reach their goals.

At the heart of Metronomics is a CEO+Leadership team that wants to win. They want to achieve their goals and are willing to learn new ways to make it easier for everyone to win. Metronomics is setup for the CEO, leadership, and the whole company. It is a regimen that meets the team where they are today and progressively promotes the best practices of growing a company until they become habits that will endure through the lifetime of the business.

I use the word *regimen* in the context of a prescribed, methodical course of action to restore or promote positive health—in this case, the positive health of both your business and your life to ensure you can achieve whatever goals you set for yourself. By following the Metronomics regimen over time— evolving in small steps day by day, week by week, month by month, quarter by quarter, year by year—the solidity of your team will be unstoppable.

I'll explain the steps you and your team can take to implement this regimen easily into your company so that it becomes second nature. The best outcome is that the regimen gets forgotten, and the focus is solely on working on your business for the very best outcome.

Metronomics is about outcomes, and its strength is founded upon 3 key components based on what I learned by being on teams and from studying the greatest teams in business and in sports.

GREAT TEAMS

The greatest teams have 3 things in common:

1. A structured, repeatable process that all team members follow.
2. Clarity of expectations of each other and a willingness to work hard to develop and maintain high cohesiveness to achieve their team goal together.
3. A coach who is an expert at the repeatable process and who ensures the team has clarity of role and position while keeping it highly cohesive and focused on the team result.

High-performing teams are cohesive, meaning that they have a shared bond to achieve the same outcome. The higher a team's cohesiveness, the higher the self-esteem of its members. Higher self-esteem brings increased morale, leading to increased performance across the whole team, and so on— time and time again.

A high level of cohesiveness drives a team's collaboration to a level of excellence through a willingness to participate together. Highly cohesive teams have a deep sense of trust; they share a strong sense of team character and have confidence in their team abilities. They also have a great sense of self-accountability, behavioral rules, and an understanding of decision-making within the team context.

Highly cohesive teams are not the result of luck. To build one requires the team to develop emotional competence together as a group over time.

If you're thinking, "So all I have to do is create a cohesive team to win," not so fast. Cohesiveness is critical to a great outcome, sure, but it will not guarantee success without a commitment to the team's organizational goals.

It's essential that the team's organizational goals are clear and understood, and the best practice is to develop these goals with the whole team. The metrics—the measurable performance indicators—must be clear, known, and visible. This allows team members to evaluate their own performance and their team's performance in a way that is clearly visible and connected to the overall metrics of the whole organization.

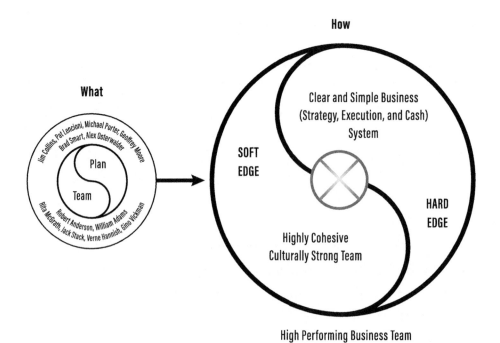

High Performing Business Team

The team learns together. They're clear on their decision-making ability to achieve the goals. They're rewarded for their success in achieving team goals. And there is an open "playing field" and culture that displays to all team members all the relevant information flowing through it.

Metronomics is founded upon the best practices. We have studied and evolved high-performing *business* teams for over 20 years while striving to implement a dynamic business system for growth and goal achievement. What we found is that you cannot achieve success without having both in place: a highly cohesive, culturally strong team and a clear and simple business (strategy, execution, and cash) system.

We have taken the "what" of all the greatest thought leaders and have pulled it together into one connected system that shows you "how"—"how" to balance your team (the soft edge) and your business (the hard edge).

Most CEOs I know run from the words *culture*, *cohesiveness*, and *human*. Instead, they focus on the business components: cash, strategy, execution. A focus on the business components—what I call the hard-edge systems—won't make it easy to grow a company over the long term. It needs to be balanced from the beginning with attention to the soft-edge systems (Culture, Cohesiveness, Human) and the hard-edge systems (Strategy, Cash, Execution). Growing up a company is a true balancing act, and Metronomics ensures that you and your team stay in balance with the business.

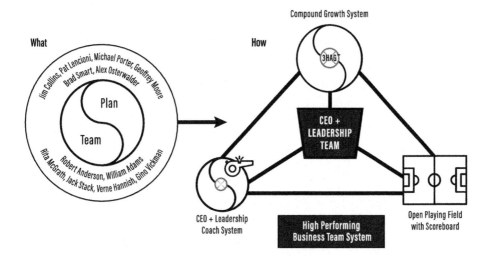

3 COMPONENTS

Metronomics is broken into 3 components:

1. A repeatable, structured process that actively balances the progression of a highly cohesive team with alignment and commitment to an organizational plan for the whole team.
2. An Open Playing Field.
3. An expert CEO+Leadership team coach who understands the playing field and the system in order to ensure the team is high performing while remaining aligned to the plan. The coach will unlock ease, speed, and confidence in the team and the plan to reach your goals sooner.

Before we dive into the rest of the book, let me give you a quick overview of the components that enable the Metronomics regimen.

REPEATABLE, STRUCTURED PROCESS

In Metronomics, the repeatable, structured process is called the Compound Growth System. It was developed over many years in my first company and validated in my second. It was then perfected in my coaching practice, both with my own clients and with those of other coaches certified in the system.

The Compound Growth System comprises seven systems that exist in every business, whether the team is aware of them or not: Cultural, Cohesive, Human, Strategy, Execution, Cash, and Coach Cascade. We'll talk about the Coach Cascade later in the book, so for now let's focus on the six systems in this diagram.

This diagram represents the balance you need to develop and grow a high-performing team to win the game. It provides the regimen to build a high-performing business team and breaks the process down into practical progressive steps, each building on the next. It clearly identifies the systems that create a highly cohesive team and the systems that align the team to a differentiated strategic plan to be executed. The result is a consistent,

COMPOUND GROWTH SYSTEM

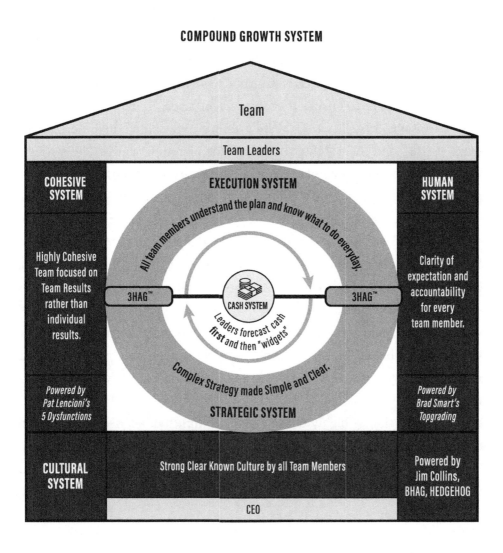

confident, high-performing business team that achieves its goals consistently and with confidence.

This house diagram, which has evolved over more than 20 years, represents six of the seven systems in the Compound Growth System.

The structure of the house is made up of the 3 systems that create a highly cohesive, culturally strong team: the Cultural System, the Cohesive System, and the Human System. These systems make up the foundation and the frame of the house. They represent the strength of the team and the ability to achieve the plan.

The CEO is represented as the ultimate foundation of the organization, with the team leaders and the team at the top of the house. In this way, the CEO and the team encompass the Cultural System, the Cohesive System, and the Human System to ensure that they are in place. If any one of these systems is missing, it will put the team's ability to become a high-performing team at risk—and their ability to achieve the plan in jeopardy. The stronger the foundation and frame of the house, the easier it will be to execute and achieve the strategy and the greater return to the organization's value.

In addition, the stronger these 3 soft-edge systems are, the easier it is to take a complex strategy and make it simple and clear so that all team members understand the plan and know what to do every day, aligned to the cash forecast. The hard-edge systems—Strategy, Execution, and Cash—are only as good as the soft-edge systems.

In other words, we can develop the greatest strategy, execution plan, and fiscal forecast but still miss our goals every month, quarter, and year unless the soft-edge systems are in place. But if we maintain a great balance between the soft-edge systems and the hard-edge systems, we will have a high-performing team that is highly cohesive and committed, aligned to their plan, and achieving their goals.

Let's review these systems in a little more detail to explain the context for the Compound Growth System before digging into the progression of Metronomics.

SOFT-EDGE SYSTEMS

Cultural System

The purpose of this system is to ensure that there is a clear, known culture that creates the team's strong belief in the Core Purpose, team behavioral values, and the very long-term 10- to 30-year goal for the organization. It's the necessary foundation of all high-performing teams. The deep learning and experience behind this system come not only from great thought leaders like Jim Collins and Pat Lencioni but also from the experience of using their principles and those of other thought leaders to create a daily, repeatable behavioral system to ensure that a company's culture is not something static on paper or up on the wall but something that pulses in the organization every day, starting with the CEO.

Cohesive System

It's difficult to develop a cohesive team while growing a company. It takes time, discipline, and focus. We developed the Cohesive System so that every day we could progress and develop further as a highly cohesive team knowing that the daily behavior of the team members could affect our level of cohesiveness as a whole. This is a practical system that is highly interconnected with the Cultural System to ensure that team cohesiveness progresses and evolves every day in an organization, not just at an offsite two days per year.

There is an abundance of great thought leaders in this area. We found Pat Lencioni's *The Five Dysfunctions of a Team* framework to be the most practical in growing cohesiveness, both in our organization and for my clients. As with all the systems, the abundance of thought leaders can be plugged in to each specialty area, helping us to evolve and progress as required.

What I love about Pat's framework is that leaders can implement it and progress with overcoming the five dysfunctions every day, working on team trust, healthy team conflict, team commitment, and team accountability, and focusing on team results. This provides a great connection to the everyday execution of the hard-edge systems: Strategy, Execution, and Cash.

All winning teams are highly cohesive and work at this together every day.

Human System

The Human System was developed and named in my first company. I wish we had come up with a better name but, funnily enough, everything about the system *is* human. Its purpose is to ensure that each and every team member is supported with the same repeatable process, from recruiting to hiring, to training and onboarding, to clarity of their functional role's Scorecard, to coaching, feedback, and opportunity for growth and rewards.

The Human System is founded upon A-Players who want to be coached and given the opportunity to grow. A-Players ooze the company's Core Values and consistently exceed performance expectations; they're attracted to being measured and held accountable for the position they volunteered to own on behalf of the team in the company.

The Human System was inspired by Brad Smart's Topgrading methodology, which ensures that you hire A-Players 9 out of 10 times by using a Scorecard that attracts top talent who want to understand what is expected of them through metrics and clear accountabilities. We have been using Topgrading since Brad released his first book with great success. We've found that, once you have a team of A-Players, you must have a practical, efficient, repeatable system to support them because they want to be coached, kept, and grown into the next opportunity. And we wanted to ensure they remained on our team for their next growth opportunity.

The Human System is highly dependent on the Cultural System, as all team members must behave according to the Core Values most of the time, ensuring the culture remains strong. The Human System ensures that all the functional roles the team requires to win are consistently filled with A-Players.

We've also learned that A-Players attract A-players. These are the team members we will develop into a highly cohesive team. There is a tight connection to the Cohesive System, ensuring we develop a high-performing team.

The Human System is also connected to the hard-edge systems, through ensuring the organization is functionally designed to align to the execution growth for current and future goals.

The team is represented at the very top of the house by the leadership team, completing the frame and filling the rooftop with the team. The team holds the reputation of the business in the marketplace in their hands. Everything that happens in the marketplace to serve the customer needs to be shared in a strong feedback system throughout the company. In order for this to work well, the cohesiveness of the team needs to be high so that team members feel confident in and committed to sharing their feedback.

You'll have noticed that the soft-edge systems and the frame of the house are made up of the people systems of an organization. The strength of these systems will determine the strength of the team—and its ability to win the game.

It doesn't matter what goes on inside the house: these systems are foundational for any type of team, whether it be a professional sports team or a beer-league hockey team, a U8 soccer team, or a business team. Without the Cohesive System, we will lose team members. Without a Human System giving clarity of expectations to each and every team member, connected to the company goals, we will lose team members. And without the Cultural System, the foundation, the team will not reach its true potential and quite possibly come to a halt or fall apart.

These 3 systems are present in every company. It's up to leaders to be aware of them and to have the discipline to implement and grow them. These systems work intensively together and with the hard-edge systems. Ironically, the soft-edge systems provide a clear and solid structure for all teams to achieve their goals.

HARD-EDGE SYSTEMS

Inside the house are the Strategic System, the Execution System, and the Cash System. These are known as hard-edge systems: they are easy to focus on and define because they have to do with strategy, execution plans, and financial and cash forecasts—hard results. These important systems depend on successful goal attainment. A highly cohesive team in itself will not guarantee success. It's possible for individuals to feel connected to other team members and yet still be completely detached from the organizational plans and goals.

Most companies only focus on these hard-edge systems, or at least on two of them. The Cash System is where every company starts—no cash, no company—and the Execution System has to work well with the Cash System in order to sustain itself and grow up the company.

The hard-edge systems are the key to building a high-performing winning team. You cannot win without clear objectives and goals, aligned metrics, continuous learning, decision-making awareness, team rewards, and an Open Playing Field. Each one of these elements needs to be in place with a highly cohesive team in order for the team to grow up as a high-performing team that wins every time.

Let's review the hard-edged systems.

Strategy System

Although business experts include strategy among the hard-edge systems, it can be quite abstract for most companies. Most leaders don't have the same understanding of what strategy is, and many find it a challenge to confidently articulate their strategy. We'll talk more about that later in the book.

In Metronomics, the Strategy System's purpose is to take a complex strategy that can be hard for the whole team to understand—even the leaders—and use it to create a clear and simple strategy that the whole team understands, can explain, and can use to make decisions. The Strategy System, like the other systems, is a progression that ensures the leadership team collaborates to create the most differentiated, confident strategy for their business.

The level of cohesiveness of the team is important to create the most impactful strategy. The more team trust, the more the team will have a healthy conflictive discussion to decide on the strategy for their business.

The Strategy System is made up of the core components and steps you need to create a differentiated strategy and, most importantly, to ensure that it stays aligned through active knowledge of the dynamics of your market as well as the internal operation of the company. The Strategy System keeps the company in a unique and valuable position, making sure its set of differentiating activities remain relevant and appealing to Core Customers.

As with all the other systems, the Strategy System is founded on the principles of strategy experts such as Michael Porter, Kaihan Krippendorff, Rita McGrath, and Alex Osterwalder, to name a few. The system connects their principles and brings them alive.

One of the key differences in how a strategy is created through the Compound Growth System is the prescriptive step-by-step method that allows a team to build up their strategy and validate it every step of the way, creating and maintaining confidence. The entire leadership team is involved, and the team has clarity through the leverage of "strategic pictures" that are created to ensure clarity, focus, and an easy and efficient way to evolve strategy and keep it alive in the company every day.

The foundation of the strategy system, and the glue that holds together the Compound Growth System and Metronomics, is the 3HAG™ (3 Year Highly

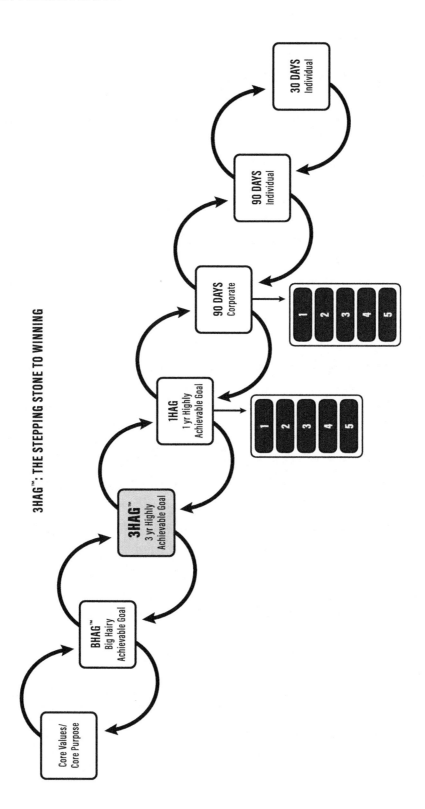

Achievable Goal). This is the stepping-stone, the evolution vehicle, that ties the plan to your cohesive team.

My team and I discovered that if you gut out where you will be in 3 years' time, as humans you will never stop validating it to make sure it is accurate, thus driving the team to stay immensely focused on the goals. And when you align the soft-edge systems with this, the balance provides a consistent way to win each and every year.

My second book, *3HAG WAY*, provides a step-by-step, prescriptive method of how to create your 3HAG in great detail. In this book, I'll also cover the progression of the 3HAG and the strategy system because it is one of the key reasons teams consistently win using Metronomics.

Execution System

The Execution System does not need much explanation, but it's worth discussing its significance in a high-performing team. An Execution System has a clear plan, of course, but when we started our first company, we thought it just had to be a 12-month plan. What we discovered instead was that if we created and leveraged a long-term goal, like Jim Collins's 10- to 30-year goal, and also had a 3HAG™, a 3-year goal, then creating a 12-month company priorities plan with metrics—both fiscal and nonfiscal—highly aligns the team and brings clarity to what they need to accomplish. Bringing that clarity together with a daily, weekly, monthly, quarterly, and annual focus on the plan with the team ensured that we made better, faster decisions to get us to the outcomes we had set as goals.

The Execution System is founded upon principles Jim Collins included in *Beyond Entrepreneurship 2.0* and on Verne Harnish's *Mastering the Rockefeller Habits*. It ensures there are clear, specific, accountable priorities that are owned by leaders and measured for the company on the basis of a 1 Year Highly Achievable Goal or annual plan (1HAG) and a Quarterly Highly Achievable Goal (QHAG) or 90-day company plan. These company priorities are then aligned through the owners to other individuals on the team, who will commit and ensure that these priorities are completed before their own individual priorities.

Company prioritization is critical. Company priorities ahead of individual priorities. Always.

The ownership and accountability of these clear priorities and metrics are vital to the Execution System interacting fully with the other hard-edge systems, but most importantly with the soft-edge systems.

Cash System

The Cash System is simple. Forecast cash first. In fact, forecast how much cash you want in the bank at the end of every month, month over month for 36 months. You don't just forecast it once and you're done. It's a system. You do this every month with the leadership team. The forecast is owned by the whole leadership team, not just the finance team.

The process is to forecast cash first and then the "widgets," the nonfiscal things that flow through your business: the things in your business that your team controls. All teams should be able to forecast their function widgets month over month through the organization before adding the corresponding fiscal assumptions associated with the widgets.

Most organizations just create a fiscal budget and base it only on past history and percentage increase year over year. It's my great hope that when you have finished this book, you will never forecast that way again.

Forecasting widgets, which team members own and control, directly connect the team to a very achievable and realistic plan that in turn connects directly to the cash balance required to grow your business. The more the team owns the forecast, both cash and widgets, the more likely the forecast will be highly achievable. The widgets are key to being able to forecast cash accurately every month.

As with all the systems, the Cash System is a progression and will be worked up with the team quarter over quarter. The initial goal is to create a 12-month widget-based forecast, then to add 12 more months—and then 12 more months after that. This creates, best practice, a 36-month widget-based rolling forecast that predicts cash in the bank first, that is owned by the leadership team, and that is based on sound assumptions about the widgets that flow through the company—not on wild-ass or frivolous guesses about "percent growth on top-line revenue."

This system creates a plan that is not only realistic but active. Clear owners will forecast the widgets they own with the rest of the team over 36 months. They map out the plan to execute their strategy all the way out to their 3 Year Highly Achievable Goal, the 3HAG™.

These are the hard-edge systems that must be connected to the soft-edge systems and progress together to create a high-performing team that achieves its goals and wins every time.

You might be thinking, "Wow, Shannon, if this is what it takes to win, it seems like there is a lot going on all at once." Right?

Well, I'm not going to lie. There *is* a lot going on. We will need to activate each of these systems together, step by step. We'll turn the dials each and every quarter to create a pathway to continue to build your team members from where they are into a high-performing team that achieves its goals and has a lot of fun doing it. The best thing I can tell you is that this book lays out a prescriptive step-by-step way for you and your team to take advantage of the progressive nature of the Compound Growth System.

It doesn't have to be painful.

When most of my new clients start out, they're not even aware that we progress each of the six systems every quarter. In some quarters we need to focus deeper on some of the systems and make significant progress, while in others we just take baby steps. As you follow the chapters year by year, and quarter by quarter, you'll get a good view of how we build up to create a highly cohesive team while creating a collaborative, differentiated strategy plan for maximum value to your shareholders.

All the systems progress every step of the way, meeting the team where they are right now.

THE SEVENTH SYSTEM

The seventh system of the Compound Growth System is the Coach Cascade System. Think of it as the rebar that reinforces the whole house. The purpose of the Coach Cascade System is to grow all leaders into coaches themselves and their teams into high-performing teams connected through the corporate

COMPOUND GROWTH SYSTEM FRAMEWORK

Team

Team Leaders

COHESIVE SYSTEM

HUMAN SYSTEM

EXECUTION SYSTEM

All team members understand the plan and know what to do everyday.

Highly Cohesive Team focused on Team Results rather than individual results.

Clarity of expectation and accountability for every team member.

3HAG™

CASH SYSTEM

3HAG™

Leaders forecast cash first and then "widgets"

Powered by Pat Lencioni's 5 Dysfunctions

Powered by Brad Smart's Topgrading

Complex Strategy made Simple and Clear.

STRATEGIC SYSTEM

CULTURAL SYSTEM

Strong Clear Known Culture by all Team Members

Powered by Jim Collins, BHAG, HEDGEHOG

CEO

COACH CASCADE SYSTEM
Grow all leaders into a coach of a high performing team.

plan. This is a part of the secret sauce that creates exponential momentum in the team's high-growth results.

The Coach Cascade System takes the leaders' and the team's behavior to the next level. It takes the team's cohesiveness to the next level of behavior and vulnerability, ensuring that every leader becomes a coach who can create other coaches within the organization: hence the Coach Cascade System.

This Coach Cascade is easiest when you work with an expert CEO+ Leadership team coach who coaches the CEO to coach the leaders, and coaches the leaders to coach their own teams, and so on. This is the progressive system that allows leaders to grow into a "Level 5 Leader," as Jim Collins has coined it, or what Robert Anderson and William Adams call an "Integral Leader" in their book *Scaling Leadership*.

In order to grow up our company, we must grow ourselves as CEOs first—and then our leaders and team—into humble coaches with a fierce commitment to the purpose and goal.

Having the willingness and desire to get to this level will exponentially transform your company's outcome and the life you live.

COMPOUND GROWTH SYSTEM

The Compound Growth System is the nucleus of every company. A conscious, disciplined awareness of this connected system is key to business success. It enables the team that will develop into a highly cohesive team and the connected plan required to achieve goals. The great news is that no matter where your team is right now, this system will meet it wherever you begin.

This core system allows you and your leaders to leverage all the great thought leaders of our time as they plug into each specific system. Those thought leaders are experts in allowing you to leverage their great research, knowledge, principles, or tools, and the Compound Growth System brings their value into one connected benefit to leverage as needed. The beauty of this connected system is that you don't have to choose any one thought leader: you can pick and plug in different tools as your company progresses.

With the Compound Growth System, you never have to choose one tool over another; you can always use both—or something else. Most thought leaders' tools provide us with a specialized outcome or a view specific to one of the systems, and they can be plugged into the respective system as needed. The diagram shows some of the thought leaders' tools and frameworks that have influenced and can be used within the core system.

We were ferocious learners and consumers of business books while we

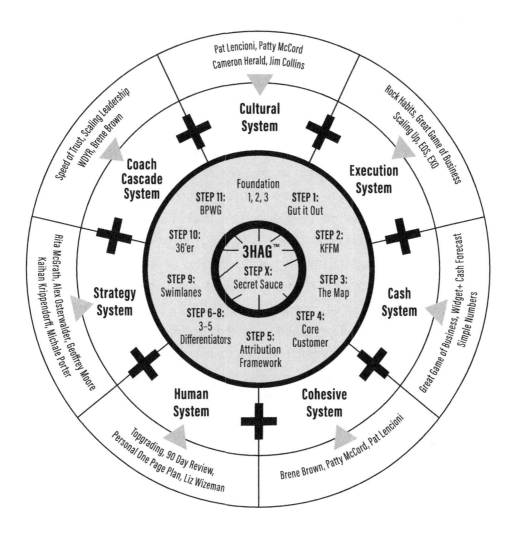

created the Compound Growth System, and we created a core system that provides a dynamic, practical way to progress and evolve, including plugging in these tools.

I'll say it again: it's always an "and," not an "or." The work of each expert thought leader can easily plug into the system wherever it relates. It will provide a validation of the current state of the company—and a connected way to grow.

The great thing about this plug-and-play is that the system and your company will continue to evolve with the latest, greatest thought leadership. That's been happening to me and my teams for over 20 years.

OPEN PLAYING FIELD

All sports teams play somewhere: a field, a court, or an ice rink. That's where they perform together to achieve a shared goal. That goal is winning the game by leveraging their individual competencies, the team's systems and processes, and their strategized plays. Every team has a culture, a level of cohesiveness, and clear expectations of the positions each individual plays. They understand how to execute a plan together for a team outcome.

In business, too, a team has a culture, a level of cohesiveness, clarity of expectations, a strategy, and an execution plan to win their game. But the playing field—or court or rink—is not always clear or open.

In my first company, the Open Playing Field was captured in the One Page Strategic Plan from Verne Harnish's *Mastering the Rockefeller Habits* execution framework. It was actually two pages printed onto one in Word. We captured the company plan in this format and then shared it through the hundreds of team members throughout the company, every quarter and year, evolving the one-page format over time to reflect a practical and efficient playing field. Everyone had the same plan, except the last column reflected their own priorities aligned to the team plan and goals.

As technology evolved, we tried different project-management and business-tracking software. The software didn't create the open, real-time playing field we were yearning for, however—so we went back to the Word version. All the project-management and business software we tried removed visible, active ownership behavior from each team member. It didn't connect the individual plan they could easily see to the whole company. The connection got lost. The visibility of playing the game together got lost.

At least with the Word version, I, as CEO, and the whole company all had clear visibility of the company plan, and everyone had their own priorities and metrics aligned to the company priorities and metrics.

It was simple but impactful.

When I became a coach, I did not want my first clients to have to put in the same effort we had into a Word-formatted Open Playing Field. I wanted them to be able to easily create an Open Playing Field for their team. Those early clients tried many virtual playing fields, but over time, each team slowly moved back off whatever software they chose—and back to Word.

I knew Word *could* work—but I also knew there must be an easier way.

I decided to build an Open Playing Field just for my clients because it was necessary to help them grow.

I engaged my friend Benoit Bourget, one of my team members for the last 20 years, to build the platform we had always wanted in our businesses but had previously been too busy to develop. Benoit launched a minimum viable platform for my clients at the end of 2015. I was very careful stepping my clients into the minimum platform, and their feedback was key to growing the Open Playing Field.

Soon, other business coaches had seen or heard of the platform and wanted to use it themselves. I refused. It was only for my clients! But they would not take no for an answer, so Benoit and I founded Metronome Growth Systems to offer the Open Playing Field to all companies and coaches who wanted the experience.

In fact, the Open Playing Field doesn't even need software. You can use wall charts and posters. The format doesn't really matter. The key to success is the commitment to the Open Playing Field and to transparent and accountable behavior. Whenever you come across the Open Playing Field in this book, know that you can decide on what type of field you would like to use with the Metronomics regimen.

The Open Playing Field is where every team member can clearly see others playing the game: their functional role, their execution, what they are accountable for, their Scorecard, and how they will be measured in the context of the company's priorities aligned to their metrics in the context of the 1HAG, 3HAG, BHAG, and the company win.

The Open Playing Field shows the team how the game is being played. It is where the team communicates at the moment about progress daily, weekly, monthly, quarterly, and annually. It creates visibility so that team members can easily ask other team members if they need help, as they would if they were playing a game together on a field, court, or ice rink. It also provides a way for team members to easily ask for help if they can see they may not achieve what needs to be done to win the game for the team.

I've already identified the Open Playing Field as one of the keys to developing a high-performing team's transparent and accountable team behavior. For a sports team, the playing field is easy to use to play together; in business, this open field is harder to create to achieve the same execution focus and accountability.

The Open Playing Field mimics the sports environment to ensure the behavior required for each individual to easily commit to a team goal and stay focused on it. It allows leaders to easily coach their team members. And it allows the CEO+Leadership team coach clear visibility of the field on which the team is executing to reach their goals. A high-performing business team needs an Open Playing Field.

THE BLIND-SPOT REMOVER

As a CEO+Leadership team coach, I am a blind-spot remover for the team on the Open Playing Field. It was only when I started writing this book that I realized that's what I do.

I consistently work with CEO+Leadership teams to help them see what they cannot see because I am observing the team executing from a different perspective.

The Compound Growth System and the Open Playing Field help me ask the most impactful questions at the right time. That's why I have learned to trust the system. It guides me to ask the questions needed exactly when my client needs to answer them to remove their blind spots.

In my own career, I relied on my own blind-spot removers. My coaches started out just coaching me as the CEO, but as time passed I realized that I needed a coach who would work with me *and* my leadership team. In order to be great, we needed to be coached together and to learn together.

My coaches knew lots of foundational business thought-leader principles and tools and had great experience. Their guidance helped us develop the Compound Growth System—but they did not understand the "how" or, even better, how to explain it. They knew the unconnected principles and had experience implementing them in a piecemeal way in their own business.

They didn't get how to tie together all the business principles into one practical, efficient, connected system that could grow up with the company. Which is, of course, what we now know as Metronomics.

I'll say again that no team goes to the Olympics without a coach for the whole team. So why would you and your team go to the Business Olympics without a CEO+Leadership coach?

Not wanting to be too blunt, but when I reflect on my own success, I can see that it's because my team and I were open, willing, and hungry to find a better way to grow for the company to "win" the gold medals.

A CEO+Leadership team coach is not a life coach. They are not an executive coach. They are not a CEO-only coach. They coach the whole team together. They are a business team coach. The CEO+Leadership team coach leads the quarterly and annual "practices"—the planning sessions—and coaches the team on the whole system to ensure the plan is solid and aligned while ensuring that the team implements the progressive regimen required, quarter over quarter, so the company grows with ease, speed, and confidence.

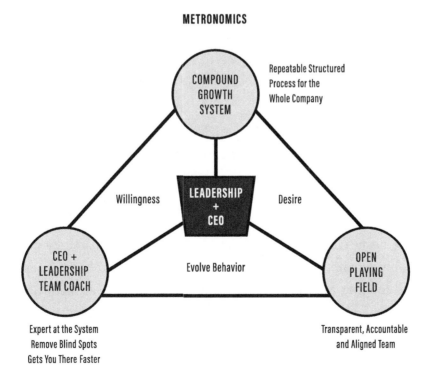

METRONOMICS

CEO+LEADERSHIP TEAM

We've already seen that the CEO+Leadership team is core to the success of Metronomics.

Without a CEO who has the willingness and desire to commit to achieving their goals and evolving their behavior, Metronomics won't work. The leadership team must also have the same willingness and desire to commit to the same goals in order to grow with the CEO and the company. They must really want to "win."

Metronomics is founded on the CEO+Leadership team's behavior and willingness to commit to the system to grow up their company while living the life they want. Each individual must be willing to evolve from the leader they are today into a continuously improving version. From Leader 1.0 to Leader X.0. If they do this, their company will follow—and so will their life.

Seems simple? It is!

You have to have the desire to grow—grow yourself, grow your team, grow your company into a high-performing business team that brings together developing cohesiveness connected to the visible elements of the collaborative plan.

GROWING UP

I don't think I've ever met a CEO or a leadership team who doesn't want to grow their company. Everyone wants to grow their company. But for many people, growing their company is one of the hardest things they've ever faced. Many thought leaders say that growing a company is like climbing a mountain.

I can relate.

I have never climbed a real mountain, but I am fascinated by mountaineers and mountain climbing. I've studied many successful and unsuccessful climbs—and they are all founded upon the same regimen as Metronomics.

There are barriers to climbing a mountain, and there are barriers to growing a company:

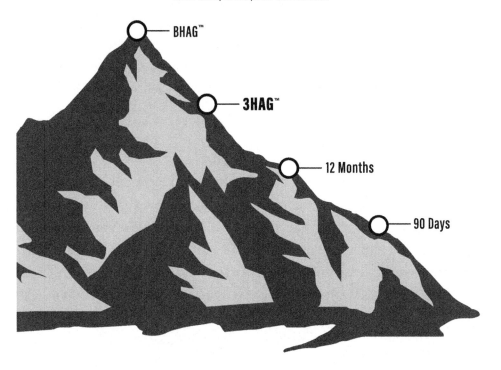

CLIMBING THE MOUNTAIN
WITH EASE, SPEED, AND CONFIDENCE

BHAG™

3HAG™

12 Months

90 Days

- The #1 barrier to growth is Leadership. It sounds harsh, but it's true. You cannot summit a mountain without a strong A-Player and a cohesive, high-performing leadership team, and the same goes for a company. The easiest way to grow up a company is to have a 100 percent A-Player leadership team. We will dig into this in much more detail later in the book.

- The #2 barrier to growing a company is the lack of deep market expertise. You must ensure that the leadership team has experts in the market and understands the market well. A team wanting to grow their company must be experts in the environment they're playing in. Just like when you're climbing a real mountain, you don't necessarily control the environment. A mountaineer can't control the weather, and a CEO building a company doesn't control the market.

- The #3 barrier to growth is lacking the right infrastructure at the right time—which is when you need it, not too soon or too late. Think of how a team of mountain climbers moves first from base camp, then to camp after camp up the mountain. They move their infrastructure as they climb. It is no different in business. If you know your long-term and near-term goals, it is easier to make infrastructure decisions now and in the future to help reach those goals.

You don't become an expert mountain climber by reading books. You start by finding other mountaineers who want to climb mountains, too, and you start climbing together. You don't go straight to Everest. If that's your ultimate goal, you start with some smaller mountains to learn and grow with your team. You train together. You become better and better, mountain after mountain, year after year. You progress together.

As a CEO and leadership team, growing up a company is very similar. In theory, quarter over quarter, you will get better and better, go higher and higher. In reality, of course, this is not always the case. Leaders can be impatient. Leaders get disenchanted, worn out, and desperate because we cannot see how to turn up the dial to grow, quarter over quarter. Grow the company. Grow ourselves. Get where we want to go.

Be patient. Human team behavior takes time to evolve—and we can only grow as fast as our behavior evolves.

CREATING THE SYSTEM

As CEO, I longed for the silver bullet. I would have done anything to make it easier to grow my company faster sooner. Anything.

After four years of looking for the silver bullet, reading every book I could find, I attended a conference where the creator of the Rockefeller Habits, Verne Harnish, was the MC. There, I learned about the One Page Strategic Plan and the specifics of tactical execution.

Verne's work showed me and my leaders the foundation to create the Compound Growth System. Every quarter, we dialed in tactical execution

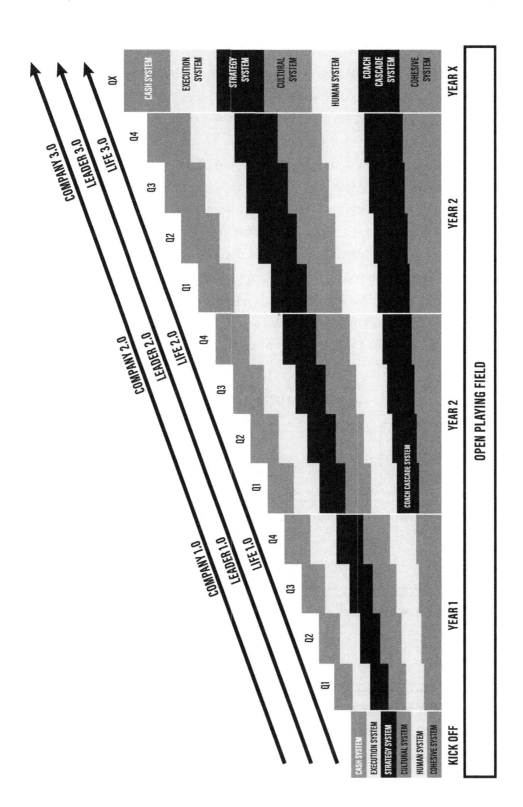

more and more—and learned more and more together. We knew we needed to go beyond execution. We learned about Culture, Cohesion, Human, Strategy, Cash, and Coach Cascade Systems to create the seven connected systems that became a practical and efficient way to grow a company.

When we sold our first company, the company that bought it adopted the Compound Growth System. This time it worked well in an even larger business, four hundred people. We validated the system in my second company from day one by growing up over 12 quarters and then selling the company for an exponential valuation based on our first 3HAG.

The Compound Growth System worked. CEOs started calling me to coach their CEO+Leadership teams to implement the system. It worked for them too. Coaches started seeking me out to learn the system and use it to coach their own clients. It worked for them too.

I *know* it will work for you and your leadership team.

QUARTER BY QUARTER, SYSTEM BY SYSTEM

2 Day Kick-Off

YEAR 1
FOUNDATION: Kick-Ass Execution and Cash with Aligned Strategy
Quarterly   Quarterly   Quarterly   2 Day Annual

YEAR 2
MOMENTUM: Work on the Business, Not in the Business
Quarterly   Quarterly   Quarterly   2 Day Annual

YEAR 3
COMPOUNDING: Grow Up and Out—It's All About Your Behavior!
Quarterly   Quarterly   Quarterly   2 Day Annual

However, you should know that it will *only* work if you have the willingness and desire to commit to evolving your behavior and your goals day by day, week by week, quarter by quarter, and year over year.

The good news? Willingness and desire are all that you need.

Are you ready to kick it off?

The quarter-by-quarter progress is an overview of how to implement Metronomics with your team. This book is intentionally prescriptive and specific. It shows you how to take each separate step.

The good news is that every step of the way leverages the foundation you have in your company today.

In the next chapter, I'll guide you through the 2-day Kick-Off Meeting that gets you and your team a Baseline Gutted-Out Growth Plan to start this remarkable progressive regimen that will grow with you and your team.

CHAPTER 2

GUT IT OUT: THE KICK-OFF

Alex wondered if it was too late to cancel the meeting.

It was a few months since he had contacted Lee, the Metronomics coach. When he agreed that he and the leadership team would attend a 2-day Kick-Off Meeting, he had warned her that it would be difficult to find two days when all six of them were free.

In fact, it turned out to be Lee who was the problem. Her calendar was so full that he was determined to grab the first available slot.

Now it was nearly here, and Alex was nervous. He'd spoken to Lee on the phone and was excited. She was a firecracker, and he knew that if anyone could get them unstuck it would be Lee. Already she was exploding with great ideas that Alex couldn't wait to share with his leadership team.

But they were not all excited, frankly.

He'd had to make Daniel, his CTO, shift a couple of off-site meetings to take advantage of Lee's window. Daniel made it clear that he was not happy. Andrew, the VP of Sales, kept popping into Alex's office with random questions about the purpose of the meeting. What was Lee going to tell them to do?

Chris, the CMO, was just as nervous. "Are you trying to shake things up?" he asked. It was obvious that he was concerned about his job.

That was the last thing Alex had intended. He wanted to take everyone forward together, but they didn't seem to understand that. It was frustrating that he didn't seem to be able to communicate with them effectively anymore.

And now the meeting was tomorrow. Kick-Off time.

Of course, he couldn't cancel. That didn't stop his lying awake at night, however. He wasn't sure whether it was because he was nervous about the team—or whether he was too excited. From the moment he had first spoken with Lee, he had felt better about the future.

She had told him, "You've done a great job getting your company this far. I know you feel stuck. But I also know that I can help you and your team move forward."

He could still remember the firmness in her voice.

All Alex heard these days in the voices of his leadership team—and his own voice—was hesitation and nervousness, a feeling that they did not know where they were going, how, or even why.

It was refreshing to hear someone with such confidence.

Tomorrow's meeting would set in motion everything OpenDoor needed to grow as he knew it could. And Lee had also promised that she would help him develop a structure that would allow him to spend more time with Lisa and the girls, work fewer hours, and regain the excitement and energy he'd felt when he started the company 10 years earlier.

Alex tried to stay patient. The first thing would be to get the leadership team onboard.

And he had to bring them along.

It might ruffle some feathers, but at this stage, Alex was ready to try anything. He wanted OpenDoor to grow, he wanted a life outside of work, and he wanted his leadership team to be excited and working together to put a cohesive strategy into action.

The next morning, Alex could barely eat his breakfast. Lisa watched him and squeezed his shoulder. "Don't worry," she said. "It can't be worse than it already is."

That's right, thought Alex, as he walked into the Kick-Off Meeting. It can't be worse. At the very least, we'll walk out with what Lee calls a Baseline Gutted-Out Growth Plan.

All eyes were on Alex as he introduced Lee to his team.

The first thing she did was ask each team member 5 questions designed to give Lee a sense of what they believed their functional roles were in the company, what they believed they were accountable for, and understanding how they measured success:

1. What's your name?
2. How long have you been with the company?
3. What is your functional role, not your title?
4. What is the number one thing you are accountable for?
5. How do you measure success in your role?

Next, Lee asked questions everyone could answer easily, such as "Where were you born?" and "What number child are you, and out of how many?" and "Describe a memorable event from your childhood under 12 years of age." Lee answered first and then Alex. She already told him that the questions were the foundation of the Cohesive System and started a great journey of team trust. Alex could see that some of the leaders weren't comfortable with talking about themselves. They work together, he thought. It doesn't mean they want to be friends.

As Lee took a few moments to introduce herself further, talking more about her family, schooling, training, hobbies, and passions and how she was once an exhausted and stressed CEO before developing Metronomics and the coaching system she now used, Alex looked around, trying to get a read on his team. Chris, his CMO, Jen, his COO, and Andrew, VP of Sales, were learning forward in their seats and hanging onto Lee's words.

Good, he thought to himself, knowing he'd made the right decision hiring Lee. At least some of the team members were as eager as he was to hear what she had to say. He was sure they knew as he did that this new start or reset would take the company forward.

But then he saw Alison and Daniel sitting farther back. It was hard to tell for sure because a seat blocked his view, but Alison was looking down and seemed to be reading her phone. Daniel drummed his thumb on the arm rest like he was bored. Alex didn't know why he'd expected them to act differently, why he'd expected they would stop thinking the company was doing fine and didn't need a plan, why he thought they would suddenly come around and be ready to evolve and eager to participate.

No, he thought. He did know. They had been with him from the start, and he really, *really* wanted them to feel the same excitement he did—because then he wouldn't feel that perhaps he'd made a mistake hiring them in the first place.

But if they didn't stop holding everyone back, that would force him to choose between his loyalty to Alison and Daniel on the one hand and the company on the other.

He desperately wanted to avoid that choice.

Determined to make this work, he refocused on Lee as she discussed what they would cover in their next two days together, how companies and organizations who had gone through this process continued to grow and achieve or surpass their goals, quarter after quarter, year after year. Why? Because their clarity, focus, and ability to work together as a team had gotten better with time.

Alex couldn't wait to get down to work. Even Alison and Daniel seemed to pay a little more attention when Lee introduced the Organizational Function Chart and the Key Function Flow Map (KFFM). Together, they laid out clearly the functional positions within OpenDoor and who owned which function and then mapped out graphically how the functions worked together to make money, with the owners of each function displayed clearly on the map along with the things that flowed through the map, the widgets.

The team was excited to see their organization depicted in such a clear, simple way. The owners of the functions couldn't help but feel proud to see clearly how they contributed to the company's success.

From there, Lee moved them on to their Core Purpose and their 10- to 30-year goal, which Jim Collins calls the Big Hairy Audacious Goal, the BHAG™.

The BHAG provides a company their North Star. It maps out where the company wants to end up in 10 to 30 years' time.

Jen, the COO, and Andrew, the VP of Sales, immediately pushed back. Thirty years was ridiculous, they protested. Even a 10-year forecast was nothing but a guess. Surely, none of them would even be at the company ten years from now. They were truly uncomfortable with the idea of creating a goal that might be impossible to achieve.

Lee reassured them that was fine. It didn't have to be perfect, she said. Frankly, it couldn't be, anyway.

"From your gut, write down where you believe the company will be in ten or more years with a sharpie on a post-it note. You don't have to think it all through. Just gut it out! It's okay! There are no wrong answers, just great discussions."

She urged them, "Don't worry. It will be good enough for right now."

Jen and Andrew looked bemused but seemed to accept what she said—but Daniel and Alison made a big sigh and pulled faces as they wrote down their best guess. Everyone shared their BHAG statements, then discussed them until they came up with the best one they could all agree on for now. This was good enough for now.

Then they used the same process to set their 3HAG.

At the end of the day, Lee asked Alex, "How do you think your leadership team performed?"

"I'm not sure what's going on with Alison and Daniel, and I'm so sorry they gave you a hard time."

"Oh, that's okay. How long has this been going on?" Lee asked.

Alex crossed his arms. "They're high performers and they achieve their numbers. They've always delivered."

Lee nodded. "Yes, but you're here to grow your company, and you've got two members of your leadership team who don't seem to be bought into the team."

Alex thought for a minute before replying, "I know. I've actually known this for a while."

"I understand," Lee said. "These things aren't easy, especially when they've been a part of your team for so long. But these are the things we need to address if we are going to grow the team and the company."

"Okay," Alex said. "I get it."

"Good. I have some homework for you. It's an A-Player Leadership Team Assessment, and it should put things more into perspective and help you with your decision-making process and action plan."

"Sounds good," Alex said. "I'll start on it first thing tomorrow morning."

2-DAY KICK-OFF

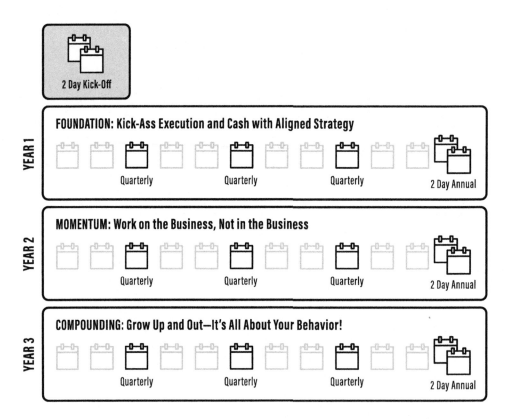

The key objective of the 2-day Kick-Off is to get the CEO and leadership team aligned:

- Aligned to the Core Purpose of their 10-plus year goal (BHAG)
- Aligned to their 3HAG
- Aligned to their 1HAG

- Aligned to corporate 90-day priorities (QHAG)
- Aligned to the individual team members

The team is excited to have this clarity, as they have never before all felt that they were on the same page, seeing the same path forward. Achieving this visible company alignment allows the team to agree on the plan and start to work on the team development. This will create a great foundation and an arena for significant discussions on moving the company forward.

It's just the Kick-Off, but it includes starting or restarting all six systems in the Compound Growth System.

PREPARATION FOR THE MEETING

There's always preparation or homework before each meeting. It helps make the meeting day itself far more effective in less time. Have your leadership team—and yourself—prepare for the Kick-Off Meeting like this:

1. Everyone should have read my book *Metronomics* or watched the introduction video at *www.metronomicsthebook.com*. This usually happens well in advance of the meeting as this is how the team has decided to schedule and complete the Kick-Off Meeting.

2. Everyone attending the meeting should review the current business plan in whatever state it is in. If you are working with a coach, send it to the coach to review.

3. Have all attendees fill in the Kick-Off Preparation Survey. Send this survey out to the leadership team at least 10 days before the meeting, and share the results with everyone, including the coach, prior to the start of the meeting. Completing the Preparation Survey allows each individual leader to consider and reflect on the Kick-Off Meeting and to start preparing for the transformation on which they are embarking. It will also give them the ability to share their

STAY FOCUSED ON WHERE WE ARE GOING

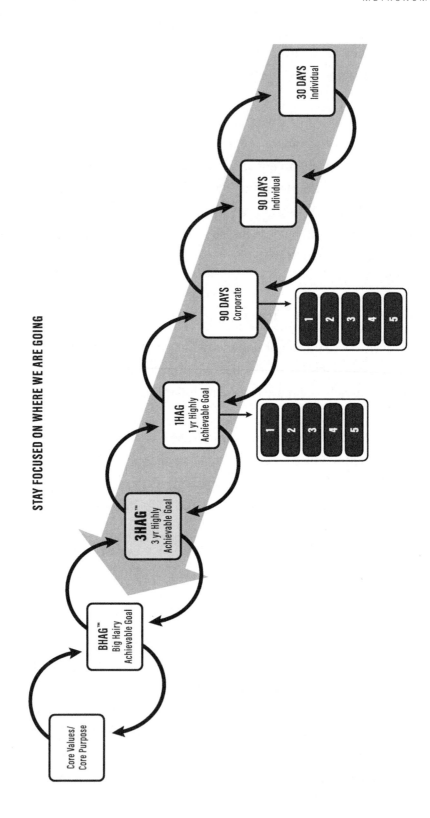

thoughts with the other leaders prior to the meeting. This is a key step. It saves so much time in the meeting, encourages attendees to prepare well, and gives you a way to understand individuals' current thinking. These surveys can be found as templates in the Meeting area of the Metronome software or as downloadable templates at *www. metronomicsthebook.com.*

KICK-OFF DAY 1: STRATEGY

AGENDA

Compound Growth System	Day 1
Cohesive System	• Intros, including functional questions • Good news • Where were you born et al questions
Human System	• Organizational Function Chart • KFFM
Cultural System	• Core Purpose • Core Values • BHAG™: Gut It Out
Strategy System	• 3HAG™: Gut It Out

The Kick-Off sets the stage for your journey on the Compound Growth System. Over the two days, you will turn on 6 of the 7 systems to start the journey.

The first day looks as if it is mainly focused on strategy. You'll cover 4 of the 7 systems, starting with the Cohesive System, and the key objective is to end the day with the Cohesive, Human, Cultural, and Strategy Systems turned on with a Gutted-Out 3HAG.

You'll notice as you read through this book, by the way, that every meeting follows the same structure. That way, we can be sure that we're progressing and balancing each system and ensuring we are building on where we are every time we meet.

The idea behind "Gut It Out Is Good Enough" is to get your team to a place each time that is a good enough platform to take the next step. If we try for perfection in any one of these areas, we will never get any forward momentum. (And what is *perfect* anyway, right?)

The work you do with your team just needs to be good enough. Lots of teams have trouble with this concept at first, but they slowly come to understand that iterative progression rather than perfection is key to the success of Metronomics.

COHESIVE SYSTEM

Every meeting begins by working to evolve the cohesiveness of the team. It's the best way to keep team cohesion alive all the time, rather than pushing it once a year at an offsite or a retreat.

Introductions

Introductions are unique to the Kick-Off. We start with introductions to learn more about each other and about each individual's view of their roles, their accountabilities, and how they measure success.

1. What's your name?
2. How long have you been with the company?
3. What is your functional role, not your title?
4. What is the number one thing you are accountable for?
5. How do you measure success in your role?

This is done in a round-robin format with each leader answering each of the 5 questions. This is a great way to understand the current level of functional clarity, accountability, and measurable success in the company.

Good News

Good News is a great way for team members to recognize other team members for living the Core Values and achieving company goals. This is accomplished in a round-robin format with each leader taking 5 to 10 seconds to share the Good News.

Get used to it. Every meeting starts with Good News—and there's going to be lots of it! Good News allows every meeting to start by connecting with the team, recognizing others, celebrating wins, and ensuring that the day opens on a positive note.

Five Dysfunctions Framework

Each quarterly and annual meeting will include an individual or team assessment exercise, in which you and the leadership team explore your own work style and each other's. The fastest-growing leaders have a strong sense of self-awareness and team awareness. There are thousands of assessments out there, and we'll leverage the best to keep our awareness and growth high.

In the Kick-Off, I always use these adapted questions from Pat Lencioni's *Overcoming the Five Dysfunctions of a Team* framework. They're a great way for the team to get to know one another without much effort. Most business teams do not know much about the other team members. Understanding where teammates come from is key to developing a highly cohesive team.

1. Where were you born?
2. What number child are you out of how many?
3. Describe a memorable event from your childhood under the age of 12.

If you are working with a coach, they will go first, followed by the CEO. Then you have a round robin of everyone at the meeting.

HUMAN SYSTEM

At every meeting, we will review and update the Organizational Function Chart that we've adapted and simplified from Verne Harnish's *Mastering the Rockefeller Habits*. And we will review and update the Key Function Flow Map (KFFM). The KFFM is the foundation of everything.

3HAG™: ORGANIZATIONAL FUNCTION CHART

Functional Role	Name
Head of Company	Alex
Marketing	Chris
Sales	Andrew
Operations	Jen
Development	Daniel
Finance	Alison
Treasury	Alison Alex
Controller	Alison
HR/Learning/People	Alex Alison Daniel Chris Andrew
Information Technology	Daniel
Customer Success	Jen

Adapted from Rockefeller Habits

Organizational Function Chart

The key to the Organizational Function Chart is to ensure we have identified the top-level functions that exist in your company. They might include Sales, Marketing, Manufacturing, Finance, People/Learning, and IT, to name a few. We give them names that make sense—they can be as simple as those I just listed—and we make sure we understand who owns what function. In many cases, owners have many functions or one function has many owners; there may be functions with no owners. This simple chart provides great clarity to every team I work with. It seems simple, but the first time we go through it also provides a great in-depth discussion as the team gets clarity about these functions.

All you're trying to do is gain clarity about where you are today.

Key Function Flow Map (KFFM)

The KFFM is a simple graphical representation of how your company makes money.

It shows the nonfiscal things that flow through each of the functions of your company in order for you to put cash in the bank.

The KFFM is the foundation of everything because it ties so much together in one great active view. It is a live scoreboard that gets updated daily so the whole team can see if the company is winning or losing.

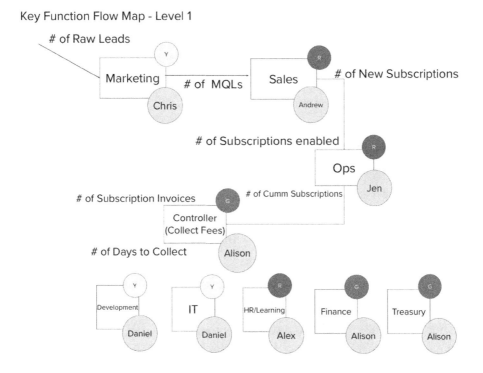

Key Function Flow Map - Level 1

The KFFM is simple to build. The first step is to identify all the high-level functions in your business with their associated accountable person. From the list of functions in your Organizational Function Chart, identify the 3 to 5 key functions that are involved in making the company money. Once you've identified them, draw them in the order of how things flow through each function. Resist the temptation to get too detailed. Stay very high level. Keep it to the key functions only.

You may well look at the KFFM and think, "What's the big deal? Why are we doing this now, and is it really the foundation of everything?"

Well, here are 10 reasons to create an active KFFM—and to do it *now*:

1. It provides functional clarity for your business.
2. It identifies clearly who owns each key function in your business.
3. It's a way to measure a daily score for your business in real time.
4. It allows functional owners to easily share the key challenges or celebrate the wins in their functional area.
5. It provides a strong foundation for nonfiscal forecasting in your business.
6. You can use it as a foundation to design forward.
7. You can use it to design deeper into the organization in a connected way.
8. It represents each functional Scorecard.
9. You can create a 36-month forecast based on the nonfiscal things that flow through the KFFM.
10. It provides a visible score for the whole company every day to make better decisions sooner.

That's why we are creating our very first KFFM now. It will evolve and iterate as we grow forward in the system.

The KFFM is not just a view for small companies. It works for all companies, from small to huge. The KFFM is one of the best ways to connect the business systems to individual team members every day, so it makes a significant contribution to developing a high-performing team.

I have to confess that I didn't do the KFFM justice in my first two books. It may not seem like it right now, but as we progress you will see that it connects to every system in the Compound Growth System and in the team and to their impact on the Open Playing Field. The KFFM will become the live, owned scoreboard of your business. It's what shows day by day whether the team is winning or losing. It will empower them to make better, faster decisions together.

That has to be good, right?

The map will contain the 3 to 5 key functions you identified from the Organizational Function Chart that make the company money. It will specify the owners of the functions, as well as the things that flow in and out of each function. These are the widgets.

A reminder: a widget is a thing that flows through your company that is controlled and owned by a team member.

CULTURAL SYSTEM

The key to bringing the Cultural System into focus is to take the first steps in establishing the cultural foundation I described in the last chapter by getting the team members to confirm or gut out their Core Purpose and their BHAG.

Core Purpose

Most companies have a mission statement or a Core Purpose. And in most companies, they're outdated or they're too long or no one can remember them.

If you have a mission statement or a Core Purpose, we'll acknowledge it. A good check with the team is to see if they actually know it without looking it up. If they do—go to the next agenda item. If not—let's create a new one without looking at the one no one remembers. Let's gut out a new and more succinct Core Purpose. We do that by answering the question, "Why does your organization exist?"

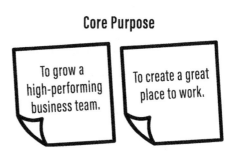

Core Purpose

To grow a high-performing business team.

To create a great place to work.

The answer is rarely, if ever, financial. If you ask a group of people to identify Disney's Core Purpose, for example, they won't say, "To make billions of dollars." They'll say, "To make people happy."

A Core Purpose that is identified, clear, and known ensures consistent belief throughout the organization.

We find it by asking each leader to gut out what they believe the Core Purpose should be by writing it down on a post-it note. We share each leader's post-its with the whole team and then have a full discussion and agree on the one that is good enough for now to proceed.

Core Values

If the company has Core Values of any sort, we acknowledge them—but we don't do any work on them *yet*. Most of the time, the Core Values that exist in a company are out of date, or are brand values, or have to be looked up because no one remembers them.

It might seem strange that we are not going to work on Core Values now, beyond acknowledging what the company has or doesn't have, but I see it like this: the Core Values already exist in your company, so we don't have to discover them today. They exist and they are active. They may not be clear to everyone, but that will come. We really need to concentrate on getting the end-to-end baseline plan mapped out to help team alignment, get some forward momentum, and see the path forward. We will come back to Core Values later. Core Values are foundational.

Big Hairy Audacious Goal

Creating a BHAG—the name Jim Collins gives to an exciting and compelling 10- to 30-year goal—may seem ridiculous. Many people scoff at the idea, and most companies do without one. But without a BHAG, you have no idea where you're going. It's like being on a bus with no destination in mind. How can you make decisions or know which way to turn?

A BHAG motivates your team. A great BHAG aligns your team. Gutting out the company's 10-plus-year goal is key to getting the team aligned today and in the future. Your aim is to have each leader gut out—write down individually—what they think the BHAG should be *without numbers*. Each leader will share their idea. A great discussion will take place, and then you'll lock in on the one that everyone agrees on for now.

Be sure the BHAG does not have any numbers in it. The purpose of the BHAG is team alignment. I've tried all types of BHAG with my companies, and from my experience a BHAG with no numbers is easiest for a team to believe in, align to, and drive toward with every decision they make every day. If the company already has a BHAG at the start of the Kick-Off, we will work through it to confirm or evolve it.

BHAG EXAMPLES

| Every book, ever printed, in any language, all available in less than 60 seconds. | A computer on every desk and in every home. | Crush Adidas. | Leading global payment service provider. |

Profit/X

Profit/X is a term coined by Jim Collins as part of his Hedgehog Concept. The Hedgehog, as shared in Jim's book *Good to Great*, brings together 3 overlapping concepts: a company's Core Purpose, its core business, and the economic engine of the core business. Jim's research showed that these overlapping concepts provide the one big thing that great companies focus on, like a hedgehog. It might sound silly, but the companies that focus on one big thing, one hairy audacious goal, are most likely to achieve it and become great companies.

The Profit/X term represents the company's economic engine and how to measure success. How the company will make money. It's basically a way to ensure that companies can make money at their core business. The Profit/X is a way to measure your BHAG. At this stage, the best "X" we have will come from the work we've done on the KFFM. It's worth identifying a few "X"s while we are very early in the process of confirming the BHAG and identifying the company "X."

The key objective of the Kick-Off with regard to the Cultural System is to get a foundation visible and activated. It's going to be the basis of many great discussions to come.

STRATEGY SYSTEM

With all the base foundational pieces in place, it's time to move onto a key piece of Metronomics. It's the glue that brings together the long term, near term, and now: the 3 Year Highly Achievable Goal (3HAG). The 3HAG flows through every system in the company and keeps them all connected. It's where strategy, execution, and cash stay aligned and relevant.

The afternoon of the first day of the Kick-Off is one of my favorite times as a coach. This is when we gut out the company's 3HAG for the first time (this is Step 1 in my book *3HAG WAY*).

Don't be misled by the diagram: we are only going to take the first step. (And we've already covered Foundation 1, 2, and 3 in the morning in the Cultural System.)

Before we get going, ensure that all team members understand the same definition of strategy. I use the definition given by Michael Porter:

Strategy is "the creation of a unique and valuable position, involving a different set of activities."

STRATEGIC ANALYSIS AND EXECUTION
MICHAEL PORTER

```
Industry (External)
Analysis  ─────┐
               ▼
          ┌──────────┐        Strategy        ┌──────────┐
          │ Strategic │       · Scope          │          │
          │ Evaluation│ ───▶  · Positioning ──▶ │ Execution │
          │          │       · Stance          │          │
          └──────────┘        · Fit            └──────────┘
               ▲              · Logic
Firm (Internal)─┘
Analysis
```

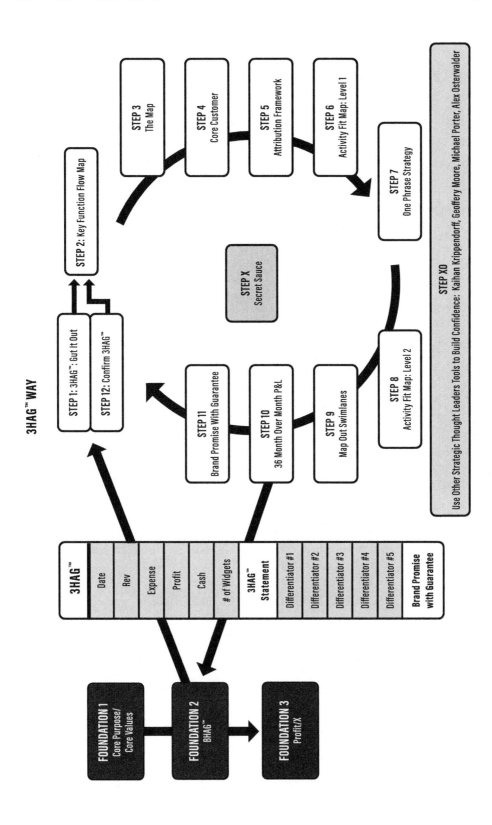

Once you've agreed on a definition of strategy, we look at Porter's view on Strategic Analysis and Execution, which we started to follow in my first company.

We found that Porter's analysis and evaluation only went in one direction, however, and that was not realistic to the speed at which markets were evolving in the late 1990s. We knew we needed feedback from the team executing in the market in order to continuously create and evolve our strategy aligned to execution.

STRATEGIC ANALYSIS AND EXECUTION
3HAG™ WAY EVOLVED

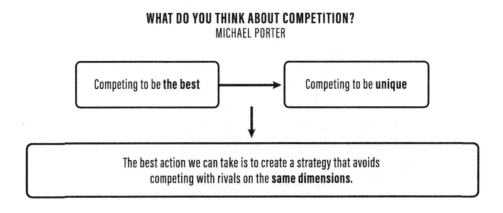

In our Strategy System, we evolved Porter's process from a less dynamic to a highly interactive process where the arrows go both ways, creating a flow of information to ensure the strategy is aligned to the execution plan and vice versa.

WHAT DO YOU THINK ABOUT COMPETITION?
MICHAEL PORTER

| Competing to be **the best** | → | Competing to be **unique** |

The best action we can take is to create a strategy that avoids competing with rivals on the **same dimensions.**

Michael Porter's work was impactful in resetting our views on strategy in another way. We had always assumed we were competing to be the *best*, like a sports team. Porter showed us that, as a business team, we should be competing to be *unique*!

The best thing we could have done was to create a strategy that would put us in our own unique, valuable dimension. If you're in your own dimension, you avoid competition with your rivals.

This revelation completely evolved our approach. (To dive deeper into this, read *3HAG WAY* or any of Michael Porter's work.)

One Word

The afternoon kicks off with you asking each of the team to write down and then share one word that represents their company's current strategy. It is asked in a vague way on purpose. The answers are likely all over the place. That's to be expected as most teams are not aligned on strategy—yet!

THE 3HAG™: GUT IT OUT

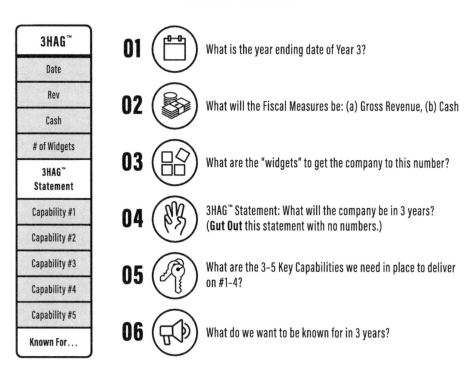

3HAG: Gut It Out

The team is keen and excited about their first 3HAG. This is when they learn the not-so-subtle art of "gutting it out."

Work through the questions in the diagram on the previous page in order. Have each leader write down their answers, then share them together. For each question, the goal is to collaborate to agree upon a "good enough" answer.

01	What is the year ending date of Year 3?	December 31, 2023
02	What will the Fiscal Measures be: a) Gross Reveue, b) Cash	· Gross Revenue: $30M · Cash in the Bank: $2M
03	What are the "widgets" to get the company to this number?	· New subscriptions: 12,000 · Cummulative subscriptions: 30,000
04	3HAG Statement: What will the company be in 3 years? (GUT OUT this statement with no numbers.)	To Be the Leading North American Messaging Platform.
05	What are the 3–5 Key Capabilities we need in place to deliver on 1–4?	· Highly Available Platform · 24x7 Support · Support Any Message Type · Easy Setup of a Subscriber
06	What do we want to be known for in 3 years?	Making Messaging Easy

The key idea is to gut it all out. Draw a line in the sand and start from there. As the saying goes, "You got to start somewhere"—and whatever the team guts out will be a great place.

Most teams are uncomfortable at this stage. They're uneasy as to how to deliver. At the same time, they feel good that they have had a full discussion of things people often talk vaguely about in the company and that everything is now clearly laid out in front of them. So even if the team members are uneasy, they will be humanly motived to validate the 3HAG.

That's the beauty of the gutted-out 3HAG. The team won't want to be wrong, so they will work together to make it right and to validate the fiscal numbers and widgets. The widgets are the things the company needs to create in order to achieve the fiscal numbers forecasted in the 3HAG.

For example, the widgets mentioned previously are:

- New Subscriptions: 12,000
- Cumm. Subscriptions: 30,000

Widgets are what link the plan to the team members: they make the system as human as it gets. No individual or team wants to be wrong. Once the 3HAG is written down, it sparks everyone on the team to find a way to validate it, evolve it, and achieve it.

OUTCOMES

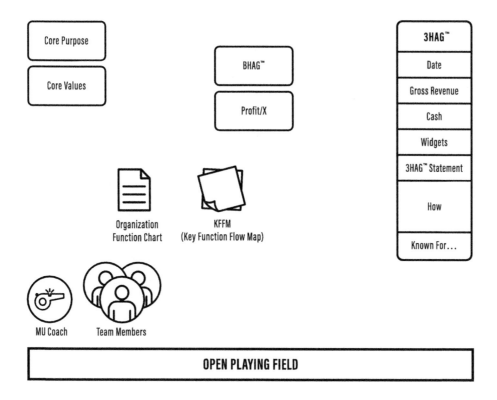

Wow. That was quite a day. But it was so rewarding!

The team is excited to have a great view of the KFFM, including a widget or two, plus a gutted-out BHAG and a 3HAG. They've never had such a clear view of the future as you've just put together (the KFFM is always one of the clear highlights of the day for leaders). This outcome will set them up perfectly for Day 2, which is all about creating a prioritized Execution Plan aligned to where they are going.

KICK-OFF DAY 2: EXECUTION

AGENDA

Compound Growth System	Day 2
Cohesive System	• Day 1 Reflections
Execution System	• 1HAG • QHAG • Aligned Individiual Priorities • Meetings • Cascade 3 Key Messages
Cash System	• Identify Company Widgets • Understand Current "Budget" to Actual
Coach Cascade System	• n/a

Day 2 is all about execution. It ensures that everyone understands the agreed company priorities, metrics, and owners, and focuses on them by setting up a regular meeting cadence to ensure the plans you created on Day 1 are achieved.

The focus is on the 1HAG, the corporate annual plan that sets priorities and metrics, and the QHAG, the corporate 90-day plan that also includes aligned priorities and metrics. The priorities and metrics will have clear owners and understood outcomes.

COHESIVE SYSTEM

The day starts by asking all attendees to share personal Good News. This is a great way to learn more about the team and each other. It's also a great idea to ask each team member to think for a minute to come up with and share one reflection from the day before.

EXECUTION SYSTEM

1HAG

The rest of the morning is spent with the team working toward a 1HAG. You'll work through the same basic process at every annual meeting, and you'll keep the 1HAG aligned by reviewing and updating it as needed at every quarterly meeting. This will become a familiar process, and you and your team will get very good at it.

Start by working through the following questions:

1. What is your *gross* revenue for the upcoming fiscal year?

2. How much cash will be in the bank on the last day of the year?

3. How many of what—think widgets—do you need to deliver in order to ensure that answers #1 and #2 are correct?

4. Who owns revenue, cash, and the widgets? Put the name beside each number for clarity of ownership and accountability.

5. What is the #1 Corporate Priority that the company must accomplish in order to ensure the numbers are achieved and to line the company up nicely to move four quarters closer to its 3HAG? Each leader answers this question individually and then shares their answer with the team. The team has a full discussion in order to agree on the #1 Corporate Priority. That priority should be specific, measurable, achievable, realistic, and timely. A priority that is written well is one that allows everyone to know clearly when and why to celebrate its achievement.

6. What are the other Corporate Priorities for the company, from #2
through #5? Use the same process, with each leader writing down
what they think individually, then sharing with the team to agree on
the order. (When it comes to company priorities, fewer is better. This
allows the company to "do less and obsess," as Morten T. Hansen so
eloquently shared in his book Great at Work.)

7. Once the Corporate Priorities are agreed on, ask who owns each one,
from #1 through #5. The best practice is that each priority should only
have one owner—and, frankly, fewer priorities are better. That way,
the team can obsess over the most important priorities to move the
company forward.

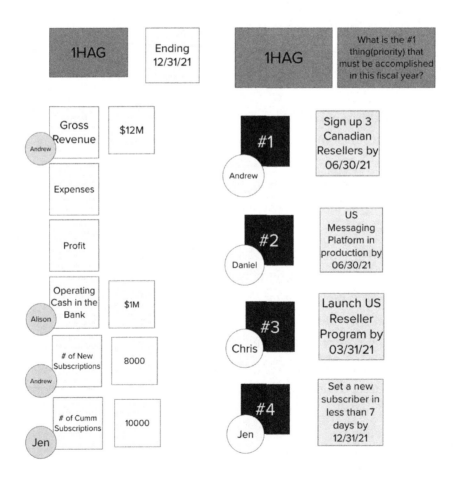

QHAG (*90 Day Corporate Plan*)

The afternoon is spent with the team working through a similar set of questions to establish the QHAG, the company's 90-day plan. Again, this basic process is repeated at every quarterly meeting to keep the QHAG aligned, so again, you'll get very familiar with it and good at it.

1. What is your *gross* revenue for the quarter? (Preferably show this month over month, with a quarterly total.)

2. How much cash will be in the bank on the last day of the quarter? (Preferably show this month over month.)

3. How many widgets do you need to deliver in order to ensure that answers #1 and #2 are correct for the quarter?

4. Who owns revenue, cash, and the widgets? Put the name beside each number for clarity of ownership and accountability.

5. What is the #1 Corporate Priority that the company must accomplish for the quarter to ensure the numbers are achieved and line the company up nicely to their 1HAG? Each leader answers this question individually and then shares their answer with the team. The team has a full discussion in order to agree on the #1 Corporate Priority.

6. What are the other Corporate Priorities for the company, from #2 through #5? Use the same process, with each leader writing down what they think individually, then sharing with the team to agree on the order. Remember, fewer is better for the focus of the team.

7. Once the Corporate Priorities are agreed, ask who owns each one, from #1 to #5. The best practice is that each priority should have only one owner.

8. Each owner should identify the team responsible to work with them and create a plan to ensure they can achieve the corporate quarterly priority. That way there will be no surprises.

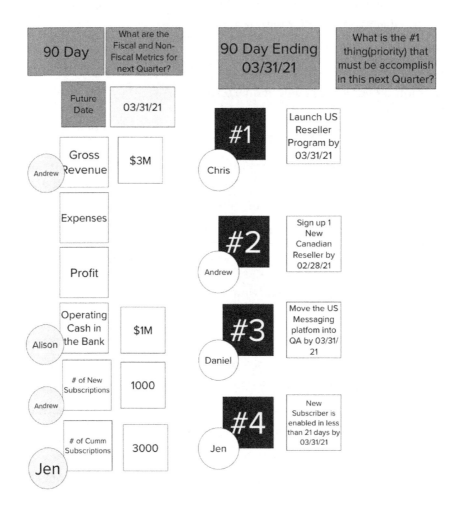

ALIGNED INDIVIDUAL PRIORITIES

Up until now, we've been dealing with Corporate Priorities. When a team member volunteers to own a Corporate Priority, it most likely also becomes their number one individual priority. If they own more than one Corporate Priority, they fall in the same order in their individual priorities as they do for the company. Not all team members will have a Corporate Priority in any given quarter.

If this is the case, the individual should establish what they feel are *their* top priorities that are aligned to the corporate 90-day priorities. In the meeting, ask each leader to take the time to write their priorities down and share them.

This is key to understanding how the team thinks about individual priorities and how well they see their alignment to the Corporate Priorities. It also ensures that everything the team members will focus on fits within the Corporate Priorities plan and targeted results.

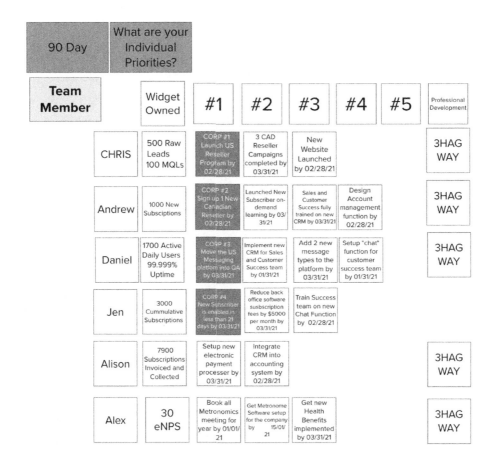

In this example, at the top of the matrix is the team member who owns the #1 corporate quarterly priority. It's the company's #1 priority, and it's the individual's #1 priority too. We can see the individuals responsible for corporate priorities #2 and #3, and so on. We can also see that they may have other individual priorities, and that team members who don't own a corporate quarterly priority have individual priorities the team feels are the best ones for that team member—but always in alignment to the corporate priorities.

This is one of the most enlightening parts of the second day of the Kick-Off. It shows how individual team members align to the corporate quarterly priorities, which align to the corporate annual priorities—which align to the 3HAG.

The compounding—quarterly, annual, 3 years—makes this super powerful.

MEETINGS

Meetings are executional in nature, but they are also tightly tied to the Cohesive System. As I've already mentioned, at every meeting we will evolve the Cohesive System, the Cultural System, and the Human System. We will also focus on strategy, execution, and cash plan, the hard-edge systems.

In most companies, meetings are seen negatively for a whole range of reasons. In Metronomics, meetings are the key to saving team members' time, keeping the team focused, consciously developing cohesiveness and healthy discussions, keeping the culture alive and well, and ensuring that whatever plan is created is focused on and achieved. In order to have an effective and efficient meeting, all team members must prepare beforehand—every time.

TIMING	PURPOSE/TYPE	WHO	HOW LONG?
Daily	Connect Meeting	Leadership Team	15 minutes or less
Weekly	Tactical Meeting	Leadership Team	1 hour or less
Weekly	Email	CEO	1 page
Monthly	Confirm Strategy / 90-Day Execution Plan	Leadership Team	4 hours or less
Monthly	Townhall Meeting	Entire Company	1 hour or less
Quarterly	Confirm Strategy / Plan Execution 90 Days	Leadership Team	8 hours or more
Annual	Strategy Planning Meeting	Leadership Team	2 days offsite

The meeting rhythm has been adapted from *Mastering the Rockefeller Habits* over many years to ensure the most efficient and impactful use of time.

Over the 90 days after the 2-day Kick-Off, the CEO and leadership team will meet once a week for a weekly meeting and on all the other days for a 15-minute meeting, or a daily huddle. Each meeting has a standing agenda, which makes it possible for all attendees to prepare effectively beforehand.

The meetings are effective because the strategic execution plan was developed and agreed upon with the team. The agenda is set up so that the alignment of the six systems in the Compound Growth System to the team develops in every meeting. The standing agendas ensure the Cultural and Cohesive Systems are covered in Good News, the Human and Cash System are covered in the Metrics section, and the Priorities keep a clear focus on the plan and accountability in play. The Dynamic section is where the team members will continue to hone their cohesiveness by sharing stucks, asking for help, or offering help. The discipline of the standing agendas ensures continuous development as a high-performing team by activating the Compound Growth System.

The meeting rhythm and the standing agendas are not a recommendation but a must. I will not coach a client who does not huddle every day utilizing the Open Playing Field. (Chapter 8 of my book *The Metronome Effect* gives a full explanation of each meeting and agenda. The Metronome software also fully supports meetings through consistent scheduling, the recommended standing agenda templates, as a way to prepare for each meeting, and through the execution of the meeting with your team.)

Daily Connect	
Compound Growth System	Topic
Cohesive & Cultural	Good News
Execution	Metrics
Execution	#1 Thing in the Next 24 Hours to complete
Execution	Dynamic: Stucks, Questions

Weekly	
Compound Growth System	Topic
Cohesive & Cultural	Good News
Execution	Metrics/KFFM
Execution	Top 3 Priorities for the Week
Strategy	Feedback: Team, Customer, Partner, Competitor,
Execution	Dynamic: Stucks, Questions

Monthly	
Compound Growth System	Topic
Cohesive & Cultural	Good News
Cohesive	Opening Cohesive Question
Human System	KFFM/Team View
Execution	Metrics
Execution	Review/Celebrate QHAG Plan
Execution	Top 3 Priorities for the Month
Strategy	Feedback: Team, Customer, Partner, Competitor,
Execution	Dynamic: Stucks, Questions
Cohesive	One Phrase Close

Monthly Townhall	
Compound Growth System	Topic
Cohesive & Cultural	Good News
Human System	KFFM/Team View
Execution	Metrics
Execution	Review/Celebrate QHAG Plan
Strategy	Feedback: Team, Customer, Partner, Competitor,
Execution	Dynamic: Stucks, Questions
Human System	Core Value Recognition
Cohesive	One Word Close

Quarterly	
Compound Growth System	Topic
Cohesive	Good News Opening Cohesive Question
Human	Function Chart/KFFM/Team View
Cultural	Core Purpose/Core Values/BHAG
Strategy	3HAG
Execution	Review/Celebrate 1HAG &QHAG New QHAG 3 Message Cascade
Cash	Rolling Widget Based Cash Forecast
Coach Cascade	If ready – follow the progression.
Cohesive	One Phrase Close

Annual	
Compound Growth System	Topic
Cohesive	Good News Opening Cohesive Question
Human	Function Chart/KFFM/Team View
Cultural	Core Purpose/Core Values/BHAG
Strategy	3HAG
Execution	Review/Celebrate 1HAG &QHAG New 1HAG New QHAG 3 Message Cascade
Cash	Rolling Widget Based Cash Forecast
Coach Cascade	If ready – follow the progression.
Cohesive	One Phrase Close

Cascading Messages

At the end of the two days, the best practice is for the leadership team to agree on 3 Key Messages from the meeting. We learned this from a great book of Pat Lencioni's, *The Four Obsessions of an Extraordinary Executive*. The reason is simple. The rest of the team will be curious as to what happened in the 2-day Kick-Off, and it's important that the leadership team shares the same messages about the key events and learnings at the same time. This will keep the team together and excited as we move forward with the plan, but the messages shared by each leader with their teams must be exactly the same. This ensures all team members have the same information at the same time.

It also ensures that the leaders are starting the practice of cascading out messages from meetings to their teams.

One-Phrase Close

These have been two big days for the leadership team, and we want to ensure before we close the meeting that we check in with each team member. Ask each team member in turn, "From your *gut*, how do you feel right now in 5 words or less?" It's a chance to check in with each leader and find out exactly where they are, after having been through this Kick-Off.

CASH SYSTEM

When I'm coaching, before everyone leaves the room at the end of the meeting, I ask for a quick discussion with the person who owns the annual fiscal plan. It's usually the CEO, the chief financial officer, or the director of finance.

I ask them to take the current fiscal forecast or budget, or whatever they call it, and to insert the widgets we've identified in the last couple of days. This is the first step we have to take in order to get clear month over month on what widgets the company needs to deliver in order to achieve the fiscal forecast. It's a reasonability check.

It's unlikely the team doesn't already have a budget or a forecast, but if they don't I ask the person responsible to take the fiscal numbers and incorporate them into a 12-month plan with the widgets shared in the Kick-Off Meeting.

The goal for the cash system at this stage is to get the owner of the forecast or budget comfortable with the idea of widgets and to get them to add widgets to their spreadsheet model. I also want to ask if we can add a simple cashflow calculation to the bottom of the profit and loss statement. The goal is not to make too many shifts to how the team currently forecasts but to get the current model set up to handle widgets and cash. We just want to start the process of evolving the framework we're using to measure our ultimate success. It will progress meeting by meeting.

OUTCOMES

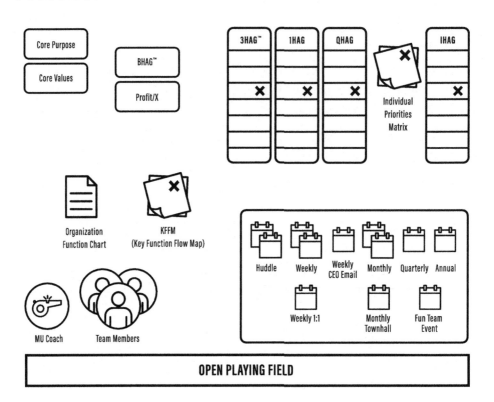

The outcome of the 2-day Kick-Off Meeting is a Baseline Gutted-Out Growth Plan with a lot of foundational components to set the company up for success. All the elements are incorporated on a single page of the Open Playing Field: Core Purpose, BHAG, 3HAG, 1HAG, QHAG; corporate and individual priorities; the Organizational Function Chart and the Key Function Flow Map; and the commitment to the meeting cadence for planned execution and team development.

All the pieces are in place. The important question now is what we do with them.

In the life of most companies, there have been so many great 2-day planning sessions where everyone gets excited about the Best Plan Ever and… nothing ever happens. That is not what will happen with Metronomics. We have now activated each system in Metronomics: Cohesive, Human, Culture,

Strategy, Execution, and Cash—and it is up to the leaders to keep these systems alive through their homework and next steps.

HOMEWORK/NEXT STEPS

No meeting ends when everyone walks out of the room. At the end of every meeting, we spell out the follow-up steps that need to be taken. I like to call this your "homework."

1. **Open Playing Field:** Decide with your team what platform or software you will use to input details of the plan you have created. I've already mentioned that there are many possibilities, but my strong recommendation is to leverage a platform that helps to create the team accountability behavior required to achieve your plan and develop a high-performing team with ease.

2. **Input the Plan:** Input your Gutted-Out Growth Plan into the Open Playing Field you decide to use. Whatever that is, ensure that you and your team can clearly see the alignment in the plan, the ownership, and the metrics, both fiscal and widgets.

3. **Schedule Meetings:** Schedule the daily and weekly meetings, together with weekly 30-minute 1-on-1 meetings with each of your leaders. Recommended best practice is to have one meeting day each week, when you would have your weekly leadership team meeting plus your 1-on-1 weekly meeting with your leaders. This saves time and compresses the focus of the meetings. In my old company, we had meetings on Mondays because it got us fired up and focused for the rest of the week. Then we could go off and do whatever we needed to get done.

4. **Support Meetings:** The Open Playing Field platform you choose may support meetings, so you can schedule them there. This allows

all team members to use the same standing agenda and have the key elements of the plan visible live in every meeting, from metrics to priorities and immediate action items. Supporting your meetings on the platform ensures that you all stay focused on the plan there. At a minimum, it ensures that everyone looks at the plan once a week, although in best practice the team is looking at the plan every day. Think about how that will affect the successful execution of your plan.

5. **Meeting Follow-Through:** Once the meetings are scheduled, it's important to hold the schedule. The CEO and the leaders need to show up for every meeting. They need to be prepared to discuss the plan and to put the brutal facts on the table. They need to be prepared to make better, faster decisions before the quarter runs away from you. Every meeting is an opportunity to improve cohesiveness. That's why every meeting kicks off with Good News.

6. **Leadership:** After the 2-day Kick-Off, the CEO should carry out an A-Player Team Assessment to gain an objective view of each leader and understand if they have a 100 percent A-Player leadership team. This review takes all of 5 to 10 minutes, but it does need a plan of action to follow through on the results. If you're not familiar with an A-Player Team Assessment, you can learn more at *www. metronomicsthebook.com.*

7. **Financial Forecast/Budget:** Make sure the current financial forecast/budget is updated to back in the widgets from the plan created in the 2-day Kick-Off. This is important both to confirm the reasonableness of the plan and to ground it to the things you and your team control in the company.

READING AHEAD

Everyone should read my book *3HAG WAY* to be ready for the first quarterly meeting.

These next 90 days—the first quarter of your 3HAG—are critical to putting some disciplined habits in place for the Strategy System, the Execution System, the Cash System, the Cohesive System, the Human System, and the Cultural System. This quarter is about laying the foundations for and expectations of behavior in the first 90 days, which is important to the success of the first year of implementing Metronomics. That's how you lay a strong foundation of execution and get it cranking well, quarter over quarter, as you move forward and continue to map out a strategy for the organization.

Let's get ready for the next meeting by laying out a strong foundation for Year 1!

YEAR 1:
THE FOUNDATION YEAR

There was no avoiding it. After all Alex's nagging doubts, there it was in black and white.

Alex had done the homework Lee gave him: the leadership team assessment. He placed himself and the others on the graph that depicted A, B, and C players. Only two names fell in a C placement on the graph: Daniel and Alison.

Alex had to face facts. They didn't seem to fit on the team.

Deep down, as the organization grew, he had always known that they didn't fit. Their behavior was not consistent with his own or that of the rest of the team. They preferred to get things done themselves. He'd noticed it in the past, but he'd always told himself that was the price you paid for their consistently great performance.

Every day brought a new reminder that they weren't on board. That they didn't fit. They skipped the daily huddle or didn't engage. If they did engage, the meeting ran way over the allotted 15 minutes because they weren't prepared. Their behavior was clearly not aligned with the rest of the team.

TEAM ASSESSMENT

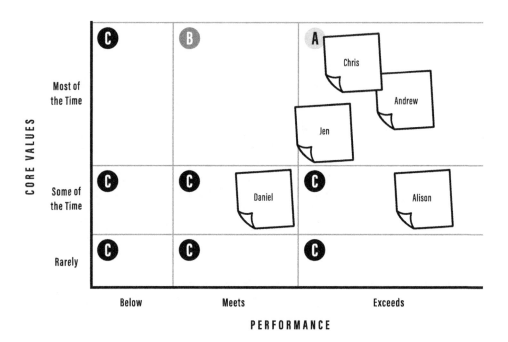

It was holding the others back as well as the team. Alex could see how excited Chris, Jen, and Andrew were to connect with the team, share Good News and their metrics, and the one thing they needed to complete in 24 hours. They came prepared, raised stucks and questions, shared solutions, and knocked through the agenda. At almost every meeting, someone repeated: "Every day is a play."

That was Lee's mantra. She put the daily huddle at the heart of evolving the company's culture and a high-performing business team. Cohesiveness, and focus on outcomes. It was a question of behavior, she told Alex. She refused to coach any company where there wasn't a daily huddle. Teams that connect every day win!

Alex was excited. More than half his leadership team was on board, he reasoned, so he could let things ride. Once they saw the benefits, Daniel and Alison would come on board. They wouldn't be able to resist.

The 2-day Kick-Off had left Alex buzzing. It was months, perhaps years, since the team had had such a strong view of the path to growth. He'd brought home pizza for his family, and after the girls were in bed, he and Lisa had a glass of wine while he talked excitedly about their Core Purpose, their BHAG, and 3HAG.

She said, "It sounds like Lee is just the right person to tell you what you need to do."

Alex said, "That's the thing. She didn't actually tell us anything. She asks great questions, provides recommendations, and explains logical, team-oriented ways to build a team, plan and measure our performance, and then everyone comes up with ideas."

Lisa said, "So are you happy you took Mark's advice and hired a coach?"

Alex said, "I'm kicking myself that I didn't do it sooner. I've already texted to thank him. Listen: 'Mark, you were right. I wasn't crazy to believe the business could grow. I was just working so hard I couldn't see how much I was missing. But now Lee has shown me.'"

"Did he reply?"

"He said, 'Just wait until you build out the Open Playing Field platform further. You won't believe how it brings everyone together.'"

At his first 1-on-1 monthly review with Lee, Alex raved about how energized he and the leadership team felt. They had their BHAG, 3HAG, and 1HAG. They were building out the Open Playing Field platform as she had suggested and checking in on the widgets every day and week, aligned to the month and quarter. They were focused on the plan and evolving their behavior.

Lee told Alex, "That's because you're evolving your own behavior as CEO. You're showing them how to work together. Well done!"

Alex said, "They're each stepping up to take ownership of the company metrics—the widgets. It's amazing. Everyone is so committed without me having to push like I used to."

Lee said, "How about Daniel and Alison? Are they on board?"

"Well, it's taking them a bit longer than the others."

"What's your plan to remove them?"

"Remove them? I don't know if I can. They've been with me for many years. They do things their own way, sure, but they always have. I can't repay their loyalty by removing them."

Lee was quiet. Then she said, "Listen, Alex. In order to achieve your 3HAG, you need a 100 percent A-Player leadership team. That's the biggest barrier for any CEO to grow up their company. By delaying evolution, you will be delaying the achievement of the company's goals. That's why you brought me in. You wanted me to work with you and the team to achieve the goals you set. I would be doing you a great disservice if I didn't strongly recommend you create an A-Player leadership team plan."

As the next monthly meeting approached, Alex felt a familiar gnawing feeling in his stomach. It was how he used to feel all the time. By now, he could see Chris, Jen, and Andrew updating and sharing their progress on the Open Playing Field. He saw at the meetings the behavioral accountability for the Corporate Priorities and metrics. Not only were they owning the widgets; they were all on the same track. But not Daniel and Alison.

On the morning of the meeting, Alex's email dinged: Alison, explaining that she couldn't make it because of an urgent client problem. There were no client issues Alex was aware of, but the message came as no surprise.

Daniel did attend, but before the meeting even started, he dismissed the agenda. "This is always the same. We talked about this stuff yesterday in the huddle, and in last week's meeting. Lee needs to let us set our own agenda. She doesn't know how we work."

Alex said, "The whole purpose of the standing agendas is to allow everyone to focus in on the current priorities and metrics, and those of the rest of the teams, and to be prepared to discuss it all at the meeting. If we stay focused on what we said we would do, we'll achieve as a team. I am convinced of that. These agendas are set up to keep us focused as a team and aligned to our plan."

Alex could see the frustration of the others. Chris wanted to back Alex up but instead looked down at the table, doodling on his pad. Jen was gazing out of the window, hoping the confrontation would go away—and probably Daniel too. She just wanted to get into the meeting and knew it would be better without him, even if she did not have the courage yet to say so. Andrew had apparently found something interesting at the bottom of his coffee cup.

The energy had gone out of the room, and he didn't want to fight Daniel here, even though he knew he should. He was frustrated and exhausted from the constant battle.

With great regret, he abandoned the meeting—but now his mind was made up. When he spoke to Lee next, he said, "I can't go on like this. They're slowing down the team and our progress. Things will be a constant fight, an energy suck, and it won't evolve until they're gone."

Lee said, "I know this is a tough decision, but it's one you will not regret. It won't be pleasant, for sure, so think about what you'll get in return. This will give you the opportunity to put A-Player leaders in the right seats with the rest of the team. One of the big goals of this first year is to ensure we have a strong functional design for the company so that we can put the right players in the right seats at the right time to grow up. A 100 percent A-Player leadership team is a must to achieve that."

Once Alex had made the decision, the weight lifted off his shoulders, although in the pit of his stomach he knew how hard it would be to let people go. He knew he had to be rigorous with his decision and action and to ensure respect was maintained for each of them.

While he was dreading the meetings, in fact, it was easier to give Alison and Daniel the news than he had expected. Neither complained. Alex thanked them sincerely for all their work, but he knew they didn't fit anymore—and so did they. They'd both get other jobs easily.

While Alex started the process of hiring the right people, the rest of the leadership team was as liberated by the shifts as he was. And they quickly pulled together as a team to cover the areas left open by Daniel and Alison.

What a difference the shifts made! Everyone was ready to hit it out of the park.

At their Q2 meeting, Alex enthused to Lee: "Any homework I give them, they do it so fast they ask for more! Not only are they hitting their metrics, they're all aligned. On the Open Playing Field platform, they can see what each other is doing, so they really take pride in reaching their goals sooner and helping the others do the same. They're ready to bring their own teams into the huddles."

Lee smiled. "Slow down, Alex. Behavior doesn't evolve overnight. 99 percent of Metronomics is behavioral, so you all need to be patient—starting with you. One of your most important jobs this year is to be patient with the rollout. Everyone always wants to go faster, but we can only go as fast as the team behavior develops and builds. Get your leaders' understanding and confidence in the Execution System nailed. And align the widgets and cash. Don't miss out on any of the steps. This year's all about building your foundation for growth and endurance by connecting the team and the plan. Get execution cranking, aligned to cash, and with a strategy mapped out like the team has never seen before!"

By Q3, Alex was thrilled. The new CFO and CTO were in place, and they were both A-Players. He told his colleagues at his next YPO forum meeting, "I can't believe how far we've come. I've got so much more time to think about the business now, rather than just firefighting. This time last year, there was no time to get anything done in the office, and I'd come home feeling shattered. I couldn't even start thinking properly about the business until everyone else was in bed."

"Ah yes," said a woman Alex knew ran her own startup. "Strategy in the dark by yourself. Been there, done that."

As so often happened, Alex could see other people nodding in recognition of what he was describing.

That evening, his inbox dinged with a message from Mark, who had also been at the meeting: *Hey, did you book your meetings with Lee for next year? I usually book my meetings with her on a rolling basis so I always have four quarters booked out, no matter what, so I always get the best options on her calendar.*

WTF?

Alex hadn't thought of that, and the message threw him into a blind panic. No way was he going back to trying to do everything himself.

Now those monkeys were off his back, they weren't getting back on.

He fired off an email, then spent a few anxious hours waiting for a reply. He'd rarely felt more relieved than when Lee confirmed the bookings out to the end of the following year.

They laughed about it during their last 1-on-1 of the year. Alex told her, "We're so far ahead of where we were, I can't believe it. I should have gotten a CEO+Leadership team coach years ago. The team members all have their huddles and meetings; we are living it on the Open Playing Field. Everyone is aligned; everyone knows their role and has their own widget. We're a year into our original 3HAG and BHAG, and we all love how they're evolving as we tighten things up.

"I can't believe the success we've had. We're executing better, and revenue and cash are up. But it's not just the numbers. The whole team is working together much better. I finally know that we have a collaborative shared BHAG, 3HAG, and 1HAG. And we own them together!! Everyone can explain it and share it with others. I feel like we're finally starting to make it! At last!"

Lee nodded. "You've had a very good year, for sure. Congratulations!"

"Then why are you smiling?"

"Because even though you've had a great year, there is so much more to accomplish to continue your journey. You have just scratched the surface. You have formed and stormed this with your team, there's no doubt. We are ready to really turn the dials up more next year. You're going to really see what it's like to have the company you dreamed of—and the life you always want to share with Lisa and your family."

Alex thought about that the next morning while he went for his run along the river. He had time to run more regularly now that he wasn't exhausted every day. It helped him stay sharp—and trim. What Lee said was exciting, though he wasn't sure much more improvement was even possible. But it was cause for a small celebration. After he came home, he offered to make breakfast: "Who wants pancakes?"

Lisa said, "Are you sure you have time?"

"Sure. I can get to the office a little later. Everyone knows what they have to do. They're getting on with it."

"I remember when you used to have to go to the office so early you just took a coffee in the car."

"I know. It seems so long ago. Remember how I used to fall asleep on the couch I was so tired? That wasn't why I wanted to be a CEO and grow up a company. Pancakes with my family on a beautiful morning. Now *that's* why I wanted to grow my own business—not so I'd be beholden to it."

YEAR 1: QUARTER BY QUARTER

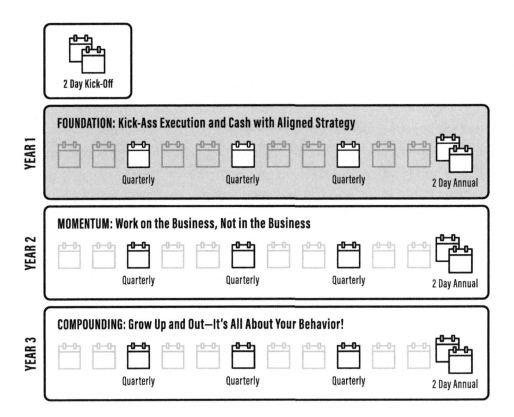

The first year of Metronomics is all about laying the foundation for growth. You're taking your first steps to get the business where you want it to be. You'll see results quite quickly, and there will be times when it will be frustrating. You're going to feel you can go much faster, but you have to resist the temptation. At the end of the day, this is a behavioral system to develop a high-performing business team—and that will take time. This is the year you put in the effort that is going to enable you to reach your 1HAG, your 3HAG, and ultimately your BHAG and give you more time back to work *on* the business rather than *in* the business. But first, you need to set a strong execution foundation with the team.

The focus is on the hard-edge systems of execution and cash. They're the absolute priority. Having the best 3HAG in the world is useless if the business can't execute and doesn't have enough money to survive long enough for it to come into play to execute on your mapped-out strategy.

Even though Year 1 is heavily focused on execution and cash, it won't be a success if you don't also further develop your team's behavior to form a highly cohesive team. You need to end the year with the leadership team tight and cohesive, which will set us up to continue the momentum of Year 1 in Year 2. All the soft-edge and hard-edge systems will continue to be progressed with the team, meeting by meeting.

So, Year 1 is the year of getting kick-ass execution and cash in place, while mapping out your strategy aligned to the 3HAG you gutted out in the 2-day Kick-Off.

The plan for the first year, like our fiscal year, is divided into quarters, with each quarter having a different focus:

- Q1: Clear and accountable leadership
- Q2: Aligned widgets and priorities
- Q3: Forecasting cash and evolving strategy
- Q4: Aligning the 1HAG to the 3HAG

In each quarter, you'll turn the dials of each system a tiny bit, adjusting and refining. In some quarters, we will turn a dial on one system more than the others. By the end of Q4, though, these tiny turns will have allowed the team to evolve in a big way. You will not only have a new 3HAG and a new 1HAG but also a fully developed and mapped-out strategy. Your leaders will have functional clarity, and you'll have a great foundation for spreading Metronomics into the rest of the business.

I would be doing you a disservice if I did not mention again that implementing Metronomics is easier and faster with a CEO+Leadership coach. The quarter-over-quarter timelines I spell out in this book reflect the speed at which a team moves when they have a coach (though it's still only a guide, of course). The Metronomics regimen will meet a team wherever they are, but my experience as both a CEO and a coach is that a coach enables teams to progress at least 3 times faster to develop into a high-performing team and win the game.

If you don't work with a coach, you'll take that role as the CEO. That can be successful, but it does make far more work—which is the opposite of what we're trying to achieve. It also creates some of the very problems you're trying to avoid. Because the CEO is on the Open Playing Field with the team, it's far harder to take in the big picture, see around corners, and remove the blind spots with the same clarity and speed as a coach would.

QUARTER 1: CLEAR AND ACCOUNTABLE LEADERS

This is the first quarter following the 2-day Kick-Off with your leadership team. Everyone is ready to move forward. You've set your company widgets and have had many discussions as to whether they are the right ones. That's all very natural. Your leaders have developed and implemented the meeting schedule of daily huddles and weekly and monthly meetings. The CEO is sending out the weekly email.

By now, the leadership team has input everything into the Open Playing Field platform you're using to create the behavior required for the company's growth. This might be the Metronome software platform or it might be another system, but whatever you choose, the best practice is to make sure that the Growth Plan is aligned, transparent, and visible.

On the Open Playing Field, the aligned one-page view of the plan shows the Core Purpose, the BHAG, 3HAG, and 1HAG Corporate Priorities, and who is accountable for them. The same goes for the QHAG, the 90-day corporate plan, and for the individual priorities from the Kick-Off session. The company metric, the widget you came up with together at the 2-day Kick-Off, is visible and has been aligned and tracked, too, along with the daily and weekly meetings.

It's key that the leaders are looking at the Growth Plan every day to update what they own of the plan and to prepare for each meeting. We have strong data that shows that teams who look at their plan and update it daily on the Open Playing Field achieve their plans sooner and more consistently, year in and year out. Why? Because they are referring back to the plan every day with their team, discussing it regularly while developing their cohesive team behavior, and making better, faster decisions to achieve their goals.

THE FIRST QUARTERLY MEETING

The objective of the Q1 quarterly meeting is to increase functional clarity and improve execution by raising team accountability. Evolving team behavior takes a disciplined focus and effort, so the team needs to get comfortable with these things.

PREPARATION FOR THE MEETING

There's homework before each quarterly meeting. It helps make the meeting day itself far more effective in less time. Have your leadership team—and yourself—prepare for the meeting like this:

1. Everyone should make sure they have finished reading my book *3HAG WAY*.

2. Everyone should ensure the status of the priorities and metrics they own is up to date on the Open Playing Field so everyone can review them prior to the meeting. If they're not, you'll waste time updating the plan in the meeting.

3. All meeting attendees should review the current status of the whole plan. The leaders should make notes and ask questions and be ready to discuss them in the context of building the plan for the next quarter.

4. Two weeks before the meeting, have the leadership team complete the Preparation Survey, with the results being sent out to everyone between 2-5 days before the meeting. The Preparation Survey is a great way to remind your leaders that the planning meeting will take

place in a few weeks and to start to prepare. As we progress with
Metronomics, this preparation will include preparing with their teams,
but for now, leaders will learn how to prepare themselves for each
quarterly meeting. Completing the Preparation Survey individually
allows the leader to consider and reflect on the quarter they'll be
discussing. It will give them the ability to share their thoughts with
the other leaders prior to the meeting and show whether there's
alignment in their views of where they currently are as a team and
how they are executing the plan. This is a key step as it saves so much
time in the meeting, gets attendees to prepare well, and gives you a
way to understand individuals' current thinking. These surveys can be
found as templates in the Meeting area of the Metronome software or
as downloadable templates at *www.metronomicsthebook.com*.

AGENDA

Compound Growth System	Day 1
Cohesive System	• . Good News / Key Objectives • Cohesive Question
Human System	• Organizational Function Chart • KFFM
Cultural System	• Core Purpose • Core Values • BHAG™: Confirm/Evolve
Strategy System	• 3HAG™: Confirm • Market Map
Execution System	• Status Review Annual Plan / QHAG • New Quarterly Plan • Cascade 3 Key Messages
Cash System	• Talk to Finance Leaders to create Annual Widget Based Worksheet
Coach Cascade System	• n/a

The first quarterly meeting can seem like an ordeal. These meetings last a whole day at least, and the agenda can seem overwhelming. Rest assured, it gets easier each quarter as the team gets better at understanding and implementing the process. Like sports practice, this process will become a great team habit as each team member learns how to prepare.

COHESIVE SYSTEM

Good News

Every meeting kicks off with Good News to allow team members to share and recognize great things that are happening in the organization. Do not skip this step. It is key to developing a cohesive team.

Cohesive Question

This is a short discussion to create a personal connection and help to improve team trust. For example, you might ask team members to describe Sunday night dinner at their house when they were growing up (this is adapted from Pat Lencioni's *The Five Dysfunctions of a Team*). It's a round robin, so everyone does it. Round robins always start with the coach and then the CEO.

Self-Awareness Assessment

At every meeting, try to introduce something to evolve the leaders' awareness of themselves as individuals and of the team as a whole. This is key to evolve the self-awareness of each individual team member as well as the team awareness. This speeds up the development of a cohesive team on our Metronomics journey into becoming a high-performing business team.

The assessment I recommend at this stage is one David W. Merrill and Roger Reid published in *Personal Workstyles and Effective Performance*. It's simple but impactful. You can have the attendees complete it in the meeting, and it will lead to an excellent discussion about and understanding of the work style of each leader. There is no right or wrong work style, but this view and discussion highlight the *preferred* communication style for each work style. It uses colors to make each individual aware of their dominant work style and how it compares to those of the others.

I love this view. If there are frustrations among the team, this visual approach helps to explain them and bring awareness to some of the causes. It also provides great guidance for improving communication while everyone works together on the Open Playing Field.

It often also provides a chance for a few laughs—and that's always welcome.

For more info on this assessment, visit www.metronomicsthebook.com to download.

HUMAN SYSTEM

Organizational Function Chart

The next step in the meeting is to review the Organizational Function Chart, as you did in the Kick-Off Meeting. You'll work through this chart at least every 90 days. Why? Because in a high-growth company this allows you to design the functions required to grow the company and understand who is the best person to own each function as you grow forward.

The function chart is a dynamic strategic picture. It will evolve quarter over quarter as you get clearer on what is required to execute your plan for the current year and beyond. It is a key tool to ensure that the whole team, rather than just the leadership team, is clear on who owns what function. This year is about accountability as much as clarity of expectations, so it's critical to review the function chart at least once a quarter from here on in. We will not build it from scratch every time, but every quarter we will discuss and make adjustments as needed. As a CEO, I spent a lot of time with this view designing forward.

If you're in a high-growth situation, I strongly recommend you look at the Organizational Function Chart at least every month. Best Practice is to keep this up in your War Room.

The War Room is where you make visible all the strategic pictures of the components of Metronomics that we create and evolve at each meeting. It's the place where we see the results of our team discussions and plans. The War Room might be a physical space, say on a wall or a virtual space or folder—or both.

*Key Function Flow Map (**KFFM**)*

You'll review the KFFM for the organization and have each leader update the others on how their functions are operating. If you have identified widgets (the inputs and outputs of each function), you can review the actual/forecast. If you have not identified your widgets yet, spend time talking about the things that flow in and out of each function in the KFFM with the leadership team. The KFFM is the foundation of execution: the more intimate, aligned, and known the KFFM is, the clearer your team will be.

The KFFM at this stage is still quite rough, but it is shaping up into a great active map for the company. The KFFM gets clearer with each quarter of the first year—not because we are better at mapping the flow, but because the behavioral ownership of the functions and the widgets in the map progresses as each leader gets better clarity about how to work together as a team.

The KFFM is the active daily scoreboard that all high-performing business teams require.

A-Player Team Assessment

At every 90-day meeting, leaders will assess their direct reports on the A-Player Team Assessment graph for everyone to review and discuss. In this first quarter, we are not able to complete this assessment because we haven't yet discovered or confirmed the team's Core Values. Still, the CEO should have used the A-Player Team Assessment to review the leadership team on their own, even without the clarity given by having defined Core Values. That helps create the speed required to get an A-Player leadership team in place as soon as possible.

CULTURAL SYSTEM

Core Purpose

Quickly review and confirm the Core Purpose from the last meeting, which is visible on the Open Playing Field. If needed, evolve it based on the discussion. Don't get too bogged down, however. Remember: good enough, not perfect.

Core Values

Acknowledge the Core Values you have, or acknowledge that you don't have any yet. You'll work on them in the coming quarters.

BHAG

By this first quarterly meeting, the team has had 90 days to sleep on the BHAG, the 10- to 30-year goal, and decide if they love it or hate it. Maybe they just want to tweak it a bit. Whatever they feel, this is the time to get the feedback, the brutal truths of how the members of the team feel about the BHAG. If it just needs some wordsmithing, take it offline. If it is fundamentally not correct, however, then spend time now getting the next BHAG version in place.

At this point, many teams are still struggling with the idea of "good enough." Don't get caught in the rabbit hole of perfect. The discussion is key. An agreed-upon good-enough view will be enough to progress the team forward.

Let go of perfect. It will always be "good enough."

Make sure that what your team is doing is good enough and keep moving forward. Trying to pursue perfection in any of these steps will bog your team down and stall its forward movement.

Profit/X

Check in on the Profit per X developed at the Kick-Off Meeting. It's really a check in on the "X," the company widget. As we have just completed the second round of reviewing the whole KFFM with the team, we may have a more confident view of what that "X" should be right now. We also just had another discussion on our Big Hairy Audacious Goal, and the Profit/X is a way to help measure this 10- to 30-year goal. The clearer we get on our KFFM and BHAG, the clearer we will be on how we make money, which can be simply reflected in Profit per Widget (Profit/X).

There is no need for a deep dive, just an acknowledgment of the X and elimination of any that don't make sense at this time.

STRATEGY SYSTEM

3HAG

At this point, you need to do a quick review of the 3HAG—but don't get hung up on it. If the fiscal metrics or widgets are not the right numbers but are close, leave them be for now. They will be fully validated through this process. If the widgets are not the correct widgets, correct them. That's important to help anticipate what things will be flowing through your company 3 years from now.

Check in on the 3HAG statement in the same way as you just did the BHAG statement. Review the 3 to 5 Key Capabilities and what you want to be known for in 3 years' time. And keep moving.

What you have for your 3HAG is good enough for where we are in developing our plan and our team.

3HAG: Market Map

The next step in your strategic 3HAG system is to create the Market Map. The Market Map is a strategic picture that we created in our first company. It's a key view for the team to leverage as an active external analysis of the marketplace.

Remember, the #2 barrier for any company to grow is the lack of deep market expertise by the whole leadership.

The Market Map allows the leadership team to get on the same page and understand not only where the company fits into the market now but also how the other players evolve over time. This is a visual way to represent the arena in which the company is playing, and to map out all the players in that arena, whether or not you have a relationship with them. It's a view of your entire marketplace that shows on the left side how your company goes to market and other players in the arena. On the right side, it shows where your company has relationships and spends significant amounts of money. You should also add the top competitors you talk about most as a leadership team, as well as any business associations, memberships, or groups that exist in your marketplace.

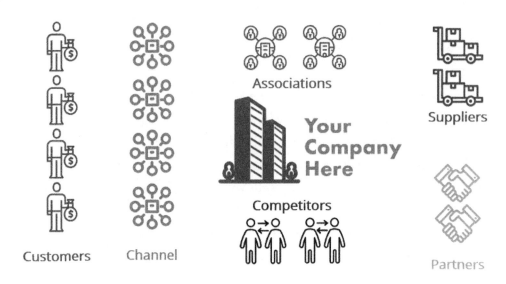

For a full explanation on how to create your Market Map, please go to *www. metronomicsthebook.com.*

Your team will be super excited to see the Market Map. Most people have never seen their company positioned in the marketplace in this way. It's the first time they can see all the players they hear about in the marketplace in a single place and understand the relationship between them and your company.

It is best practice to keep the Market Map up to date and to review and discuss it on at least a monthly basis. Ensure it is completely reviewed on a quarterly basis.

It's only useful if it's up to date. Keeping it up to date at each meeting takes minutes, but it saves time and keeps the team focused.

The Market Map is like the Google Map of your business arena. There are so many overlays you can add to get different useful perspectives, from overlaying the dollars that flow through the map to showing strategic partners or where the next best step might be for your organization to get to market.

By the time you've finished the Market Map, it's only lunchtime. You've covered a lot for a single morning. In fact, you're likely wondering how you did it so quickly. In order to be efficient, you must be able to keep the meeting moving forward, having just "good enough" progression and discussions. Avoid the rabbit holes and keep the forward momentum moving.

There will be times you will absolutely get stuck in a rabbit hole. It's inevitable. Acknowledge it and learn from it both from a team perspective and from a planning perspective.

Remember: "good enough" is "good enough."

EXECUTION SYSTEM

The second half of the day is all about execution. We have the whole afternoon to learn to get better at this process. I love this part of the meeting. It's as much about developing team habits and behavior and progressing the team's cohesiveness as it is about defining the next quarter's plan. We will follow a similar process as we did in the Kick-Off to create our quarterly priorities. Since we already have our annual priorities, we'll have a quick check in on them too. We will also do a review on how we did completing and achieving last quarter's priorities and metrics.

1HAG and Current QHAG

Over time, this review of the annual priorities and the current quarterly priorities will become quicker and quicker. As this is the first time we are reviewing the annual priorities and quarterly priorities, however, it's a great opportunity to review what went well and what did not go so well, and what we might do differently, as well as to create the next set of priorities for the next quarter.

New Quarterly Plan (QHAG)

Spend the afternoon with the team working through questions to create a clear 90-day corporate plan for the next quarter. These are much the same as the questions you asked at the start of the first quarter about revenue, cash, widgets, and priorities, with a couple of additions:

1. What is your gross revenue for the quarter? (Preferably show this month over month, with a quarterly total.)

2. What are your total expenses for the quarter? (Preferably show this month over month, with a quarterly total.)

3. What is your profit for the quarter? (Preferably show this month over month, with a quarterly total.)

4. How much cash will be in the bank on the last day of the quarter?

5. How many widgets do you need to deliver in order to ensure that answers #1 to #4 are correct for the quarter? (Preferably show this month over month, with a quarterly total.)

6. Who owns the fiscal levers shared in #1 to #4, and the widgets? Put the name beside each number for clarity of ownership and accountability.

7. What is the #1 Corporate Priority that the company must accomplish for the quarter to ensure the numbers are achieved and line the company up nicely to its 1HAG? Each leader answers this question individually and then shares their answer with the team. The team has a full discussion in order to agree on the #1 Corporate Priority.

8. What are the other Corporate Priorities for the company, from #2 through #5? Use the same process, with each leader writing down what they think individually, then sharing with the team to agree on the order. (I always recommend there are no more than 3 Corporate Priorities at one time. I know this is hard, but focus, focus, focus.)

9. Once the Corporate Priorities are agreed on, ask who owns each one, from #1 to #5. The best practice is that each priority should have only one owner. As you can imagine, when one team member owns more than one corporate priority, it will be hard to get both completed. I know this is difficult to avoid in smaller organizations, but it is key to growing the company.

What is the 13-Week Sprint Lane Plan?

The 13-Week Sprint Lane was developed from the framework in *Mastering the Rockefeller Habits*, which introduced the "13-week race" for each corporate quarterly priority. We found this to be useful in breaking down week by week the ability to achieve our Corporate Priorities, but we also discovered that the process was not visible or transparent to the whole team. So we created a strategic picture called the 13-Week Sprint Lane Plan. (As before, the process of creating the plan is as much about developing the team as it is about the plan itself.)

Each Sprint Lane represents a corporate priority for the quarter, broken into 13 weekly tasks. The Plan maps out week over week each task that needs to be completed in each lane in order to achieve the priority by the end of the quarter. This makes your corporate quarterly priorities not just aspirational but achievable. It also maps out the company quarterly widget metric on a weekly basis, again ensuring that number is achievable, not just aspirational.

The 13-Week Sprint Lane allows a team to take a step back and review the whole plan to ensure it is achievable and that they have the resources to achieve it. It ensures team members progress their execution ability as well as their team ability to focus. And it shows the team how to achieve their most important priorities aligned to the direction they want to progress.

If you need more guidance on how to create 13-Week Sprint Lanes with your team, please go to *www.metronomicsthebook.com*.

Once the 13-Week Sprint Lane Plan is complete, ask each of the leaders to work through their individual priorities aligned to the corporate quarterly priorities in terms of resources required, just as they did in the Kick-Off Meeting.

Check-In

The meeting ends with a check-in on how the leaders are getting on with the Metronomics regimen. How are the meetings working for them? Is there anything they need to be adjusted, including the Open Playing Field?

Do not skip this step and assume all is well. This step was important in how I and my leaders developed Metronomics through innovating and iterating the process and making sure it worked for the team.

FY2021-Q2			Qtr Beginning Balance	WK1 04/02/21	WK2 04/09/21	WK3 04/16/21	WK4 04/23/21	WK5 04/30/21	WK6 05/7/21	WK7 05/14/21	WK8 05/21/21	WK9 05/28/21	WK10 06/04/21	WK11 06/11/21	WK12 06/18/21	WK13 06/25/21	FY2021-Q2
Widget (Andrew)	New Subscriptions			100	100	125	125	125	130	140	150	180	200	200	200	225	2000
Widget (JEN)	Cumm. Subscriptions		3000	3100	3200	3325	3450	3575	3705	3845	3985	4175	4375	4575	4775	5000	5000
#1 (Daniel)	US Messaging Platform in production by 06/30/21			Present UAT Plan	UAT Phase 1	UAT Phase 2	Production Sandbox Platform Build Complete	UAT Phase 3	UAT Phase 4	Production Platform Complete	Promote Release to Sandbox	SUAT Phase 1	SUAT Phase 2	SUAT Phase 3	Promote Release to Production	US Messaging Platform Live	
#2 (Andrew)	Sign up 1 new CAD and US Reseller by 06/30/21			CAD Reseller Contract sent for signature	Book US Reseller final Present and Demo	Follow Up with CAD Reseller	New CAD Reseller signed contract	Confirm final requirements with US Reseller	Send Proposal to US Reseller	Negotiate Proposal US Reseller	Proposal Agreement	Us Reseller Demo Meeting	US Contract sent for Review	US Contract Updated with requests	US Contract sent for signature	New US Reseller Signed Contract	
#3 (JEN)	New Subscriber is enabled in less than 14 days by 06/30/21			Success Team trained on self serve setup	Success Team using self serve for internal setup	Setup is now 20 days	Self Serve setup ready for subscribers	Self Serve ext training launched	All new subscribers use self serve setup	Setup improves by 3 days to 18 days	Automated messaging integration started	Automated messaging integration Dev	Automated messaging integration Dev QA	Automated messaging integration Prod QA	Automated Messaging integration complete	First subscriber turned on in 14 days	

Cascading Messages

Use the same process you used at the end of the Kick-Off to create the top 3 messages coming out of the meeting. Make sure that all the leaders understand the messages and have written them down to share them with their teams the next day. This allows the teams to stay aligned with the key messages and plans in the organization.

One-Phrase Close

Ask everyone, "From your gut, how do you feel right now—5 words or less?" Either you or the coach asks the question, and it's a round robin. Everyone has to answer, with the CEO going last, and answers are limited to 5 words or less. Only the CEO and coach get more than 5 words because they need to assimilate and react to what they have heard.

The feedback may be positive, such as "Energized," or negative, such as "Overwhelmed." When there is negative feedback, the CEO has the responsibility to check in with that leader after the meeting to understand their feelings and support the leader and their team.

CASH SYSTEM

As the company widgets are the foundation of our cash system, we have been implicitly focusing on the Cash System without the team even realizing it. At the end of the last meeting, we asked the owner of the cash forecast or budget model to back in the company widgets. Now, the next step is to ask them how backing in the widgets went, as well as adding the mini cash-flow statement or calculation at the bottom of the forecasted profit and loss statement. From there we want to take the current annual budget or forecast and create an annual widget-based forecast. This will show a month-over-month view of the company widgets for the current year, providing a great perspective on the actual-to-forecast as you move forward. Remember—the widgets are the things that flow through your company that you control. They are tightly tied to cash as well as to your fiscal results. For more info see *www.metronomics thebook.com.*

NEXT STEPS/HOMEWORK

Again, homework and active behavior are key to making sure the plans and the system are not simply forgotten about but continue to be brought alive:

- Leaders should update the Open Playing Field as much as possible with the evolved plan.

- Each leader should add to the Open Playing Field the Corporate Priorities, including the 13-week subpriorities from the Sprint Lanes developed with the team, as well as their own individual priorities.

- Add the Market Map to the physical or virtual War Room so it is visible to everyone.

- Continue to run all company meetings through the Open Playing Field.

- The CEO will create the company's very first function Scorecard, starting with a Head of Company function that is the very first function shared on the Organizational Function Chart.

- The Scorecard in Metronomics is much simpler than the Scorecards used in the Topgrading methodology. Over time, we simplified the Scorecard so that it was more practical and usable every day. Each function Scorecard contains the purpose of the function, the 3 to 5 key accountabilities the function owns, the one to 3 metrics the function owns, the key competencies required for the owner of that function to be successful, and the Core Values of the organization. This is the recommended template for all function Scorecards. This template can be found at *www. metronomicsthebook.com.*

- At this stage, we want the owner of the Head of Company function, which is currently the CEO, to gain experience creating the company's first function Scorecard. This allows the CEO to understand and get comfortable with the process, and ultimately to share an example to others of the function Scorecards they have committed to the team to own. The Scorecard is foundational to the Human System and tightly tied to the KFFM.

- To learn more about how to create Scorecards for the functional roles in your company, please go to: www.metronomicsthebook.com.

- All leaders should cascade 3 Key Messages from the meeting to their teams.

- Everyone should read *The Four Obsessions of an Extraordinary Executive* by Patrick Lencioni before the next quarterly meeting.

OUTCOMES

Looking back at each quarterly and annual meeting, you should be able to see clearly what progression you have achieved, both in your clarity of the plan and in the development of the team. In this case, the progression is:

- Cohesive: The cohesiveness of the team is progressing, with the team gaining trust. The accountability of the team and individuals is visible and progressing. The team is settling into the rhythm of the meetings and liking the feeling of connectedness.

- Human: The Organizational Function Chart and KFFM have improved the understanding of functional clarity as well as accountability. Widgets are becoming clearer and connected.

- Cultural: The habit of recognizing team members through Good News in the daily huddle is keeping the accepted behavior of the team in focus. Leaders are being thoughtful about the Good News they share.

- Strategy: 3HAG validation has started with the external analysis of the Market Map. The team is excited about this view and moving to the discussion of the Core Customer in the next quarterly.

- Execution: The next iteration of the Growth Plan will be visible and clear on the Open Playing Field. The active meeting cadence will keep achieving the plan in focus.

- Cash: Team members' habit of forecasting and tracking the company X week over week will be active and visible on the Open Playing Field and through the 13-Week Sprint Lanes.

The cohesiveness of the team is progressing, with stronger, healthier discussions. The evolution of the team's behavior is noticeable.

Overlaying each of these systems together can be overwhelming, but it is necessary. Remember that the key to moving through Metronomics is to break it down step by step and quarter by quarter. Working 13 weeks or 90 days at a time is the best way to get your head around the progress of each system.

That's why this book gives you a prescriptive guide for each quarter. It gives you the best sense of how to move the dials forward on each system while you are trying to grow a company.

QUARTER 2: ALIGNED WIDGETS AND PRIORITIES

Heading into Q2, you have an evolved Growth Plan and the team's behavior is changing. You have your updated Market Map in good view. The team has kept the active plan alive and well on the Open Playing Field. You and your leadership team have a good meeting cadence and are leveraging the standing agendas. You have better functional clarity with team accountability.

PREPARATION FOR THE MEETING

1. Everyone should make sure they have finished reading *The Four Obsessions of an Extraordinary Executive* by Patrick Lencioni.

2. Have each team member complete the Gallup StrengthsFinder 2.0 assessment. The team members should share the results with the coach and CEO and be ready to discuss them at the meeting. To learn more about the StrengthsFinder 2.0 assessment and Metronomics, please go to *www.metronomicsthebook.com*.

3. Everyone should ensure the status of the priorities and metrics they own are up to date on the Open Playing Field so everyone can review them prior to the meeting. If they're not, you'll waste time statusing the plan in the meeting.

4. All meeting attendees should review the current status of the whole plan. The leaders should make notes and questions and be ready to discuss them in the context of building the plan for the next quarter.

5. Two weeks before the meeting, have the leadership team complete the Preparation Survey, with the results being sent out to everyone between 2-5 days before the meeting. The Preparation Survey is a great way to remind your leaders that the planning meeting will take place in a few weeks, so they should start preparing!

You start the Q2 quarterly meeting with professional Good News. You also do a round-robin get-to-know-you question again. For sample questions, visit *www.metronomicsthebook.com*. You'll review the Organizational Function Chart and the Key Function Flow Map and update them as necessary. They are getting better and better.

Everything is up to date. The team is getting to understand the process and they are well prepared. This always puts a smile on my face, because this makes it easier for everyone to create momentum. We are ready for a great meeting.

Everyone is happier with the idea of looking for "good enough."

AGENDA

Compound Growth System	Day 1
Cohesive System	· Good News · Cohesive Question · Self-Awareness Assessment
Human System	· Organizational Function Chart · KFFM
Cultural System	· Core Purpose · Core Values · BHAG™: Confirm/Evolve
Strategy System	· 3HAG™: Confirm · Market Map · Core Customer
Execution System	· Status Review Annual Plan / QHAG · New Quarterly Plan · Cascade 3 Key Messages
Cash System	· Talk to Finance Leaders to work back "Widgets" in their current "Budget"
Coach Cascade System	· n/a

COHESIVE SYSTEM

Good News

By now, the team is getting good at delivering their Good News and recognizing their peers, and it's a fun, positive way to kick off the meeting.

Cohesive Question

We always have personal get-to-know-you questions or icebreakers. It's a round robin, as usual, and you start with the coach and the CEO. This creates more personal connections to continue to improve team trust. Don't skip this step because you think it is too squishy and soft. Remember, these simple steps are a key step in building your cohesive team and take no time at all.

Self-Awareness Assessment

At every meeting, we try to bring in something to evolve the leaders' awareness of themselves and the team as a whole.

This time, I recommend Gallup StrengthsFinder 2.0, which helps each individual identify their top strengths. I love being able to map the leadership team's strength in the context of the 34 StrengthsFinder themes across the four domains of executing, influencing, relationship building, and strategy. This provides a great view of your leadership team and is important in developing cohesiveness. For more info, please go to *www.metronomicsthebook.com*.

HUMAN SYSTEM

Organizational Function Chart

The next step in the meeting is to review the Organizational Function Chart, as you did in the Kick-Off and in the last quarterly meeting. You'll work through this chart every 90 days at minimum. You will discuss what actions have been completed and what actions are needed next to evolve the functional design as the company grows. For efficiency, you will continue to evolve the view that was created in the Kick-Off Meeting, with the adjustments from the last quarterly meeting.

Key Function Flow Map

Now review the Key Function Flow Map, led by each functional owner. This is what the KFFM should look like by now.

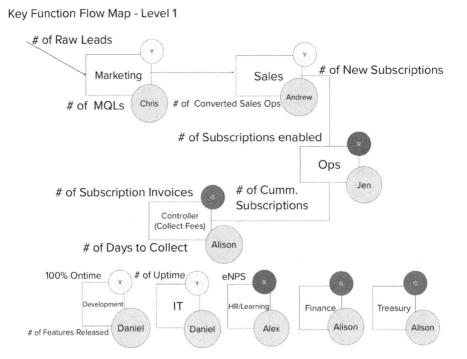

Key Function Flow Map - Level 1

A-Player Team Assessment

At this time, only the CEO will do the A-Player Assessment, because the Core Values haven't been discovered and shared yet. We'll start the Core Value process this quarter.

(If you already have rock-solid Core Values for your team, don't wait to do the A-Player Assessment. Please go to *www.metronomicsthebook.com* for more info.)

CULTURAL SYSTEM

Core Purpose

Quickly review and confirm the Core Purpose. Good enough.

Core Values

Acknowledge the Core Values you have or acknowledge that you don't have any yet. Review and put a plan in place to work with the team to discover the team's Core Values. The process I recommend is based on Jim Collins's Mission to Mars exercise. Introduce the concept here with the goal to follow the process over the next quarter.

Core Values are the foundation of your culture and the accepted behaviors of your team. They're the way we establish if there is a "fit" with a team member. We need to ensure all team members possess the team Core Values—but first, we must have clarity of what those values are and what behaviors they entail from the team.

Jim's Mission to Mars is one of the best ways I know to discover or confirm your team's Core Values. I used it as the basis for the exercise that follows, which aims not to have only the CEO+Leadership team discover the Core Values but also the larger team. This will ensure accuracy, a 360-degree view, and the whole team's buy-in to the process and the team Core Values.

This approach will work for any size team, but in this case, it's written for a team of 20 or more people.

1. Explain the situation: "You have been asked to provide team members from your company to go to Mars and be observed by the Martian culture. The Martians want to observe people who most accurately illustrate your company's culture and what is right, best, and noble about it. You are to choose 3 team members that best illustrate what you believe are the Core Values of the team. BUT the Martians cannot speak or understand human language. They can only learn about your Core Values by observing your team members living them."

2. Have each team member in the room individually come up with 3 people *outside* of the team in the room to send to Mars and write them down.

3. Break the team into equal groups for discussions.

4. Have each individual in the group share who they chose and why.

5. Have each group agree on the top 3 people they choose and the Core Value they each represent. Write the name of each person and their Core Value on a post-it note, so each group has a total of 3 post-its.

6. Have each group present who they chose and why, sticking their post-it notes on a whiteboard or easel at the front of the room.

7. Let all groups present, with the moderator grouping notes with similar Core Value descriptions together.

8. Once all the post-its have been presented and grouped, see if you can come up with a word or phrase to represent the Core Values identified on the board, or at least a few words that represent a certain behavior or Core Value that has been identified.

9. Give all team members in the room 3 votes they can use to vote for what they believe are the 3 people on the board who best represent the behaviors or Core Values in the company. They can choose individuals who are all linked to one Core Value identified on the board or who represent different Core Values.

10. Get all team members to come up to the board to vote. This can be done by checking the post-it notes for their selections with a marker.

11. Tally up the score of all votes per Core Value or behavior.

12. Identify the 3 with the most votes.

13. Discuss anything the team feels has been left out of the top 3 and see if it warrants further discussion.

14. Conclude the session by acknowledging that we have discovered or confirmed the 3 key areas for the Core Values focus. The next step is to have a smaller group draft names and a key descriptor phrase that describes the behavior.

15. Once this is complete, the draft will come back to the group for review and confirmation.

It is best practice to include more than just the CEO and the leadership team in this process. This shows the rest of the team that the company is committed to its team Core Values as the foundation of both the business and a high-performing team.

This is a great team-building and feedback session, and I would recommend that all leaders, including the CEO, take part. There is nothing more important for any company than getting clarity on its team Core Values.

The leadership team must understand the importance of committing to this process because it's not to be rushed and might take more than one quarter. The focus and follow-through are critical to developing a highly cohesive team on our journey to becoming a high-performing business team.

For more information on the process of discovering the team Core Values please go to: *www.metronomicsthebook.com.*

BHAG

A quick review of the BHAG should confirm that it is good enough for now.

Profit/X

Check in on the Profit per X, which really involves a check-in on the "X," the company widgets. As we have just completed the third review of the whole KFFM with the team, we may have a clearer view of what "X" should be right now. There is no need for a deep dive, just an acknowledgment of the company widgets and the elimination of any that don't make sense at this time.

STRATEGY SYSTEM

3HAG

At this point, do another quick review of the 3HAG. Again, there's no reason to get hung up. Check in on the 3HAG statement in the same way as you just did on the BHAG statement. Review the Key Capabilities and what you want to be known for. And keep moving.

3HAG: *Market Map*

Review the Market Map and update any shifts that have taken place in the market in the last 90 days or any movement of the other players.

3HAG: *Core Customer Analysis*

The Core Customer is the foundation of your strategy. Ensuring that you know your Core Customer, right down to the level of the individual buyer, is important to create a highly differentiated and valued strategy that will serve

	Reseller			Subscriber					
Description 30-50 words	35-65 years old	Predominantly Male	Married/kids	Age 20-60	all genders	tech savvy			
	Work as little as possible for Max $$	Lifetime sales person	Reseller for other brands	security conscious	university educated	wants to get things done quickly			
	Tech Saavy	little patience		no patience for repetitive tasks					
Prioritized Needs	1.	To Make Money		1.	Trusted Messaging		1.		
	2.	Easy Sale		2.	Integrated Messages		2.		
	3.	No Support		3.	24X7 Support		3.		
Prioritized Benefits	1.	Wholesale pricing is always at a 20% GM		1.	Secure Available Platform		1.		
	2.	One Click Portal		2.	Any Message from Any where		2.		
	3.	24X7 Level 1 Support		3.	24X7 Support		3.		

their *needs* at a profit. The key to this analysis is to ensure you can describe the individual, identify their top 3 prioritized needs, and discover and understand the prioritized benefits your company offers to serve these needs. For more information on how to complete the Core Customer Analysis, please go to *www.metronomicsthebook.com*.

Because the Core Customer is the foundation of strategy, it's important to have a good view of the customers that you serve. You might serve more than one type of customer—most companies do—but they are not necessarily the Core Customer, who buys at a profit. This is an important distinction because we want to build our strategy only on the Core Customer who will buy at a profit.

EXECUTION SYSTEM

The second half of the day is still all about execution. This process is getting easier and easier as the team fully embraces it.

Status: 1HAG and Current QHAG

The review will be quick as long as the team has their Open Playing Field up to date before the meeting and has been reviewing and discussing the 1HAG and QHAG on a weekly basis.

New QHAG

Spend the afternoon with the team working on a new QHAG by going through the same questions you've used before, including the 13-Week Sprint Lane and the Aligned Individual Priorities.

As this will be the second time you have created a 13-Week Sprint Lane from the QHAG priorities, take time to create the plan again as you did in the last meeting. Don't skip this step, as it's key to your team's belief in the achievability of the plan, their accountability, and their confidence as a team to work together to deliver. The Sprint Lanes allow the team to increase their execution efficiency, make decisions sooner, and celebrate wins each and every week. They also create momentum. The leaders need to understand this process in order for them to share it with their teams in the future.

CASH SYSTEM

The next step with the Cash System is to have the finance leader work back all the key company widgets from the KFFM in their current "budget" model. They will most likely start creating a new Excel model.

CHECK-IN

As with every meeting, check in with the team about how the meeting cadence, agenda, and outcomes are progressing. This gives you as a team the opportunity to tweak anything that needs to be adjusted so everyone stays aligned with their teams.

Cascading Messages

As at all our meetings, we will check in with everyone and note the 3 Key Messages that need to be cascaded to the rest of the organization in tomorrow's huddle.

One-Phrase Close

The day wraps up as always by asking each of the leaders for 5 words or less to describe how they feel right now.

NEXT STEPS/HOMEWORK

1. Update the Open Playing Field as necessary.

   • Each leader should add to the playing field the Corporate Priorities, including the 13-week subpriorities from the Sprint Lanes developed with the team, as well as their own individual priorities.

   • Add the updated Market Map to the War Room.

- Add the strategic picture of the Core Customer to the War Room.

- Continue to run all company meetings through the Open Playing Field.

- Leaders carry out the Core Values discovery process with teams.

- Complete Scorecards for all leaders. In the last 90 days, the CEO has created the function Scorecard for the Head of Company functional role. Over the next 90 days, the CEO will work with the leaders to create the function Scorecards for each of the functions represented in the KFFM in the same way. For more information on creating functions Scorecards, please go to *www.metronomicsthebook.com*.

- All leaders cascade 3 Key Messages to their team.

- All leaders should read the book *Overcoming the Five Dysfunctions of a Team* by Patrick Lencioni.

- All leaders with their teams carry out the StrengthsFinder 2.0 assessment and create a visual view of all team members. The team shares their results from the StrengthsFinder 2.0 assessment at the next weekly meeting of their team and, best practice, at the Monthly Town Hall meeting with the whole team. These results should be added to the company War Room. It's a great practice to create a large visual of how leaders' strengths are mapped across all areas for the whole team to review. It's also good practice to have all team members complete the assessment and then map themselves onto the same grid. This helps create team awareness and respect for each other's strengths as we grow. In my first two companies, we had this large map on the wall in one of our team meeting rooms. When new team members joined, they would do their StrengthsFinder 2.0 assessment on the first day, then map themselves on the grid with the rest of the team. It was a great way to welcome a new team member and incorporate them into the company.

OUTCOMES

- Cohesive: The cohesiveness of the team is progressing, with the team gaining trust and healthier discussions taking place. The accountability of the team and of individuals is visible and progressing on the playing field. In addition, we are now starting activities that make everyone aware of your commitment to developing a highly cohesive and high-performing business team through the simple yet powerful assessment of StrengthsFinder 2.0.

- Human: The Organizational Function Chart and KFFM are visible, with the team's understanding growing of the importance of the functional widgets and ownership and their recognition of the value of the KFFM as a company scoreboard. The more the KFFM is updated by the team, the more 'real-time' the scoreboard is for the whole company.

- Cultural: The habit of recognizing team members through Good News on a daily basis is keeping the accepted behavior of the team in focus. And the leadership will work together to discover and define the Core Values of the team, with the team, if needed.

- Strategy: 3HAG validation continues with keeping the Market Map up to date and the first iteration of the Core Customer Analysis complete. These strategic pictures are visible for all to review and explain to the whole team.

- Execution: The next iteration of the Growth Plan will be visible and clear on the Open Playing Field. The 13-Week Sprint Lanes are gaining great momentum and increasing confidence in achieving the quarterly plan and accuracy of forecasting widgets. The active meeting cadence using the Open Playing Field will keep the focus on the plan every day.

- Cash: The habit of forecasting and tracking the company "X" (widgets) by team members week over week will be active and visible on the Open Playing Field through the KFFM. There will be an agreement to create a new company widget-based forecasting model in Excel.

QUARTER 3: FORECASTING CASH AND EVOLVING STRATEGY

When you reach the Q3 meeting, your goal is to plan the last quarter of the fiscal year. It's nearly a year since the Kick-Off Meeting. The objective of the Q3 meeting is to continue to increase the planning and execution momentum through the balance and alignment of the team's cohesive behavior progression. We will continue mapping out our strategy following the *3HAG WAY* progression.

PREPARATION FOR THE MEETING

Have your leadership team—and yourself—prepare for the meeting like this:

1. Everyone should have finished reading *Overcoming the Five Dysfunctions of a Team* by Patrick Lencioni.

2. Everyone should update the status of the priorities and metrics they own on the Open Playing Field so everyone can review them prior to the meeting—otherwise, you'll waste time statusing the plan in the meeting.

3. After reviewing the status of the whole company plan, the leaders should make notes, ask questions, and be ready to discuss in the context of 3HAG, 1HAG, and building the plan for the next quarter.

4. Two weeks before the meeting, get the leadership team to complete
    the Preparation Survey, with the results being sent out to everyone
    between 2-5 days before the meeting.

AGENDA

Compound Growth System	Day 1
Cohesive System	• Good News • Personal/Get to know you question • Left and Right—Appreciation
Human System	• Organizational Function Chart • KFFM • Team Assessment (A, B, C)
Cultural System	• Core Purpose • Core Values • BHAG™: Confirm/Evolve
Strategy System	• 3HAG™: Confirm • Market Map—Review • Core Customer—Review • Attribution Framework
Execution System	• Status Review Annual Plan / QHAG • New Quarterly Plan • Cascade 3 Key Messages
Cash System	• Talk to Finance Leaders to create "Widget" based forecast for next fiscal year.
Coach Cascade System	• n/a

COHESIVE SYSTEM

Good News

As always, kick off the meeting with professional Good News. The team Core
Values that you've discovered and defined with the team over the last 90 days
means that Good News can really recognize team members who demonstrate
the Core Values of the whole team.

Cohesive Question

Follow with your get-to-know-you questions or icebreakers, starting with the Coach and the CEO. Do not skip this step. For a full list of questions, please go to *www.metronomicsthebook.com.*

Self-Awareness Assessment

At this meeting, we are going to introduce a simple Left and Right Appreciation for each leader. Starting with the CEO and working your way around the table to the left, each leader writes down and tells the person on their left what they appreciate about them. When everyone has gone, the CEO starts again with the person on their right, sharing what they appreciate about that person, and you go back all the way around the table.

This is a great way to ease the leadership team into getting used to providing feedback to their peers. Peer-based feedback is a key element in building a high-performing business team, so we need to train leaders to be good at providing feedback to each other. In order for teams to be comfortable, the cohesive level of the team must be at a level to handle this behavior. We will continue to build on this as we progress.

For more information on Left and Right, please go to *www.metronomic thebook.com.*

HUMAN SYSTEM

Organizational Function Chart

The next step is to review the organizational function chart, as you did in the Kick-Off and the last quarterly meeting. Remember: you aim to work through this chart every 90 days at a minimum. Adjust as needed.

Key Function Flow Map

Each functional owner leads a review of their part of the KFFM. This is getting easier to discuss and make decisions about, as a level of understanding has increased which in turn has increased the speed of decision making for the operation and design of the business.

CULTURAL SYSTEM

Core Purpose

Quickly review and confirm the Core Purpose.

Core Values

Over the last 90 days the team has been working together to discover the team's Core Values. Review these values now and update them as needed, but bear in mind that there might need to be further discussion with a larger team in order to confirm them.

Do not rush team Core Values discovery. The Core Values are foundational to the consistent acceptable behavior of your team.

A-Player Team Assessment

If the Core Values are now defined for the team, complete the A-Player Team Assessment.

Leaders will assess their direct reports on the A-Player Team Assessment graph for everyone to review and discuss. This is done in every quarterly meeting moving forward to ensure your leadership team stays focused on having an A-Player team.

This first time, doing the assessment will take a little longer as most leaders have never discussed their direct report on team members at this level with this peer group. The key reason you want each leader to present where each of their team members is on this graph assessment is to get feedback from others as to whether they would assess that team member the same way, to provide feedback, and to ensure there is a clear plan for each team member who falls below an A-Player Assessment. Our goal to have 90-plus percent of our team members as A-Players.

Quarter over quarter, this focus with the leadership will help achieve and maintain this level. The more you review and discuss your team members together, the easier and faster it will get to make decisions and plans from this assessment to ensure we have the best team to grow forward. For more information on A-Player Team Assessment please go to *www.metronomicsthebook.com*.

BHAG

Have another quick review of the BHAG to confirm that it is good enough for now.

Profit/X

Have a quick review of the Profit/X. There will still be a few ideas for the company X, but in most cases, it is becoming clearer each quarter as confidence increases in the KFFM and the 3HAG. By next quarter, the work we have done usually means that the Profit/X is very clear and aligned to the 3HAG and 1HAG.

STRATEGY SYSTEM

3HAG

Quickly review the 3HAG and confirm that it is good enough for now.

3HAG: Market Map

Review the Market Map and make any necessary updates based on how it's evolved.

3HAG: Core Customer Analysis

The Core Customer Analysis from the last meeting has usually progressed since then. I ask a team to get it into a good enough state to give clarity about who their Core Customer is, meaning the customer who always buys at a profit. The team will continue with the work on the Core Customer as they validate the analysis with their data and marketplace information. But for now, the visibility of the Core Customer is good enough to proceed, because the analysis can sometimes take a few months to lock-in. That's fine.

The Core Customer Analysis will never be complete, anyway, as the dynamic nature of any market will need to stay in good view and the evolving needs of the Core Customer.

3HAG: Attribution Map

In this meeting, you're going to map out a view of the industry marketplace in which your company is active. It's an analysis of your *company*, not your *product*, and how it fits into and serves the attributes of the industry.

It's not to be confused with Value Curve in the book *Blue Ocean Strategy* by W. Chan Kim and Renee Mauborgne, or the Attribute Map found in the book *Uncommon Service* by Frances Frei and Anne Morriss. These tools focus on the product and service, not the company. This Attribution Map is a view of how your whole company fits into the industry market.

As a first step, brainstorm the attributes for characteristics of the industry marketplace you play in. Aim to come up with 10 to 15 attributes (don't get hung up on whether you have them perfect). Then score how well your company serves each of these attributes, using a scale from 1 to 5.

ATTRIBUTION MAP

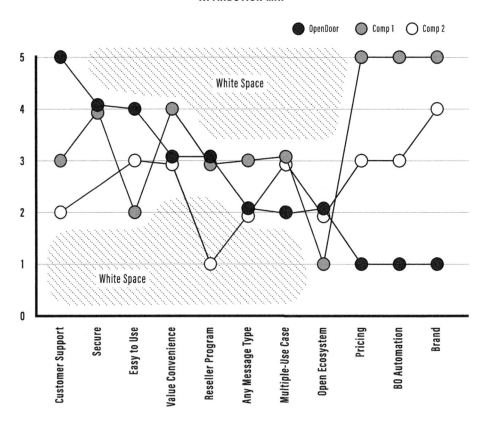

Arrange the attributes on the x-axis of the graph in order from best to worst, according to how you judge your company serves them. Start on the left with the attributes you serve the best all the way to the right, which are the attributes you don't serve as well or at all. For each attribute, chart the score you gave your company in your assessment, from 1 to 5. Join up each of your points. You should now have a line going from the top left of the graph to the bottom right.

Now carry out the same assessment for your top two competitors. Add the results to your graph.

Study the completed graph with your leadership team and have a full discussion about where the white space exists. White space is any part of the graph with nothing in it, which might be above or below your current graph's position.

The graph gives you a great view of how your company compares to others in the industry marketplace as a basis for making strategic decisions. Remember, strategy is about getting into your own unique and valuable position: you do this by occupying the white space, your own dimension without any rivals, that matters to your Core Customer.

After you've discussed the graph, decide what attributes you believe the company should maintain, improve, or remove in relation to the other players in the marketplace and the white space available. Decide what should stay the same, and decide what you could afford not to be as good at in 3 years' time. Remember: you're looking to move into white space to distinguish yourself from your competitors.

Use a different color to map out your new assessment of where you should be against each attribute, and join the points. Label this your 3HAG line. It represents where you want to end up 3 years from now.

This description doesn't do the Attribution Map justice. It's a key strategic-picture view—and a great view for your team to sleep on and discuss further.

Please don't skip this step—and please follow the directions carefully. Many teams and companies confuse this map with the others I mentioned earlier, which affects its usefulness as we move forward.

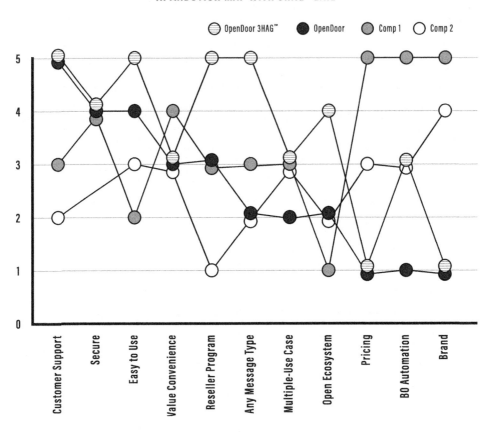

ATTRIBUTION MAP WITH 3HAG™ LINE

For a full step-by-step to implement this key strategic map, the Attribution Map, please go to *www.metronomicsthebook.com*.

EXECUTION SYSTEM

The second half of the day is still all about execution. This process is getting easier as the team fully embraces it.

Status: 1HAG and Current QHAG

Check in on your 1HAG and QHAG. This will be quick as long as the team has the Open Playing Field up to date before the meeting and has been reviewing and discussing it on a weekly basis.

New QHAG

Spend the afternoon with the team working through the usual questions to help set a new QHAG, including the 13-Week Sprint Lane Map.

CASH SYSTEM

The next step on the Cash System is to have the finance leaders take the Excel model they created for this year's budget or forecast and create a 12-month widget-based forecast for the next fiscal year. It should be ready to review for the next meeting.

This is an exciting step. With this model, the finance team will no longer have to guess at the forecast for the company. Instead, the leaders will forecast the widgets that need to be accomplished and share the fiscal assumptions associated with those widgets in the model. The model shifts the forecast ownership from the finance team that built the model to the leaders who own the widgets. Widget forecasting for the next 12 months is not to be skipped.

CHECK-IN

As with every meeting, check in with the team about how the meeting cadence, agenda, and outcomes are progressing. This gives you as a team the opportunity to tweak anything that needs to be adjusted so everyone stays aligned with their teams.

Cascading Messages

As at all our meetings, we do a meeting check-in with everyone, and take note of the 3 Key Messages that need to be cascaded to the rest of the organization in tomorrow's huddle.

One-Phrase Close

The day wraps up as always by asking each of the leaders for 5 words or less to describe how they feel right now.

NEXT STEPS/HOMEWORK

- Update the Open Playing Field as needed.

- Each leader should add to the Open Playing Field the Corporate Priorities, including the 13-week subpriorities from the Sprint Lanes developed with the team, as well as their own individual priorities.

- Add updated Market Map to the War Room.

- Add updated Core Customer to the War Room.

- Add Attribution Framework to the War Room.

- Continue to run all company meetings through the Open Playing Field.

- Review the KFFM in the Weekly Leadership Team Meeting. This will be a standing agenda item before the Metrics agenda item. The KFFM can be in your War Room —physical or virtual—or best practice for ease of use and real-time update should be in your virtual Open Playing Field, like the Metronome software, which supports a live KFFM. No matter how it is implemented, the active view of your KFFM allows your team to easily see a score for the company and the updated widgets from each leader on a daily basis. This is a key step in creating a visible, transparent score for everyone to review and to make better, faster decisions every day.

- If you are still in the Core Values discovery process, share the results with the whole team. If you are beyond this step, ensure the leaders remained focused on recognizing Core Values through Good News at every meeting.

- If the A-Player Team Assessment was completed in this meeting, leaders need to make plans or take action on any C-Player team members over the next 90 days.

- Leaders cascade 3 Key Messages to their teams.

- Since the last meeting, all leaders now own a function Scorecard, which is great for the team. As we roll up to the end of the year, the CEO can utilize the function Scorecard each leader owns to conduct an annual review on the Open Playing Field. Next year, best practice will be for these performance coaching reviews to take place every 90 days.

- All leaders should read the book *Beyond Entrepreneurship 2.0* by Jim Collins and Bill Lazier before the next meeting.

OUTCOMES

- Cohesive: Team trust has gained great momentum, with the team having a great understanding of what healthy conflict in a cohesive team is really all about. The accountability of the team and individuals is visible and progressing on the playing field.

- Human: The Organizational Function Chart and KFFM are visible with the team's understanding of the importance of the functional widgets and ownership. The function Scorecards the leaders own are now in place, with the CEO getting ready to use them for the leaders' annual reviews. This will be the last time for a *big* annual review as from now there will be performance coaching reviews every 90 days. The leaders will have their first experience in understanding the A-Player Team Assessment and the actions required to ensure the team has the highest possible share of A-Players.

- Cultural: With the great work that was done on the Core Values, the team is now clearer on the behavior expected of each team member. This makes it easier to recognize team members through Good News every day by sharing the great work team members have accomplished aligned to the Core Values.

- Strategy: 3HAG validation continues, keeping the Market Map up to date, creating the next iteration of the Core Customer Analysis, and agreeing on what more needs to be done to confirm the Core Customer. The first Attribution Map for the company is now complete, analyzing the industry marketplace.

- The team has the opportunity to take a step back and look at these key strategic pictures in order to take the next step forward, which is developing 3 to 5 differentiating activities. All strategic pictures are visible for all to review and explain with the whole team in the War Room. The great news is that, as we build up the company's strategy, these strategic pictures make it easy for all leaders to explain the same story—the same strategy—as the CEO would explain. This creates a great alignment of the CEO+Leadership team and the whole team as we continue our journey toward our 3HAG.

- Execution: The next iteration of the Growth Plan will be visible and clear to achieve on the Open Playing Field. The 13-Week Sprint Lane Plan continues to generate achievable quarterly plans. The active meeting cadence using the Open Playing Field will keep the focus on the plan every day.

- Cash: The habit of forecasting and tracking the company widgets by team members week over week will be active and visible on the Open Playing Field. The team is getting comfortable with forecasting, the process of sharing actual results, and the adjustments that need to be made. With the new widget-based forecast model for the next 12 months, this is an exciting step as the finance team will no longer have to best-guess at the forecast for the company. Instead, the leaders will own the widget forecast coupled with the fiscal assumptions. This step shifts the forecast ownership from the finance team to the leaders who own the widgets every day.

QUARTER 4:
1HAG ALIGNMENT TO 3HAG

The Q4 quarterly meeting is a 2-day annual planning session. This will be the fifth meeting the team has prepared for. They'll be excited to spend two days evolving and updating their strategy, mapping and creating a new 3HAG and an aligned 1HAG.

PREPARATION FOR THE MEETING

Have your leadership team—and yourself—prepare for the meeting like this:

1. Everyone should make sure they have finished reading *Beyond Entrepreneurship 2.0* by Jim Collins and Bill Lazier and be prepared for a good discussion around the concepts.

2. Everyone should update the priorities and metrics they own on the Open Playing Field so everyone can review them prior to the meeting—otherwise, you'll waste time statusing the plan in the meeting.

3. Have everyone complete the *Five Dysfunctions of a Team* Assessment.

4. After reviewing the status of the whole plan, the leaders should make notes, ask questions, and be ready to discuss in the context of building the plan for the next quarter.

5. Everyone should complete the Metronomics Checklist Survey. This is a true or false survey about how well the Metronomics regimen has been implemented so far in the organization. For more information go to *www.metronomicsthebook.com*.

6. Complete the Quarterly Prep Survey and review the results before the meeting.

By this time, the team is comfortable understanding the execution process and what to expect. Their knowledge of the Core Customer is as aligned as it has ever been. The Market Map is staying in focus quarter over quarter. The Open Playing Field is being utilized every day by the leaders.

The objective of this 2-day annual meeting is execution momentum and mapping out a full strategy, including rolling out a new 3HAG and 1HAG. The meeting will follow the same flow as the 2-day Kick-Off Meeting from a year earlier, with strategy focus on Day 1 and execution focus on Day 2.

DAY 1: STRATEGY

COHESIVE SYSTEM

Good News
As always, kick off the meeting in a fun and positive way with professional Good News. Do not skip this step.

Cohesive Question
Have your usual round-robin of personal questions or icebreakers to keep improving team trust. Remember: always start with the Coach and then the CEO.

Self-Awareness Assessment
Do the exact same Left and Right appreciation as you did in the last meeting, so the leaders can continue to learn how to provide feedback to their peers.

AGENDA

Compound Growth System	Day 1
Cohesive System	• Good News • Personal/Get to know you question • Left and Right—Appreciation • 5 Dysfunction Assessment Review
Human System	• Organizational Function Chart • KFFM • Team Assessment (A, B, C)
Cultural System	• Core Purpose • Core Values—Review Team Discovery and Update as needed • Hedgehog with Simon Sinek's Golden Circle • BHAG™: Confirm/Evolve
Strategy System	• 3HAG™: Evolve out + 1 Year • Market Map—Review • Core Customer—Review • Attribution Framework—Review • 3–5 Differentiators • Swimlanes
	Day 2
Execution System	• Status Review Annual Plan / QHAG • New 1HAG • New QHAG • Meeting: Check In • Cascade 3 Key Messages
Cash System	• Review Widget-based 12-month Forecast • Put Metrics into Rolling Metrics in MGS
Coach Cascade System	• n/a

Team Assessment

I recommend doing the *Five Dysfunctions of a Team* assessment with your team at least once a year. Everyone has already read Lencioni's book, so you should use it as the basis of a discussion regarding your framework and principles. This assessment is a great way to get a handle on where the team should focus on improving their cohesiveness in the next quarter and the next year. It gives your leaders self-awareness of how well they are interacting with each other for the good of the team.

The results of this assessment indicate where your team is on their development to being a highly cohesive team and developing into a high-performing business team. This assessment aligns with the work you have been doing in each of the 3 soft-edge systems. It will point out key actions and behaviors to focus on and set a benchmark to grow from into the future. I've been using these assessments since they came out with my teams and my clients' teams. They are invaluable for creating a great discussion with the team around the next steps in their cohesive behavioral growth.

To learn more about the *Five Dysfunctions of a Team* assessment and how to lead the discussion with your leadership team go to *www.metronomicsthebook.com*.

HUMAN SYSTEM

Organizational Function Chart

The next step in the meeting is to review the Organizational Function Chart. Remember, you should aim to work through this chart every 90 days at minimum.

Key Function Flow Map

The KFFM will be reviewed led by each functional owner. It's natural, now that the KFFM is well understood and ingrained in the company, that leaders want to create a KFFM for their own functional area because they understand its value. Indeed, some leaders might have already done this.

The reason I want you to stay focused on the original KFFM, or Level 1, for now, is that we need to ensure that the functions we have are correct, the owners are correct, and the widgets are correct, and that team behavior is such that they make decisions based on this active and live scoreboard for the business. In the next quarterly meeting, we will develop KFFM Level 2 maps, which will dig into and map each functional area, showing their key functions, owners, and widgets.

Team View

The Team View is a functional organization view similar to a traditional organizational chart. I'm not a fan of traditional organization charts, however, because they only show a person's name and title. The Team View, in contrast, shows the function, the person who has volunteered to own the function, and their title, and it shows all the functions and owners in one view. When team members own more than one function, that's also visible, as are planned functions for the future. That's important because it will provide opportunities for team members to grow into their next role.

This is a key view to create and keep up to date. The War Room and the Open Playing Field are great places for the team to review the Team View; you should also ensure you share it with the whole team at least once a month at the Townhall Meeting.

If you would like to learn more about the Team View, please go to *www. metronomicsthebook.com.*

A-Player Team Assessment

Leaders assess their direct reports on the A-Player Team Assessment graph for everyone to review and discuss. The way I do this with my clients is to have the assessment graph up at the beginning of the meeting. As the meeting progresses, each of the leaders can individually add their team member assessment to the graph. Later in the meeting, once everyone has updated the graph, take a moment and have a good discussion around the outcome and what actions need to be taken. Do not skip this step. This keeps your focus on an A-Player Team with your leaders.

CULTURAL SYSTEM

Core Purpose

At least once a year, I recommend you utilize a great tool created by Simon Sinek called the Golden Circle[1]. This tool allows you to easily answer questions that will ensure that you have accurately captured the Core Purpose of the organization.

The Golden Circle allows you to create a picture by getting everyone to answer these 3 questions:

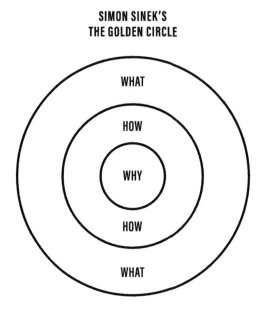

- What does the company do?
- How does the company do it?
- Why does the company do it?

Have each leader answer these questions individually and then share their answers one by one, question by question, starting with "What?" It's quite

---

1   Simon Sinek. "The Golden Circle Presentation." https://simonsinek.com/commit/
     the-golden-circle

normal to see a lot of the current Core Purpose show up in the answers around *what* or *how*. But the team will likely be forced to think deeply about *why* the company exists.

This discussion will have created a new Core Purpose or will have tweaked or confirmed the current Core Purpose. It's a great way to validate your Core Purpose. The Golden Circle is one of the most useful tools I used in business and now use as a Metronomics coach.

Core Values

Review the new and confirmed Core Values from the Discovery Process from the last two quarters. Make sure you celebrate the great work the team accomplished to get the Core Values clearly defined because that's a task only the team can accomplish.

A reminder: these are not brand Core Values or Core Values to go on your website for your customers. These are Core Values representing the consistent behaviors that your team expects of each other. Current team members who do not have the Core Values will need to be removed or will self-select and leave. We also need to ensure that our A-Player hiring process includes a strong assessment of how to identify Core Values in candidates we interview.

BHAG

Jim Collins created the Hedgehog concept to define a company's one big thing, its BHAG. If you know Jim's BHAG concept, you might have wondered why it has not come up sooner. The answer is because I like to wait to make sure the other key pieces are in place before we go deeper on the BHAG. What we've gutted out to date was good enough to create the execution momentum aligned to the BHAG and 3HAG that we gutted out a year ago and to create the cohesive confidence the team now has to really have a full discussion around the BHAG.

Now we want to dig deeper and answer 3 key questions, which we've adapted over the years to really line up with an organization.

The first question to ask your team is, "Why does the organization exist?" We just finished answering that same question using the Golden Circle, so we'll use the answer you agreed upon from that part of the meeting. That's your Core Purpose.

The second question is, "What is your core business—the thing that you can be best in the world at?" (It may not be that you can truly be best at it, but it's an *understanding* of what you can be best at.) Ask each leader to write down what they think the core business of your company is.

The answers we get can be very interesting, to say the least. Lots of leadership teams are challenged to articulate the core business they are in. After much discussion, you will land on an agreed-upon description of the core business of your organization.

The last question, which goes back to something we considered a few meetings ago, is really about describing how the company will make money: "What is the company's economic engine?" or, "What is the company's Profit per X?" or "How will the company make money at its core business?"

You've spent a lot of time and work reviewing the key functions by understanding the things that flow through your organization, so you should now have a better understanding of what your X should be in your Profit per X thanks to the great discussion around the core business married with the deep understanding of your KFFM.

We usually find that X is a widget that is in your current KFFM or a future KFFM. You and your team will identify it from your current KFFM or your 3HAG.

Once you have your 3 answers, write them in 3 circles, as shown. You can see that each of the circles intersects with the others, creating a place in the middle. This is where the BHAG lies. It's the intersection of the Core Purpose of your core business and your economic engine.

Now, ask all your leaders individually to write down what they believe the company's BHAG should now be, based upon the detailed work you've just done. Once all leaders have presented their ideas, have a healthy discussion and collaborate to agree on what the BHAG for your company should be. At this point, you will either have a new BHAG or a well-validated BHAG.

For more information on the Hedgehog concept, the BHAG, and Metronomics, please go to *www.metronomicsthebook.com*.

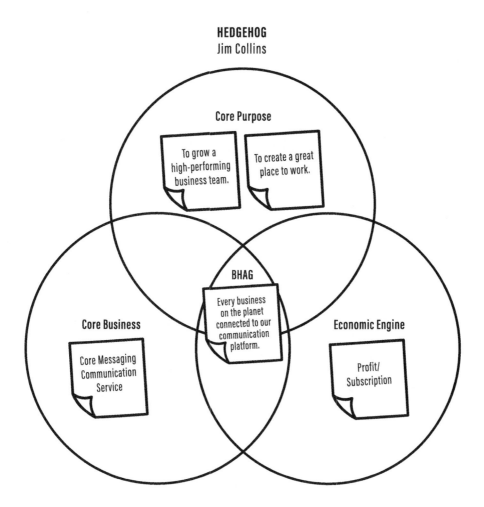

Profit/X

We just did a great deep dive into the Profit/X with the Hedgehog. We should now have eliminated any guesswork and be quite clear on our company "X."

STRATEGY SYSTEM

3HAG

You'll create a new 3HAG at this meeting. You will follow steps 1 to 4 as you did in the 2-day Kick-Off (you won't need to answer question 5 as the work we will complete in this meeting will have us focusing on the 3 to 5 differentiators, and will help progress us past the Key Capabilities at this time).

3HAG™
Date
Rev
Expense
Profit
Cash
# of Widgets
3HAG™ Statement
Differentiator #1
Differentiator #2
Differentiator #3
Differentiator #4
Differentiator #5
Brand Promise with Guarantee

THE 3HAG™: EVOLVE

01 What is the year ending date of Year 3?

02 What will the Fiscal Measures be: (a) Gross Revenue, (b) Cash

03 What are the "widgets" to get the company to this number?

04 3HAG™ Statement: What will the company be in 3 years? (**Gut Out** this statement with no numbers.)

05 What are the 3-5 Key Capabilities we need in place to deliver on #1-4?

06 What do we want to be known for in 3 years?

The team will gut out or have already forecast the fiscal numbers as well as the widgets for the 3HAG year. And the team will review and confirm the 3HAG statement or create a new one.

3HAG: Market Map

Review the Market Map and make any necessary updates based on how it's evolved.

3HAG: Core Customer Analysis

Review the Core Customer Analysis and make any necessary updates based on how it's evolved, or validate further if needed.

3HAG: *Attribution Map*

Review the Attribution Map. When this was created in the last meeting, it was a big discussion, with people feeling unsure of many things. Stop here and have a discussion around the Attribution Map and ask for any thoughts leaders may have now. This is a great way to stay focused on the players in your marketplace related to your current position in the marketplace. It allows you to make any key updates that are needed. The Attribution Map is also a great reflection of a leadership team's market expertise. It is important that the leadership team is feeling confident in the Attribution Map. That the 3HAG line is agreed upon by the leadership team before progressing to building the company's 3 to 5 differentiators.

3HAG: *Differentiators*

The definition of strategy, according to Michael Porter, is the creation of a unique and valuable position involving a different set of activities. The Attribution Map is so valuable because it shows a company graphically where a unique and valuable position might be into which it could move. The 3HAG line shows how the company could move into that white space—but it's just a line. The real secret to any company executing its strategy is deciding upon what activities it should do and what activities it should not do. A company's differentiators move it into a unique and valuable position or maintain the unique and valuable position it is already in. The activities Porter refers to in his definition are an interdependent set of activities the company decides to perform in order to move into the white space available.

In this meeting we will build up a *set* of 3 to 5 differentiating activities your company will put in place or maintain to make the 3HAG line you identified in the Attribution Map true.

The key question to start the brainstorming is: "What activities need to be in place in order to make the whole 3HAG line true as it is represented in the Attribution Map?"

Ask each leader individually to brainstorm 5 to 7 activities they think should be in place to make the 3HAG line true, and write each on a separate post-it note. Have each leader present their ideas one by one and put them up on the board. Once all the leaders have shared, group their ideas into similar activities. Then work with the whole group to try to name each group of activities you have created. There are usually anywhere from 3 to six groups of related activities to name.

BRAINSTORM ACTIVITIES TO MAKE THE 3HAG™ LINE TRUE

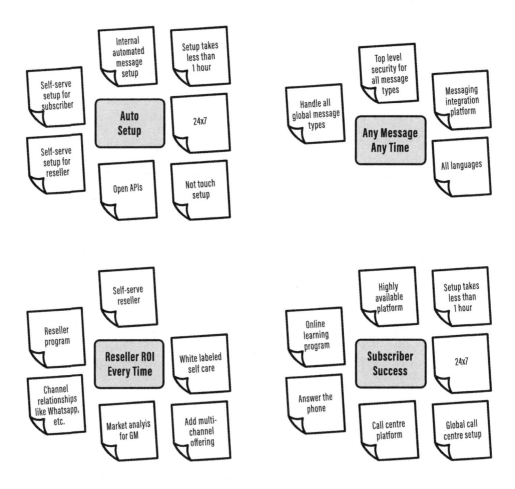

The next step is to discuss with your leadership team which of these 3 to six activities are dependent upon the others. It's very rare to get this far and not have these activities be interdependent.

Discussing these interdependencies is key to ensure that all of these activities are dependent on the others, creating a single set of interdependent, differentiating actions that creates the company's unique and valuable position. This is not necessarily the position the company is in today. It's one that you and the leadership team will aim for quarter over quarter, year over year, as you drive toward your 3HAG.

3-5 DIFFERENTIATORS (ACTIVITY FIT MAP: LEVEL 1 & 2)

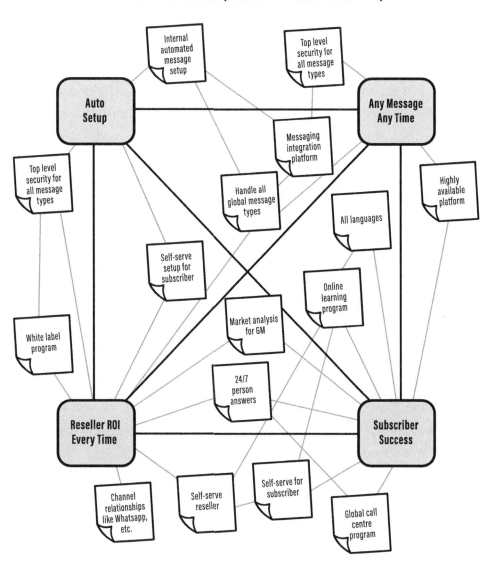

Using the Attribution Map and brainstorming activities is how you build a strategy from the ground up. It's a much stronger way to create strategy than top-downing it, which usually leaves the team with a vague understanding and little confidence. Because everyone has built the strategy together from the ground up, they absolutely understand what decisions need to be made in order to make the strategy happen.

I am always very careful working with companies creating their strategy to ensure that we're validating each step along the way. The steps we've taken so far have been careful, have been taken over time, and have been created while the cohesiveness of our team is increasing, thus creating a truly collaborative strategy.

Critics might say this process takes too long, but creating a company's truly differentiated strategy with a team like this requires many systems to be aligned before it becomes possible. Don't skip this step, and take the time you need to map out the strategy clearly and confidently. (You can definitely take the steps explained in *3HAG WAY* and complete them in a shorter period of time if needed—which sometimes it is. Just be sure to recognize that validation of the strategy is required, that to be most effective the whole team needs to have collaborated on its creation and that the strategy is clear and simple for the whole team to understand.)

A strategy is never complete because the world around us never stops moving—and our company never stops shifting internally, either.

To learn more about how to define your company's 3 to 5 differentiators, go to *www.metronomicsthebook.com* or read *3HAG WAY* for more details.

3HAG: Swimlanes

Swimlanes are a fantastic view for any team looking to create an actionable and realistic strategy. Swimlanes bring strategic execution alive. They show a team how to achieve their strategy and allow them to plan for this execution and have full discussions through planning both resources and cash. Swimlanes are a strategic picture that represents the key *milestones* required to achieve each differentiating action alongside the others.

If you imagine a pool with swimlanes, each lane represents a differentiating action stretched over 12 quarters. Within each lane, the team will brainstorm 3 to 5 big milestones that need to be accomplished in order to achieve

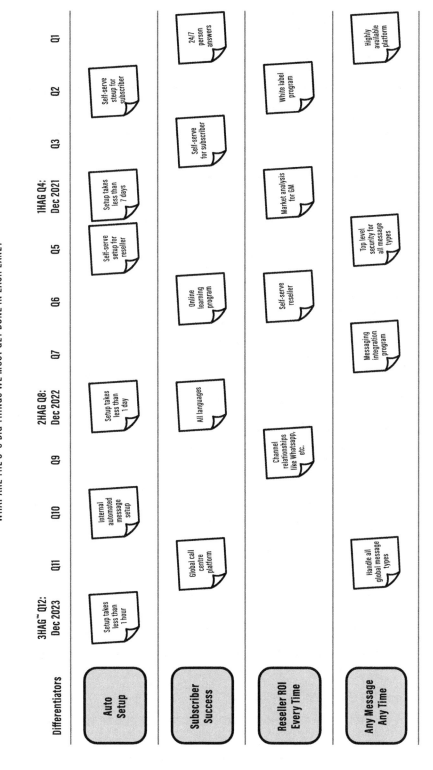

SWIMLANES
WHAT ARE THE 3–5 BIG THINGS WE MUST GET DONE IN EACH LANE?

that differentiating action. Break the leadership team into groups, each of which takes a differentiating action and brainstorms 3 to 5 milestones for that lane on post-it notes. Each group will explain the milestones to the whole team and discuss the critical path of timing across the Swimlanes. This will show the interdependency of the differentiators, which is completely normal.

Fewer milestones are better, so that you see a clear, critical path and how to implement your strategy—but also how you can keep it fluid because the environment you're playing in will evolve by quarter or year, and so must you.

Swimlanes enable the creation of a 36-month widget-based forecast, given that you have already made your key assumptions and set your timing according to what you know right now.

It's a great way to move this forward...but I am getting ahead of myself.

This first day of the 2-day annual is a *big* day. It's completely full. If you run out of time to complete the Swimlanes on Day 1, don't worry. Start with them on Day 2. As you'll see, they give you a great view of the four quarters of your next annual plan and the big milestones that must be achieved in the next year. Whether you do them on Day 1 or Day 2, you'll have completed them before you create the annual plan for execution.

For more information on how to create your Swimlanes, please go to *www.metronomicsthebook.com*.

DAY 2: EXECUTION

EXECUTION SYSTEM

The second day of the 2-day annual is dedicated to the Execution and Cash Systems, but we kick off with personal Good News, reflections from Day 1, and any wrap-up items from Day 1. If you run out of time on the Swimlanes, complete them right at the start of the day before any of the items below.

Status: 1HAG and Current QHAG
The review will be quick as long as the team has the status and is up to date before the meeting and the team has been reviewing and discussing it on a weekly basis.

AGENDA

Compound Growth System	Day 2
Cohesive System	· Day 1 Reflections
Execution System	· New 1HAG · New QHAG · 13 Week Sprint Lanes · Meeting: Check In · Cascade 3 Key Messages
Cash System	· Review Widget-Based 12 Month Forecast · Put Metrics into Rolling Metrics in MGS
Coach Cascade System	· n/a

New Annual Plan (1HAG)

The morning should be spent with the team working through the same questions you used at the Kick-Off Meeting to agree on a new 1HAG. This time round, after you have decided upon the annual priorities with your team, it is best practice to review your Swimlanes, looking at the first four quarters that you just finished creating. This will bring together a great view and validation of your annual priorities. Make any adjustments as required.

The great news is that the team has worked hard with finance to create their first 12-month widget-based forecast, so this part of the meeting is really about putting these numbers up in lights and ensuring there is clear agreement and ownership.

New Quarterly Plan (QHAG)

The afternoon should be spent with the team working through the same questions you used in the last quarterly meeting to create a new QHAG. Don't skip the 13-Week Sprint Lanes.

CASH SYSTEM

This is an exciting time for the finance team and the leadership team. For the first time, they have a widget-based forecast where the leaders have created the forecast based on the widgets in their functional area. The finance team's contribution has purely been creating the model and inputting the numbers, rather than creating the actual forecast itself. This allows ownership of the widget-based forecast to go to the next level, instilling behavior where the leaders and their teams want to keep the forecast up to date and aligned month over month in the coming year.

CHECK-IN

As with every meeting, check in with the team how the meeting cadence, agenda, and outcomes are progressing. This gives you as a team the opportunity to tweak together anything that needs to be adjusted so everyone stays aligned with their teams.

As we will in each annual planning session, review the results of the Metronomics Survey results and have a good discussion about them. Make a plan as to what needs more focus or a different approach. As the team continues to become more self-aware during the process, they will assess themselves with more vigor.

Cascading Messages

As at all our meetings, we will do a meeting check-in with everyone and take note of the 3 Key Messages that need to be cascaded to the rest of the organization in tomorrow's huddle.

One-Phrase Close

The day wraps up as always, asking each of the leaders for 5 words or less to describe how they feel right now.

NEXT STEPS/HOMEWORK

- Update the Open Playing Field as necessary, adding Core Purpose, BHAG, 3HAG, and so on.

- Each leader should add to the Open Playing Field the annual Corporate Priorities and the quarterly Corporate Priorities, including the 13-week subpriorities from the Sprint Lanes developed with the team, as well as their own individual priorities.

- Add updated Market Map to the War Room.

- Add updated Core Customer to the War Room.

- Add Attribution Framework to the War Room.

- Add Differentiators to the War Room and the Open Playing Field.

- Continue to run all company meetings through the Open Playing Field.

- Review KFFM in Weekly Leadership Team Meeting.

- Leaders to make plans or take action on any C-Player team members.

- Leaders cascade 3 Key Messages to their teams.

- Everyone should read *The Speed of Trust* by Stephen M.R. Covey.

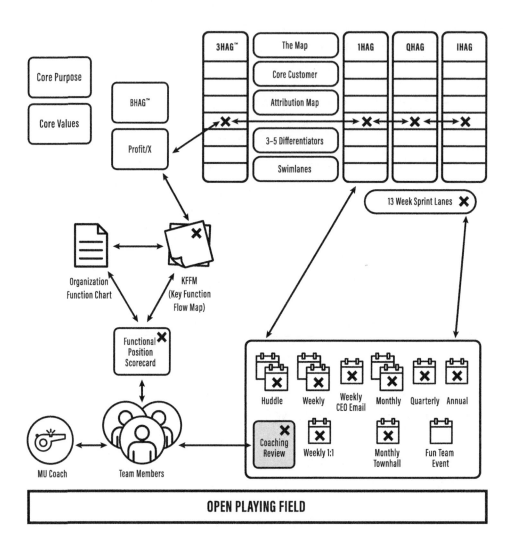

OUTCOMES

- Cohesive: The team has a good understanding of the current level of team cohesiveness and clear actions they need to take to progress. The team has a clear view of what more they can do to improve cohesiveness through the *Five Dysfunctions of a Team* assessment results and discussion. The accountability and commitment of the team and individuals are visible and alive on the Open Playing Field.

YEAR 1: FOUNDATION—KICK-ASS EXECUTION AND CASH WITH ALIGNED STRATEGY

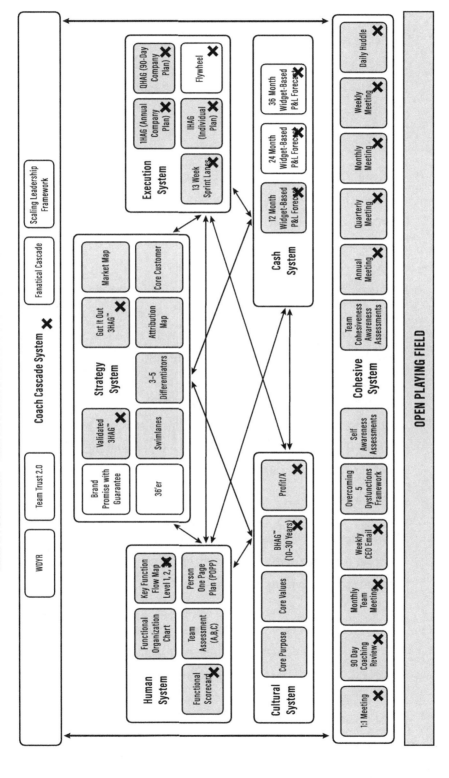

- Human: The Organizational Function Chart and KFFM are visible, with the team's understanding of the importance of the functional widgets and ownership. The CEO has completed the performance coaching reviews with all leaders, both giving and receiving feedback. All team members are focused on what they own on behalf of the team.

- Cultural: The evolution or confirmation of the Core Purpose and the BHAG bring the team's belief and commitment to a new level. The Core Values are visible and alive in the company without the need for writing them on the walls or website.

- Strategy: The team is excited to have a fully mapped-out strategy that aligns with their BHAG and 3HAG. The next 12 quarters have never been clearer, and their commitment to the plan is strong and confident. The strategy is clear, simple, and easily shared.

- Execution: The company has a new 1HAG and QHAG. The team is efficient at this process, allowing for more time for strategy. The Growth Plan is visible and clear on the Open Playing Field. The active meeting cadence using the playing field is keeping the focus on the plan every day.

- Cash: The leadership team has created the 12-month widget-based forecast together, with the leaders creating the forecast and the finance team providing the model.

- Coach Cascade: This system has been activated slightly through the CEO and leaders completing their performance coaching reviews based on the function Scorecards. In addition, the Left and Right exercise at the beginning of each meeting will improve peer-to-peer feedback. The dial on this system will be turned on starting in the next quarter.

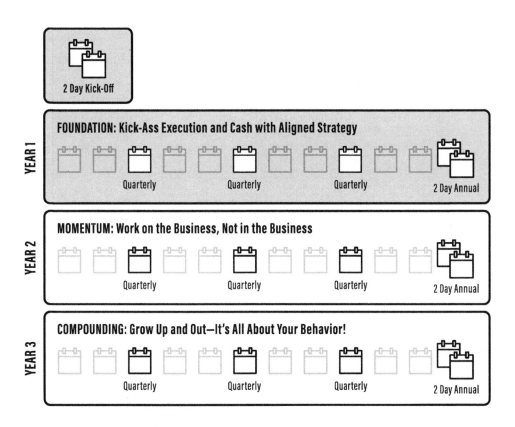

The team has now been using Metronomics for 5 quarters. *Wow!!* They have fully bought in to the regimen. They are proud of their accomplishments thus far, and they're keen to move forward into the next four quarters.

They are proud of their success to date and eager to get even better. They are developing into a cohesive team and are creating the clarity required to commit to the path forward in order to become a high-performing business team.

Don't forget: without clarity of and commitment to the key elements of the plan—goals, priorities, widgets, an Open Playing Field, and team rewards—a highly cohesive team is only a highly cohesive team; it won't necessarily translate into a high-performing business team. This can only happen with clarity and simplicity that enables you to commit with your team to the plan. Commit to the team results.

When a highly cohesive team commits to the team results, the outcome of their performance transforms them into a high-performing team, or in this case a high-performing business team. And if you've been following along, your team is in a great position to develop into an enduring high-performing business team that consistently "wins."

YEAR 2:
THE MOMENTUM YEAR

t couldn't have gone any better. It was a year since Alex had first brought Lee onboard as a CEO+Leadership team coach, and the 2-day annual meeting convinced him that he'd never made a better decision in business.

OpenDoor had come so far.

That was clear when they went back to the BHAG. Lee had told them not to dive too deep in the first year—and no one had time to do that anyway. But just a year later, something that had seemed scarily ambitious didn't just hold true. It was already getting easier to imagine it being possible. By adjusting some of the language about their core business during the great discussion around their "Hedgehog," Alex and his leaders made it even more concrete.

Alex could already foresee how parts of the BHAG aligned to the 3HAG.

They had gone back to Simon Sinek's Golden Circle to confirm their Core Purpose. What does the business do? How does the business do it? And why does the organization exist?

The team kept putting forward ideas, and each time Alex thought, That's it. That's as good as it can be. But that thought only lasted until the next iteration. And the next.

Alex felt vindicated. With the new CFO and CTO settled in, the whole team turned fast to any areas in execution, strategy, and cash that needed adjusting.

Everyone was using the Open Playing Field and could see how the company was progressing each and every day. With 12 months of metrics behind them, they'd been able to come up with a new 3HAG, too, mapping it out on the first day and talking about how to execute it on the second day.

At lunch on the first day, Alex strolled outside with Chris, the CMO. He couldn't help grinning as he asked, "How do you think it's going?"

Chris said, "We're smashing it. When you look back to last year, we knew nothing. This time it's much easier."

Alex replied, "Not easy, maybe. I just think everyone's more confident in the process and the how."

"Clarity. That's what Lee calls it. All of us are clear on where we are going, what our roles are, and what is expected of us."

The excitement was contagious. With the momentum they'd generated, the performance widgets they had, and their analysis of the market, they'd come up with an evolved strategy to grow their membership.

It was right there in front of them after they worked through the Attribution Map and built the 3 to 5 differentiators from the ground up. And it was nicely confirmed on the Swimlane build-out.

To start with, they'd been far more long-winded in how they explained it, but Lee kept pushing them to reduce the strategy to a single phrase. Now they had it. "Make messaging easy."

Everyone could learn it. Everyone could explain it. Everyone was dialed in.

These activities were all interdependent. They were mapped out over 3 years. That clearly differentiated the *company*.

Alex was relaxed about the second day of the meeting, which was devoted to execution. Execution was their wheelhouse. After the last 12 months, they'd nailed it down.

At the end of the 2-day, they had the best plan they'd ever had for the future of the company. Everyone was pumped. The team was so well aligned. Alex was so pleased he had removed Daniel and Alison. This new leadership group had improved as a team—and as individuals too.

At his usual YPO monthly forum meeting, Alex couldn't wait to explain how well the meeting had gone. Everyone congratulated him, knowing about his earlier frustrations. But a couple of his colleagues were surprised. Why did he *still* have a coach? It must be expensive. Surely the point of a coach was to come in, solve problems, and step back again.

Alex felt defensive. "It's true, we've solved lots of problems and removed a lot of barriers. But more importantly, we have implemented the Metronomics system, which we cannot live without. We're so far ahead of where we were last year. I just feel the coach can help us achieve even more within the system. Every time we meet with her, it's as if she peels back another layer of the onion. I am wondering why we would ever stop doing this."

"I don't know, Alex. It sounds like it's time to cut the strings. You don't need someone looking over your shoulder."

When a text came in as he was driving home, Alex knew it would a message from Mark. "Don't listen to them. I know what you're saying because it's how I feel about coaching too. We are building and growing a high-performing business team. And just like any of the high-performing teams in basketball, soccer, football, whatever, they all have a coach with a system."

Over the following weeks, however, some of the leadership team's excitement about the strategy wore off. They were wanting to dig in a little more. Also, Alex wanted more clarity.

As the Year 2, Q1 meeting rolled around, Alex shared his anxiety with Lee.

"I can't see the problem, but I think the strategy just isn't as strong as we thought it was."

Lee said, "This is completely normal for this point in the journey. We just finished a 2-day annual where we mapped out a clear strategy. We now need to validate that strategy. And validate it. And validate it. This year, every quarter, we will dive deeper into validating the strategy. In the meantime, though, it would not hurt to go back and review your Core Customer before our next meeting. Do that, and we can use it to create our Positioning Statement and Value Proposition that will help validate the work we have already completed."

When Alex talked to the leadership team, they all realized they needed to go deeper into a detailed analysis of their Core Customer.

Matthew, the new CFO, said, "I've always assumed we have four types of Core Customer, anyway."

Alex thought that sounded reasonable, but Lee encouraged them to do the deeper work to really validate who their real Core Customer was: the customer whose top 3 needs they served and who bought at a profit every time.

So they did, and they got down to two Core Customers to analyze. On the one hand, individual subscribers. On the other, resale companies that would brand OpenDoor's SaaS products to serve their own membership of customers.

Matthew argued that they were both essential. Alex silently agreed, but Lee said, "Let's use the Core Customer Analysis for both."

The map soon revealed that the individual subscriber who had been OpenDoor's original customers were not only hard to define, but they also didn't raise enough cash and would take too long to grow at scale. The companies who would rebrand their products were a far more profitable enterprise. Even though those companies ultimately brought more individual customers on board, it was the *resellers* who were OpenDoor's Core Customer, not the individual subscribers.

The figures were clear. That was where they should focus. And it aligned well with their 3HAG.

Matthew was looking down at the table. Alex asked him, "Happy, Matt?"

Matthew nodded slowly. "I was mistaken in my assumptions, and I can see that now. This was a great process to get all the facts and feedback in front of us for a solid discussion. I know to be patient and trust the system!"

Alex was relieved. He didn't want to lose another CFO so soon.

That was the most difficult part of the year, but in overcoming the bump, Alex knew they'd validated their strategy with confidence. They kept tweaking the execution, and they could see the strategy flow through the company via the widgets on the Open Playing Field.

Before Alex knew it, it was time for another 2-day annual.

It was awesome.

Execution was working, and the financial results were outstanding. OpenDoor signed up more reseller companies, and the resellers brought thousands of individual customers, so the membership rocketed.

The evolved validated strategy had become the basis for a new 3HAG. The leadership group had made their Key Function Flow Map more detailed, plugging in where each person fit, and they had more detailed widgets to help forecast accurate results. And each of the functions represented in the KFFM had its own Level 2 KFFM.

The whole team was aligned. They all knew what the next part of the story would be.

But that wasn't all. The leadership team was more empowered. They didn't look to Alex to solve problems so often—because they'd trained their teams to come to them with recommendations, not questions.

That freed up the leadership team to spend more time thinking about the business, which is why Alex had hired them in the first place. The teams had their own widgets now, that they owned, and they were excited to be able to have their own priorities.

It had been an awesome year. But when Lee asked the leadership team to do the Metronomics Assessment—in which each leader answered true or false to a set of questions to assess how they felt they were doing—the results were worse than Alex had anticipated. Lee was not surprised: she had seen this trend before.

Alex said, "Guys, we had the best year's results we've ever had. We killed it! You're performing better than ever."

Jen, the COO, said, "That's true. The thing is, last year we thought we'd got it cracked. Remember? Looking back, we had no idea about how much more there was for us to learn and evolve. So it's hard to be satisfied with ourselves now when we don't even know how much further there is to go."

Andrew added, "That's right. The most important thing we've learned, even though we've definitely moved forward this year with our execution, strategic validation, and coaching and empowering the team, is that we *still* have a long way to go. And with our growth year over year, our team is growing, too, and we have to keep the whole team aligned. So yes, we are better than we were. But we still have lots of room for improvement."

Alex had to admit that they were right. He shared the same feeling that he knew there was more to get done and he was excited about the challenge.

He said to Lee at the end of the meeting, "I feel a bit sheepish. At the 2-day last year, we were so full of ourselves. You must have been rolling your eyes."

Lee said, "Not at all. You weren't wrong to celebrate. But now Metronomics has made you all more aware of your true potential as a high-performing business team, what more you can accomplish to increase the ease, speed, and confidence with which you perform. You also are very aware of where the bar is and of your commitment to growing your team and your company. When people are dissatisfied, it just shows how eager they are to achieve more."

YEAR 2: QUARTER BY QUARTER

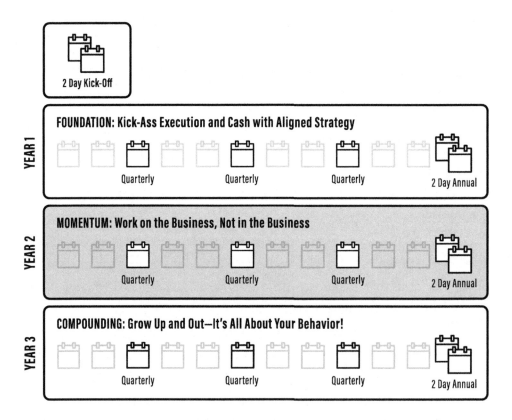

In Year 2, you and your team will pick up momentum through validating the strategy you've mapped and gain the confidence you need to make better, faster decisions to move in the direction of the 3HAG. With your team understanding the execution process and having implemented it strongly, and with visibility of your metrics all the way through to your cash forecast, the leadership team now has the opportunity to focus more on a confident strategy and on coaching the team. This year builds on both strategic execution excellence and team cohesiveness.

Picking up from where you finished Year 1, you will have evolved and/or confirmed your BHAG. You will have a new 3HAG with a fully mapped-out strategy, even though it needs further validation. Your team understands the ease of execution utilizing the process. They are fully committed to the system. And you have a regular A-Player Team Assessment in place, resulting in a higher share of A-Players on the team.

QUARTERLY MEETINGS

Again, the year is built around turning the dials on each of the seven systems through 90-day intervals. As we did in the first year, we will focus on the systems every 90 days, probably focusing on some a little more than others at different times but never abandoning any. They all need to stay active. Metronomics is focused on the connectedness of the systems to the team's behavior—so it can only move forward if the team is ready.

As in Year 1, we will turn the dials of the systems each quarter, with each quarterly meeting homing in on specific areas:

- Y2, Q1: Validating strategy
- Y2, Q2: The 36'er (don't worry if you're unfamiliar with the phrase; I'll explain shortly)
- Y2, Q3: Increasing team confidence
- Y2, Q4: Aligning the BHAG, the new 3HAG, and the new 1HAG (as in Q4 of Year 1)

The excitement is palpable. The team is stoked by the progress and the commitment of the entire leadership team.

Keeping Confidence

Once you have great momentum with strategy and execution, some companies are happy. They might feel they've come far enough or think there is no farther for them to go because they made so much progress in the first year. They decide they just want to keep what they had going in Year 1. They can do that, of course. But they don't realize how much better it can get. The execution momentum from Year 1 alone won't create the strategic confidence required to know where you are going with confidence. It doesn't guarantee the predictability that your team, your shareholders, and your buyers are looking to see. Ultimately, the team will want the visible strategic confidence of knowing where they are going and driving toward it.

Confidence is so important you must continue to build it with your team quarter over quarter. We will never stop validating the strategy, the 3HAG, and the whole plan.

As you continue this journey of growth for yourself, your team, and the company, this will get easier with each and every step you take. The speed at which the team moves gets faster, and the team's confidence continues to grow. As the seven systems grow in your organization, so does the momentum, creating the ease, the speed, and the confidence you are starting to experience.

What the team has experienced in the process so far is very human. They're attracted to the system because it appeals to human nature. It makes business entirely human. Even the 3HAG, the glue that holds this whole system together, is founded upon human behavior. Step by step, you are turning the dial or dials a little each quarter. By now, that process is becoming a habit for the whole team, coupled with their commitment to the team and to the team results—and this is what will set you free to grow your business.

By the end of Year 2, everyone will have great confidence in the strategy, which will bring better, faster decisions that will drive faster growth. You're going to take the momentum from your kick-ass execution and cash, aligned with strategy, and you're going to leverage them to build more confidence in the team, the board, and the customers.

Let's go through the second year, quarter by quarter.

QUARTER 5: VALIDATE STRATEGY

The first meeting of the second year sets out to keep the momentum of the execution going and to validate the strategy.

Before the Y2 Q1 meeting, you or the coach gives the team homework. Reading, surveys, and assessments should be shared in plenty of time prior to the meeting, and, as usual, everyone is responsible for making sure the Open Playing Field is up to date.

PREPARATION FOR THE MEETING

Have your leadership team—and yourself—prepare for the meeting like this:

1. Everyone should have completed reading *The Speed of Trust*.

2. Everyone should bring the status of the priorities and metrics they own up to date on the Open Playing Field so everyone can review them prior to the meeting—otherwise, you'll waste time updating the plan in the meeting.

3. Complete the Quarterly Prep Survey and review the results prior to the meeting.

4. After reviewing the status of the whole up-to-date plan, make notes or questions and be ready to discuss the context of building the next quarter's plan.

As in your previous quarterly meetings, there is a set agenda with sections that each focus on 1 of the 7 systems. This agenda highlights the key areas of focus; the rest of the process and system will remain constant.

AGENDA

Compound Growth System	Day 1
Cohesive System	• Good News • Cohesive Question • Left and Right • Speed of Trust Review
Human System	• Organizational Function Chart • KFFM • Team Assessment (A, B, C)
Cultural System	• Core Purpose • Core Values • BHAG™: Confirm/Evolve
Strategy System	• 3HAG™: Confirm • Market Map—Review • Core Customer—Review • Positioning and Value Prop Statement
Execution System	• Status Review Annual Plan / QHAG • Next QHAG • Swimlanes—Review • Meeting: Check In • Cascade 3 Key Messages
Cash System	• Widgets Act / F/C to P/L F/C • Book Monthly F/C Review Meeting
Coach Cascade System	• WDYR • Speed of Trust Review

COHESIVE SYSTEM

As usual, we start with activities that build the Cohesive System, Good News, and cohesive get-to-know-you questions.

Left and Right

We will evolve the Left and Right process that we started in Y1 Q3. This time, it includes not only what you appreciate about the person on your left and right but also one thing they could improve upon. We have been warming up to this, as everyone needs to be comfortable providing feedback to team members. As the cohesiveness of the team has been improving quarter over quarter, the leadership should be ready now for this important next step. For more information on this process, please go to *www.metronomicsthebook.com*.

COACH CASCADE SYSTEM

Although we have been working through the Cohesive System and building for the Coach Cascade System, we haven't really worked in this area. We will ramp up the Coach Cascade System over Year 2 and have it in full swing for Year 3. The Coach Cascade System is the key to taking human behavior to the next level of high cohesiveness, ending up in a high-performing team. I am excited to get to this point. We can now build on the great foundation you have and take it forward. And as you know, this all starts with the CEO and the leadership team.

Speed of Trust Review

The team has read *The Speed of Trust*. They're excited about where they are with their team cohesiveness. A full discussion based upon the ideas of Stephen M.R. Covey helps everyone look at their collaboration and credibility using Covey's four cores of credibility:

- Integrity
- Intent
- Capabilities
- Results

Covey's approach is a methodology of putting together vulnerability and credibility in order to move much faster—not just toward achieving vulnerability as individuals but also moving the team toward overall success at a greater speed.

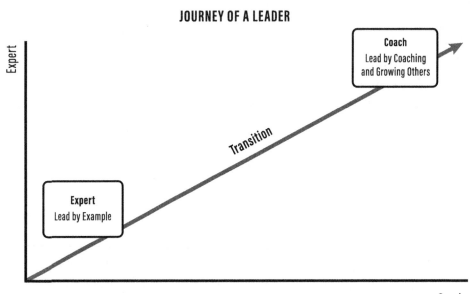

JOURNEY OF A LEADER

This is part of the effort to move your team from being Expert Leaders to Coach Leaders, so they can cascade Metronomics through the rest of the company. The meeting explores what is needed to become a Coach Leader and assesses whether it is happening in the company. If not, it determines how to make it a reality. This is a great awareness discussion to identify the key actionable steps for leaders to move themselves through the transition.

For more detailed information on how to lead this session and have a great discussion with your leadership, visit *www.metronomicsthebook.com.*

WDYR

The next step is to continue the discussion and focus on adjusting all the leaders' behavior together in a key area—and perhaps a surprising one.

Most Expert Leaders answer all questions their team members ask them. They want to because they feel that's their role. In order to grow from an Expert Leader to a Coach Leader, however, we need, as a leadership team together, to *stop* answering the questions the team is asking. This may sound counterintuitive, but in fact, the team usually knows the answers to their own questions—especially now, since we have a clear and simple connected strategy execution plan.

This is a habit we call "What do you recommend?" or WDYR. We came up with it based upon feedback from my own coach. I was exhausted trying to answer all the questions I was being asked as a CEO. Quite frankly, I shouldn't have been answering most of them anyway. I didn't really know the answers. What was more, the people asking the questions was normally the experts in the area.

Again, you are probably wondering why we're just adding this to the meetings now. The reason we can introduce it now is that we finally have a clear, known, and aligned plan that the team understands. A year ago, it wouldn't have been much use to ask the team "What do you recommend?" without a clear understanding of where we are going, coupled with our new level of cohesiveness. Now they have a clear understanding of the path forward, it is much easier for them to identify areas that we need to evolve and recommend their own solutions. And with increased cohesiveness, they have more confidence to provide recommendations as they know they will be well received.

This is a great thing because now we have the experts who work in functional areas every day recommending solutions rather than waiting for answers. This also frees time for your whole leadership team, once they see that they do not need to answer questions but to understand the expert-recommended solutions and allow the experts to execute.

Leaders are more than likely experts in their areas as well. That's why their team will come and ask them questions. And why the leaders normally answer the questions. The leaders on your team need to evolve their behavior to stop answering questions from their own team, focusing on the next 90 days.

Ask your leaders to keep track every day of how many questions they answered and how many they responded to by saying, "What do you recommend?" At the weekly leadership meeting, ask each leader to share how many questions they answered in the past week and how many they responded to with WDYR. This is a great way to get the behavior ingrained into the organization and speed up both execution and the development of high cohesion.

The more the leadership team asks their team members for recommendations, the more their team members will stop asking questions. They'll just bring recommendations. You'll see the tally evolve in the weekly leadership meetings.

The organization will get better solutions from the team rather than from the leaders.

For more information, please go to *www.metronomicsthebook.com*.

HUMAN SYSTEM

Organizational Function Chart
As at every meeting, review the Organizational Function Chart for any adjustments and ensure we are looking forward and planning out toward our 1HAG and 3HAG.

Key Functions Flow Map
By now, the KFFM should be fully visible and active for the whole team on the Open Playing Field. Carry out a full review and discussion, getting each leader to discuss the functional area they own, sharing how the function is operating—red, yellow, or green—and then discuss the metrics/widgets associated with their function, rating them red, yellow, green, or super green. The leaders are comfortable and efficient with this process. Do not skip it.

KFFM Level 2
Now we prepare to introduce a new level to the KFFM: KFFM Level 2. Each leader will build a KFFM for their function by identifying the 3 to 5 subfunctions of the function they own with their team. Do this in the same way as the KFFM Level 1, sticking to the highest-level functions of their area and identifying the inputs and outputs of each subfunction, so that the KFFM Level 2 shows the things this function area owns and controls and which member of the team is accountable.

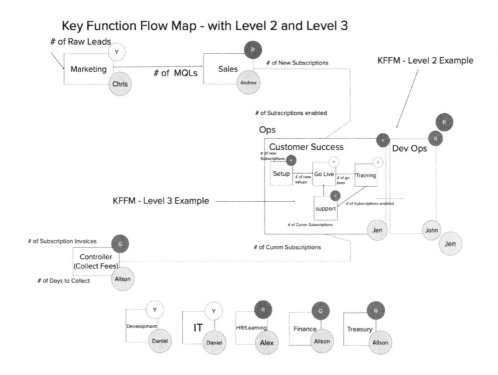

This is a powerful view of each function and really gets the team engaged and fired up. They are finally on the "scoreboard," making them further aligned with the company, and they can see the widget-based forecast being brought to life.

As a CEO who has done this a few times, I love getting to this point. The team is so excited that the energy and momentum increase tenfold. The visibility of connecting the widgets to the function to the company is a huge step forward in helping team members clearly understand what they do every day and how it contributes to the company's score. The discussions and the level of ownership of the team go to the next level.

At the next quarterly meeting, we will put up on the wall a KFFM Level 2 for each function of the KFFM Level 1 and have a full discussion. I love this view and so do teams.

Team View

The Team View is another way to view the team and team members and how they relate to one another. Remember, this looks similar to a traditional organization chart, but it is a functional organization chart. This chart puts function first, so team members can be on the chart more than once, and the open functions that need to be hired are identified. This is a great view for everyone.

As a CEO, I used this view often to play with a functional design that would support the growth of our organization. Remember, in the Team View we are not just reviewing the current status. It's vital that we look ahead. That way, we can be sure that we are planning our future functional design with the 3HAG and team in mind.

A-Player Team Assessment

Leaders assess their direct reports on the A-Player Team Assessment graph for everyone to review and discuss.

CULTURAL SYSTEM

Core Purpose

Quickly review and confirm the Core Purpose.

Core Values

A quick review and confirmation.

BHAG

A quick review to confirm that the BHAG is good enough for now.

Profit/X

A quick review to confirm that the Profit/X is good enough for now.

STRATEGY SYSTEM

After the BHAG and Profit/X, look at the Strategy System. As always, focus first on the 3HAG. Review and adjust the Market Map and your analysis of the Core Customer.

3HAG

A quick review to confirm that it is good enough for now.

3HAG: Market Map

Review the Market Map and make any necessary updates based on how it's evolved.

3HAG: Core Customer Analysis

A quick review of the Core Customer.

Positioning Statement and Value Proposition

This is a great step to take with the team at this point. The strategy has been mapped out, and this process will zero in on what you and your team are truly confident about in your strategy. You'll get clearer on each of the key sections later.

I love how this step takes all the work we've done so far on our strategy and formats it into a great statement that you and your team should be very confident in saying. The great news is that working through this format will identify key areas of the strategy work we have completed and confirm whether we are confident or whether we need to dig in further for clarity.

The other reason I love this view, which was created by Geoffrey Moore in his book *Crossing the Chasm*, is that the positioning statement and value proposition are so tightly connected. They force your team to think about the same thing in a different way.

You will find that each strategic picture you create is founded upon the principles of strategy and the work you have already done. That makes it very powerful. The team's confidence will increase with their understanding of the principles and connections of strategy. This is exactly what happened with me and my team as we built confidence in our strategy. Our own knowledge of strategy increased, and the creativity of the team was outstanding.

I haven't only seen the process in my own teams. I've also seen the same thing happen with my clients. This is where the true strategic fun begins.

POSITIONING STATEMENT AND VALUE PROPOSITION
Geoffrey Moore

Positioning Statement — Template — G. Moore

For	*(Specifically describe target customer)* **CORE CUSTOMER**
Who	*(statement of need or opportunity)* **#1 NEED**
The is a **COMPANY NAME**	**PRODUCT CATEGORY**
That	*(statement of key benefit—this is compelling reason to buy)* **#1 BENEFIT**
Unlike	*(Competitors or primary competitive alternative)* **COMP 1 & COMP 2**
Our Product	*(statement of primary differentiation)* **#1 BENEFIT THAT DIFFERENTIATES**

POSITIONING STATEMENT AND VALUE PROPOSITION
Geoffrey Moore

Value Proposition Statement — Template — G. Moore

We Believe that	*(Target Company Buyer) Lines 1 of Position Statement (FOR)* **CORE CUSTOMER**
Should be able to	*(Positive Impact on critical business issues addressed) Positioning Statement—Line 2— (Who Need)* **#1 NEED**
By	*(specific measurement of KPI, #, $, %) ROI or Business Case for the Nerve that you HIT* **LOOK AT BRAND PROMISE WITH GUARANTEE PROMISE**
Through the Ability to	*(Specific Action your Enable) Line 4 of Positioning Statement (That Provides)* **#1 BENEFIT**
As a result of	*(your unique differentiated capabilities) Line 6 of Positioning Statement—Our Product* **#1 BENEFIT THAT DIFFERENTIATIES**
For an investment of approximately	*(Average Deal $$ estimated)* **DESCRIBE INVESTMENT CORE CUSTOMER NEEDS TO MAKE**

This view will help us clarify not only our Positioning Statement but also our Value Proposition. That's an important basis for the strategic analysis we will do in the next quarter, which is the Business Model Canvas created by Alex Osterwalder.

Osterwalder also created a great Value Proposition mapping tool, by the way. I prefer to start with Moore's, but if you need to create another view, leverage Osterwalder's tool next time round. As I've said already, the great thing about Metronomics is that it enables you to plug in the tools, views, and research of all the top thought leaders, as needed. This is a great example of being able to plug in another tool that will achieve the same outcome from a different perspective. This is what makes Metronomics such a powerful system.

For more info on the Position Statement and Value Proposition, please go to *www.metronomicsthebook.com.*

EXECUTION SYSTEM

Your team knows and understands the execution system part of the day. You'll follow the same process at every quarterly meeting throughout the year. The one addition this year is the Swimlanes. What I recommend is that the team members create their quarterly priorities, and then go look at the Swimlanes. That will help them see what they may have missed that is important for driving toward their 1HAG and 3HAG.

As always, this part of the meeting closes with checking in on the Metronomics system with the leaders and ensuring that 3 Key Messages are captured so they can be cascaded out after the meeting.

CASH SYSTEM

The great news about the cash system is that you kicked off this year with a widget-based month-over-month forecast. Remember, this forecast was built up by the leaders each owning their functional area and forecasting their widgets in collaboration with the other leaders and the team goals.

Now you should have the first 3 months of actuals-to-forecast for the profit-and-loss statement, including a comparison of actual to forecasted cash.

At this stage, you should start booking a monthly forecast review meeting with the leadership team that will be recurring each month. The meeting should last a maximum of one hour. The leaders review their actual results compared to their forecasted results, then look out through the rest of the months of the year to create a rolling forecast.

This does not mean that the approved forecast they started the year with shifts; the approved forecast is static throughout the whole year. Instead, it means the leaders look at their actual results and at what the current situation is, then adjust the newly created rolling forecast as required to align with the approved forecast. The rolling forecast is the actual monthly results plus the more up-to-date month-over-month rolling forecast for the rest of the year and then beyond.

Rolling Forecast at the End of Month 2

	Month 1			Month 2			Month 3			FY2021 – Q1			FY2021		
	Actual	Rolling	Approved	Actual	Rolling	Approved	Actual	Rolling	Approved	QTD Actual	Rolling	Approved	YTD Actual	Rolling	Approved
Gross Revenue	825000	900000	900000	950000	1000000	1000000		1000000	1100000	1775000	2225000	3000000	1775000	11250000	12000000

This is important for a few reasons:

1. The leaders absolutely own their functional area forecasts and come together each month to share them with the rest of the team. We know this is important because everyone can see how these functions interact at the KFFM level.

2. The process gives clear visibility into how you are tracking to your forecast, creates focus, and allows you to adjust your plan in terms of revenue, expenses, and, more importantly, cash based on your actuals.

3. This process improves the accuracy of the forecast because all the owners of the functional areas are together focusing on the

widgets—the things that flow through the company—and adjusting as necessary.

4. This process gives full visibility not only into the next month's forecast but into the quarter and the year. As we work through this year, we will extend this 12-month forecast out to 36 months. That's what we call the 36'er. We'll turn our attention to it at the next quarterly meeting.

5. This process improves the whole team's forecasting ability together.

CHECK-IN

As with every meeting, check-in with the team how the meeting cadence, agenda, and outcomes are progressing. This gives you as a team the opportunity to tweak anything that needs to be adjusted so everyone stays aligned with their teams.

Cascading Messages

As at all our meetings, we will do a meeting check-in with everyone and take note of the 3 Key Messages that need to be cascaded to the rest of the organization in tomorrow's huddle.

One-Phrase Close

The day wraps up as always by asking each of the leaders for 5 words or less to describe how they feel right now.

The meeting should achieve both team *and* personal professional growth. The team will have the next iteration of the Growth Plan, and their activities will be visible on the Open Playing Field. In addition, team members are shifting away from answering questions and solving problems to asking WDYR and evaluating recommended solutions. Decisions are more and more made by team members, not company leaders. Leaders have time to coach team members, becoming coaching leaders. And finally, there is growing confidence in the strategy and the team's behavior.

NEXT STEPS/HOMEWORK

- Update the Open Playing Field as necessary.

- Each leader should add to the Open Playing Field the Corporate Priorities, including the 13-week subpriorities from the Sprint Lanes developed with the team, as well as their own individual priorities.

- Add all Strategic Pictures to the War Room.

- Continue to run all company meetings through the Open Playing Field.

- Leaders cascade 3 Key Messages to their teams.

- The CEO ensures the Leaders' Quarterly Coaching Reviews are completed based on functional Scorecards. (For more information on Quarterly Coaching Reviews, please go to *www.metronomics thebook.com.*)

- Each leader works with their functional teams to design their function KFFM, the KFFM Level 2.

- Leaders make plans or take action on any C-Player team members.

- Leaders keep a tally of WDYR with their teams.

- Everyone should read the book *The Ideal Team Player* by Patrick Lencioni.

OUTCOMES

- Cohesive: The team is working on the key actions from the Five Dysfunctions Assessment. The accountability and commitment of the team and individuals are visible and alive on the playing field. The team members are excited to contribute recommendations, though they may be uneasy at first.

- Human: The Organizational Function Chart and KFFM are visible, with the team's understanding of the importance of the functional widgets and ownership. The KFFM Level 2 is welcomed, with the rest of the team keen to get involved and own their own aligned metrics. The CEO has completed the quarterly coaching reviews with all leaders, both giving and receiving feedback.

- Cultural: The Core Values are visible and alive in the company without the need for writing them on the walls or website.

- Strategy: Validating strategy feels good, even though there are some areas where the team may not be as confident as they thought they were. The discussion took place at another level of collaboration, with everyone having a good understanding of the strategy through the strategic pictures we have developed.

- Execution: The team is efficient at this process, allowing more time for strategy and coaching the team. The Growth Plan is visible and clear on the playing field. The active meeting cadence is utilizing the Open Playing Field to keep the focus on the plan every day.

- Cash: The leadership team has now had 3 monthly meetings discussing the actuals vs rolling forecast (actuals to date + current forecast) vs the approved forecast from the start of the fiscal year.

The leaders now understand the power of this dynamic discussion, based on the widgets in the KFFM and forecasting forward each month, for great visibility on cash actual-to-forecast, allowing the team to make great decisions with cash in mind.

- Coach Cascade: The understanding of *The Speed of Trust* and the discussion that ensued allows the team to take cohesiveness to the next level. I call this Team Trust 2.0. This is where the level of cohesiveness of your team must be high to have the buy-in to take it to the next level.

- There's an awareness of how the cohesiveness of the leadership team impacts the cohesiveness of the rest of the team. The simple question, "What do you recommend?" has a huge positive impact on the team. It also gives leaders great feedback on whether the plan is clearly understood or not. By the end of this quarter, the team should significantly decrease the number of questions they ask, as long as the plan is understood. That gives leaders more time to coach team members.

QUARTER 6: THE 36'ER

Months pass. The leadership team gathers with the coach for the second quarterly meeting of Year 2. Everyone has done their prep work, and the Open Playing Field is up to date.

PREPARATION FOR THE MEETING

Have your leadership team—and yourself—prepare for the meeting like this:

1. Everyone should make sure they've finished reading *The Ideal Team Player* by Patrick Lencioni.

2. Leaders should have the KFFM Level 2 ready for review.

3. Leaders have reviewed the information provided on *www.metronomicsthebook.com* on the Business Model Canvas and are ready to take on a new strategic picture.

4. Everyone should bring the status of the priorities and metrics they own up to date on the Open Playing Field so everyone can review them prior to the meeting—otherwise, you'll waste time updating the plan in the meeting.

5. Complete the Quarterly Prep Survey and review the response prior to the start of the meeting.

6. After reviewing the status of the whole plan, make notes, ask questions, and be ready to discuss the context of building the next quarter's plan.

The agenda for this meeting follows the same system flow as the last quarter. The key focus is on taking the discussion about the KFFM Level 1 and 2 to the next level of understanding of accountability, metrics, and how the organization works. From a strategic validation perspective, we will map out our first Business Model Canvas, starting with the Value Proposition developed in our last meeting. A good discussion on the 36'er to get ready to add the next 24 months to the forecast model will take us right out to our 3HAG, which validates the achievability. From there, we'll wrap up the day as always, digging into getting a strong execution plan for the next quarter with the team. We will also continue our work on the Coach Cascade System, doing the Team Trust 2.0 Assessment from the *Speed of Trust* work we did last quarter.

The team is getting better and better at the process, as they understand it and are enthusiastic about the growth they are seeing. This time, however, there are several tweaks to turn the dials for certain systems.

AGENDA

Compound Growth System	Day 1
Cohesive System	· Good News · Cohesive Question · Left and Right
Human System	· Organizational Function Chart · KFFM Level I and II Review · Team Assessment (A, B, C)
Cultural System	· Core Purpose · Core Values · BHAG™: Confirm/Evolve
Strategy System	· 3HAG™: Confirm · Market Map—Review · Core Customer—Review · Business Model Canvas
Execution System	· Status Review Annual Plan / QHAG · Next QHAG · Swimlanes—Review · Meeting: Check In · Cascade 3 Key Messages
Cash System	· Widgets Act / F/C to P/L F/C · Add Next 24 Months to Widget P/L
Coach Cascade System	· Team Trust 2.0 Assessment and Team Plan

COHESIVE SYSTEM

As usual, we start with our activities to build the Cohesive System, Good News, and cohesive get-to-know-you questions.

Left and Right

We will continue this process as we did in the last meeting, getting the leaders to provide specific feedback about the people beside them—but this time only from the last 90 days. Leaders generally will try to stick to high-level "safe" feedback. We focus on the last 90 days because it's important to push the leaders to get specific with examples this time round—and every time from here on.

COACH CASCADE SYSTEM

As we work through this year, we are looking to take the leadership team's trust to the next level.

Team Trust 2.0

In this work, we will do the *Speed of Trust* "Increasing Your Personal Credibility and Influence—The 4 Cores Quiz" assessment from Stephen M.R. Covey's work. Once the leaders have individually filled out the assessment, they will share their results with each other. Each leader will then commit to 3 actions or behaviors they will put in place over the next 90 days. In addition, the whole team will commit to one team behavior they will evolve over the next 90 days.

The specific behaviors the team or individuals identify do not have to be elaborate. For instance, one of my teams committed to going to Orangetheory—an intense fitness workout—3 times a week for the next 90 days. The team was working on commitment and follow-through. I couldn't have predicted how impactful this simple action was. It had a huge impact on the team's comradery and cohesiveness. Don't skip these steps. These are as important as strategy, execution, and cash.

For more information on Team Trust 2.0, please go to *www.metronomics thebook.com*.

WDYR

The team has been implementing WDYR ("What do you recommend?") for the last 90 days. You should check in with each leader for their quarterly totals and acknowledge the leader who has had the most WDYRs. WDYRs have a huge impact on the momentum of execution, which in turn has an impact on the time the leaders have to focus in on the company and the strategy while coaching the team.

HUMAN SYSTEM

Organizational Function Chart

As always, the team reviews the Organizational Function Chart and makes any necessary adjustments.

Key Function Flow Map

After reviewing the KFFM Level 1, each leader will present the KFFM Level 2 for their function. Their map will show the key subfunctions of their functional area, how they work together, and what the things are that flow through this function, meaning the inputs and outputs of each subfunction. This process identifies the widgets of each subfunction and their rightful owners. It also gives great visibility into the operation of each function: the challenges and the wins as well as the design.

This is a big part of the meeting. It engages the leadership team as well as the functional teams. It gets each of the functional scoreboards up in lights.

The KFFM Level 2 presented will be made active in the next quarter as the functional teams leverage them in their daily huddles, and weekly and monthly meetings.

Team View

Make sure you review the current Team View with the whole leadership team.

A-Player Team Assessment

As at every 90-day meeting, leaders assess their direct reports on the A-Player Team Assessment graph for everyone to review and discuss.

CULTURAL SYSTEM

Core Purpose

Quickly review and confirm the Core Purpose is good enough for now.

Core Values
A quick review and confirmation that the Core Values are good enough for now.

BHAG
A quick review to confirm that the BHAG is good enough for now.

Profit/X
A quick review to confirm that the Profit/X is good enough for now.

STRATEGY SYSTEM

At the last meeting, we created a Positioning Statement and a Value Proposition. There is more work to be done on both, but what we did is good enough to move forward and get another great view to validate your strategy using the Business Model Canvas. To prepare for this section, we go through our usual agenda of reviewing the key strategic pictures and update and discuss as required:

3HAG
A quick review to confirm that it is good enough for now.

3HAG: Market Map
Review the Market Map and make any necessary updates based on how it's evolved.

3HAG: Core Customer Analysis
A quick review of the Core Customer.

3HAG: Attribution Map
A quick review of the Attribution Map.

3HAG: Differentiators
A quick review of the differentiators and their interdependencies.

3HAG: *Business Model Canvas*

If you are not familiar with the Business Model Canvas, it was created by Alex Osterwalder and Yves Pigneur and presented in their book, *Business Model Generation*. It is a method of creating and validating your business model through...you've guessed it...a picture.

We started using it in our company as soon as it was published. I'll never forget the day in our leadership team meeting where we started mapping out the canvas on a huge whiteboard. Over time, we created a whiteboard that mapped the whole Business Model Canvas template, using electrical tape to hold together the different sections. It creates great discussions, validates your strategy, and helps give focus.

Most people feel that innovation in a business comes from your products or services, or from marketplace innovation, or even from innovating your operation.

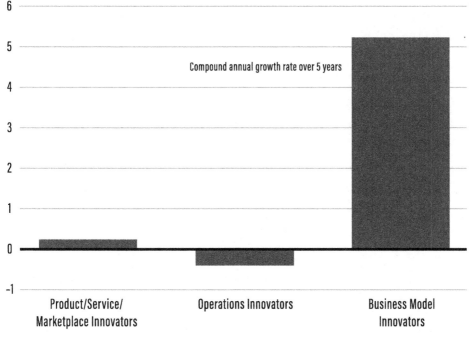

OPERATION MARGIN GROWTH IN EXCESS OF COMPETITIVE PEERS

Compound annual growth rate over 5 years

Product/Service/Marketplace Innovators — Operations Innovators — Business Model Innovators

Source: IBM, CEOs are Expanding the Innovation Horizon: Important Implications for CIOs

In fact, the most valuable area of innovation in any company is your business model.

Think about some of the most valuable companies in the last decade. What has made them so valuable? Was it new technology, new innovation? Think about Airbnb or Uber. Did they invent something new? No. Did they use new technology? No. They both created a new business model that was well received by their Core Customers and met their number one need.

In both of my companies, we were last to the market with our technology platform but exited the market with exponential value due to the innovative business model we implemented. Innovative business models will drive your valuation.

Business models are tightly coupled with your strategy and vice versa. They are founded upon a great understanding of your Core Customer needs. It's your business model that gives you the greatest opportunity for growth through innovating. Your business model married up with your strategy is one of the most powerful tools you have as a leadership team.

If you think about it, we've already been mapping out a successful map for your business that identifies sources of revenue, the Core Customer, the widgets, and the detailed forecast of cash flow. Successful business models are directly tied to the key functions in your business and how they fit together to create cash flow while having a great view of how the organization is uniquely positioned in the marketplace. A great business model takes advantage of both of these things.

In this session, you and your team will walk through the Business Model Canvas, using the last meeting's Positioning Statement and Value Proposition as a starting point. This is an example of how the work to date can be used to build the Business Model Canvas.

I could have introduced the Business Model Canvas earlier, but I've deliberately held it back until now. While we were still validating strategy, understanding the marketplace, and becoming experts in the marketplace, it's my experience that we would not have been able to leverage this view as effectively as we can now.

Your business model describes how the organization creates, delivers, and captures value. In other words, a good business model describes how the company will make money married up with how it fits strategically into a marketplace.

Thinking about our journey so far, we've become very good at understanding all the functions of our company necessary to make money, we have become experts in our market, and we have mapped out a strategy that we can validate.

THE BUSINESS MODEL CANVAS

Design Your 3HAG™ Business Model Canvas (from Strategyzer)

Key Partners 🔗	Key Activities ✅	Value Propositions 🎁	Customer Relationships ❤	Customer Segments
Insert from Market Map	Insert 3–5 Differentiators	Insert Value Proposition from Geoffrey Moore's template	Insert from Market Map	Insert from Market Map
	Key Resources 🧰		**Channels** 🚚	
	Review Swimlanes and insert the 3–5 most important resources or capabilities required to deliver		Insert from Market Map	

Cost Structure 🏷	Revenue Streams 💰
Insert the major cost lever from your Widget-based forecast	Insert your Widgets here from your KFFM and/or your Widget-based forecast	Insert the major cost lever from your Widget-based forecast

This is a great time to map out the Business Model Canvas with our leadership team. For more information on how to lead your team through the Business Model Canvas, go to *www.metronomicsthebook.com*.

EXECUTION SYSTEM

The execution system part of the day follows the same format as last quarter, including the Swimlane review. The team is very familiar with this part of the meeting by now. Close out as always with checking in with everyone and ensuring 3 Key Messages are captured so that they can be cascaded after the meeting.

CASH SYSTEM

The 36'er is a 36-month rolling widget-based forecast that is alive, utilized, and owned by the leadership team. We've been working quarter over quarter to build to this point, and now we're ready to create this view. The finance team has been supporting this endeavor since the very first meeting by working widgets into the original budget. We have come so far. The leadership team owns the widget-based forecast, finance is the keeper of the model, and the active update and review married with a strong focus on cash makes this such a big deal.

No one really seems to make a big deal out of it—but as a coach, I most certainly do! It's a big deal. Huge!

It's a great milestone in Metronomics.

The finance team has added to the 12-month widget-based forecast the next 24 months, all the way out to their 3HAG. The leaders have forecasted their widgets on a functional level for the next 24 months, too, and the finance team has included this in the model. This is the first time the leadership team can see a fully mapped-out widget-based path to their 3HAG with both a fiscal and a widget basis. This is a great and validating view.

On no account should you skip this step.

There will be a great conversation that will validate where the team and company are on their journey toward their 3HAG. Progress doesn't have to be perfect at this point, but the conversation should energize leaders to work with their teams to validate and update their assumptions based on the widgets they control and their assumptions looking out toward the 3HAG. They can marry these up with the big milestones already included in the Swimlanes.

CHECK-IN

As with every meeting, check in with the team how the meeting cadence, agenda, and outcomes are progressing. This gives you as a team the opportunity to tweak anything that needs to be adjusted so everyone stays aligned with their teams.

Cascading Messages

As at all our meetings, we will do a check-in with everyone and take note of the 3 Key Messages that need to be cascaded to the rest of the organization in tomorrow's huddle.

One-Phrase Close

The day wraps up as always by asking each of the leaders for 5 words or less to describe how they feel right now.

NEXT STEPS/HOMEWORK

- Update the Open Playing Field as necessary.

- Each leader should add to the Open Playing Field the quarterly Corporate Priorities including the 13-week subpriorities from the Sprint Lanes developed with the team and their own individual priorities.

- Add all Strategic Pictures to the War Room.

- Continue to run all company meetings through the Open Playing Field.

- Leaders cascade 3 Key Messages to their teams.

- CEO continues Quarterly Coaching Reviews with leaders based on functional Scorecards.

- Each leader works with their team to bring their KFFM Level 2 alive week by week as their function scoreboard and operational focal point in the context of the KFFM Level 1.

- Bring the Team View up to date in the Open Playing Field.

- Leaders will work with their team to create Scorecards for all the subfunctions on their functional team as shown in the KFFM Level 2.

- Leaders make plans or take action on any C-Player team members.

- Each leader keeps a tally of WDYR with their teams.

- Each leader should read the book *Good to Great* by Jim Collins.

OUTCOMES

- Cohesive: Leaders are getting better at giving each other positive and constructive feedback, not only in the quarterly meetings but throughout the quarter. The accountability and commitment of the team and individuals are visible and alive on the Open Playing Field. The team is excited to contribute recommendations.

- Human: The Organizational Function Chart and KFFM are visible, showing the team's understanding of the importance of the functional widgets and ownership. The team is excited to focus and learn more as they make the KFFM Level 2 active and visible. The focus on the functional team Scorecards takes the committed ownership of widgets further into the team. The CEO has completed the Quarterly Coaching Reviews with all leaders, both giving and receiving feedback. The Team View provides a contextual view for all team members in one concise picture. It shows A-Players a visible path for growth within the company.

- Cultural: The Core Values are visible and alive in the company without the need to write them on the walls or website. The team has a great understanding of how to leverage Good News to recognize their peers.

- Strategy: The continued validation of strategy feels good, even though the new views and perspectives the team gets can feel uncomfortable. The commitment to understand and adjust as a team is strong. The discussion continues to grow to another level of collaboration, with everyone having a good understanding of strategy through the strategic pictures we have developed.

- Execution: The team continues to stay focused on the discipline of the execution process, and continues to tweak as they learn. Their progression is still moving forward as the team grows. The Growth Plan is visible and clear on the Open Playing Field. The active meeting cadence using the playing field is keeping the focus on the plan every day.

- Cash: The leadership team is excited by the 36'er and the detailed road map it has brought into focus. The leaders trust each other's ability to forecast together as a team and focus on their goals, making the agreed-upon decisions and adjustments as needed. The 36'er will now be brought into the monthly meetings to provide long-term context for short-term decisions.

- Coach Cascade: The team members are focused on their individual commitments and their team commitment after the deep discussion on *The Speed of Trust*. The commitment to their behaviors at the leadership level is well understood and taking their cohesiveness as a team to the next stage. The leaders are loving the opportunity to coach their team members with the simple question of "What do you recommend?" It has already had a huge positive impact on the team. Leaders have more time to coach team members.

QUARTER 7: CONFIDENT TEAM

90 days pass. A mere 13 weeks. Time is flying and so is your company. The momentum of execution is strong and the focus on strategic confidence is progressing well.

This quarter we will focus on cascading execution, accountability, and the ownership of widgets further out to the team. We will also focus on understanding the company's industry profitability through Porter's Five Forces. The last thing we will cover is understanding what it takes to grow your leadership while growing your organization out and up. We'll do this by looking at the Scaling Leadership framework created by Robert. J. Anderson and William A. Adams and understanding how this can be utilized within the Metronomics regimen.

Remember: Metronomics is all about *and*, not about *or*. We can and will constantly plug in the frameworks, tools, and principles of the top business thought leaders of our time and beyond to ensure our organization continues to grow stronger and gets the best perspective to make great decisions for growth.

PREPARATION FOR THE MEETING

Have your leadership team—and yourself—prepare for the meeting like this:

1. Everyone should have finished the book *Good to Great* by Jim Collins, which should have solidified so much of the great work already accomplished by the team.

2. Leaders should have the KFFM Level 2 ready for review.

3. Leaders have created Scorecards for all the subfunctions on their functional team and are ready for review.

4. Leaders have reviewed the information on the *www.metronomics thebook.com* site on Porter's Five Forces and are ready to create a new strategic picture.

5. Everyone should bring the status of the priorities and metrics they own up to date on the Open Playing Field so everyone can review them prior to the meeting—otherwise, you'll waste time statusing the plan in the meeting.

6. Complete the Quarterly Prep Survey and review the Prep Survey response prior to the start of the meeting.

AGENDA

Compound Growth System	Day 1
Cohesive System	· Good News · Cohesive Question · Left and Right
Human System	· Organizational Function Chart · KFFM · Team Assessment (A, B, C)
Cultural System	· Core Purpose · Core Values · BHAG™: Confirm/Evolve
Strategy System	· 3HAG™: Confirm · Market Map—Review · Core Customer—Review · Porter's 5 Forces
Execution System	· Status Review Annual Plan / QHAG · Next QHAG · Swimlanes—Review · Meeting: Check In · Cascade 3 Key Messages
Cash System	· Widgets Act / F/C to P/L F/C · Review Quarterly Act/F/C
Coach Cascade System	· Scaling Leadership Intro

7. After reviewing the status of the whole plan, make notes, ask
    questions, and be ready to discuss the context of building the next
    quarter's plan.

The agenda for the meeting follows the same system flow as the others.

COHESIVE SYSTEM

As usual, we start with activities that build the Cohesive System: Good News
and cohesive get-to-know-you questions. Remember, Good News is one of
the best ways to keep the culture alive every day by celebrating team members who ooze the Core Values in the company.

Left and Right

Continue as we did in the last meeting, looking to get the leaders to provide
specific feedback about the people beside them from the last 90 days, using
specific examples.

COACH CASCADE SYSTEM

Team Trust 2.0

We will check in on the Team Trust 2.0 initiative that the team committed to
at the last meeting and discuss how well it worked or did not work and why.
The leadership team will all commit to the next initiative together.

Scaling Leadership

At this meeting, we introduce and discuss the Scaling Leadership Framework
created by Robert J. Anderson and William A. Adams. Specifically, the discussion will be around the steps needed to grow leadership capacity on a team
and to understanding the Scaling Leadership Framework. Your leaders haven't
yet read *Scaling Leadership*, so this is only an introduction to discuss a leader's
behavior and how it impacts their team in a positive or negative way. We will
also discuss a leader's reactive tendencies and their creative competencies.

In the next quarterly meeting, the 2-day annual, we will have each leader complete the scaling leadership assessment known as a leadership circle and be ready to discuss.

What Do You Recommend?

Check in and review with leaders how the WDYR is going with their teams and instigate a discussion for leaders to provide examples from the last 90 days.

HUMAN SYSTEM

Organizational Function Chart

Review the Organizational Function Chart for any adjustments.

KFFM

Fully review the KFFM Level 1 and Level 2. Take time to talk about how the KFFM Level 2 maps became active and focused on each functional team. This is key as you continue to move forward, keeping this view as an active scoreboard in your leaders' functional areas, along with the KFFM Level 1. The leaders will confirm they have created functional role Scorecards for each function on their functional team, and that they're ready to cascade them out to their teams.

Team View

Make sure you review the current Team View with the whole leadership team.

A-Player Team Assessment

Leaders assess their direct reports on the A-Player Team Assessment graph for everyone to review and discuss.

CULTURAL SYSTEM

Core Purpose

Quickly review and confirm that the Core Purpose is good enough for now.

Core Values

A quick review to confirm that the Core Values are good enough for now.

BHAG

A quick confirmation that it is good enough for now.

Profit/X

A quick confirmation that it is good enough for now.

STRATEGY SYSTEM

We've now completed a Positioning Statement, a Value Proposition, and the Business Model Canvas. This is a great time to dig deep into the forces that are pressuring our strategy and company's success. To prepare for this section, we will first go through our familiar reviews:

3HAG

Quick review and confirmation that it is good enough for now.

3HAG: Market Map

Review the Market Map and make any necessary updates based on how it's evolved.

3HAG: Core Customer Analysis

A quick review of the Core Customer.

3HAG: Attribution Map

A quick review of the Attribution Map.

3HAG: Differentiators

A quick review of the 3 to 5 Differentiators shown in the Activity Fit Map.

3HAG: Porter's Five Forces

In this discussion, we consider the Five Forces identified by Michael Porter to analyze business profitability:

1. *Competitive rivalry*. How many rivals do you have, and how good are they at what they do?

2. *Supplier power*. How many suppliers do you have, and how easy is it for them to raise their prices?

3. *Buyer power*. How many buyers do you have, and how easy is it for them to drive your prices down?

4. *Threat of substitution*. How easy is it for your customers to find a different way of doing what you do?

5. *Threat of new entry*. How easy is it for new competitors to enter your market?

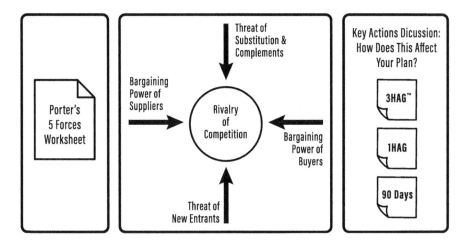

You'll assess how your company is doing in relation to Porter's theory, using worksheets and sharing your thoughts. These assessments show the team's thoughts on where the company is right now.

The most important part of the exercise is to have a full discussion about how it is affecting your current plan—QHAG, 1HAG, and 3HAG—and if there is anything you should consider doing differently.

I recently did this analysis with a client of six years at a CEO+Leadership Team Roundtable leadership session. The feedback and outcome from the discussion were critical and impacted many of the company's immediate and long-term plans. Be ready for a full discussion, as this will continue to create confidence in your plan and in your decision-making as you drive toward your 3HAG.

To learn more about how to lead this discussion, go to: *www.metronomics thebook.com.*

EXECUTION SYSTEM

The execution system part of the day is well known and understood by your team, and it will follow the same format as last quarter, including the Swimlane review.

CASH SYSTEM

Now that we have a full 36-month widget-based rolling forecast that we are reviewing monthly with the leadership team, we still need to stay focused on our actual results compared to our rolling forecasts and compared to our approved forecast for the current year. We need to make adjustments as required to this year to ensure we achieve our cash forecast out past the end of the year driving toward our 3HAG.

No matter how well you are doing on your plan, *never* skip this discussion or stop forecasting cash and widgets.

This focus increases your team's confidence that they are in control of their widgets and connected to the plan.

CHECK-IN

As with every meeting, check in with the team how the meeting cadence, agenda, and outcomes are progressing. This gives you as a team the opportunity to tweak anything that needs to be adjusted so everyone stays aligned with their teams.

Cascading Messages

As at all our meetings, we will do a check-in with everyone, and take note of the 3 Key Messages that need to be cascaded to the rest of the organization in tomorrow's huddle.

One-Phrase Close

The day wraps up as always asking each of the leaders for 5 words or less to describe how they feel right now.

NEXT STEPS/HOMEWORK

- Update the Open Playing Field as needed.

- Each leader should add to the Open Playing Field the quarterly Corporate Priorities including the 13-week subpriorities from the Sprint Lanes developed with the team, and their own individual priorities.

- Add all Strategic Pictures to the War Room.

- Continue to run all company meetings through the Open Playing Field.

- Leaders cascade 3 Key Messages to their teams.

- CEO leads the Quarterly Coaching Reviews with the leaders based on functional Scorecards.

- All leaders book and complete Annual Coaching Reviews with their team members based on their functional Scorecards. This will be the last time the team members will receive an annual review, as reviews will now be booked and completed every 90 days.

- Each leader works with their functions team weekly to bring their KFFM Level 2 alive as their scoreboard and operational focal point in the context of the KFFM Level 1.

- Leaders make plans or take action on any C-Player team members.

- Leaders read the *Turning the Flywheel* monograph and the CEO books monthly sessions to develop their first Flywheel for the company. (Go to *www.metronomicsthebook.com* to learn more.)

- Each leader keeps a tally of WDYR with their teams.

- All leaders read the book *Scaling Leadership* by Robert J. Anderson and William A. Adams for the next meeting and complete the Leadership Circle Assessment.

OUTCOMES

- Cohesive: With the continued focus on the Four Cores of Credibility individually and as a group, the cohesiveness of the team continues to increase. The peer-to-peer feedback is becoming a more natural behavior and is cascading into all the teams. The level of healthy conflictive discussions continues to increase, ensuring strategy, execution, and cash plan are as collaborative as possible.

- Human: The KFFM Level 1 and 2 are alive, active, and connected to the team and individuals. The ownership of the widgets is high and the team eager to win. The commitment to the overall team goals is in constant focus, starting with the leaders and going throughout the company. The CEO has completed the Quarterly Coaching Reviews with all leaders both giving and receiving feedback. The leaders will confirm they have created functional role Scorecards for each subfunction on their functional team and are ready to cascade them into their teams.

- The leaders will prepare, book, and complete the first Performance Coaching Reviews with their team members based on the function Scorecards created. This is a great time when the team's clarity of expectations grows immensely. The leader's and the team members' discussion and feedback are key components of these coaching reviews.

- Cultural: The Core Values are visible and alive in the company. The team has a great understanding of how to leverage Good News to recognize their peers. As teams grow, vigilance must remain focused on Core Values.

- Strategy: The discussion about the forces in the market is always great for any team. With the team looking to get new perspectives on their strategic confidence and what they are feeling but are not necessarily able to articulate, Porter's Five Forces is a great framework for this discussion. The continued validation of strategy feels good, and everyone knows they must stay knowledgeable as experts in their market. The discussion continues to grow to another level of collaboration, with everyone having a good understanding of the strategy through the strategic pictures you have developed. This is a great place to be—but don't get too comfortable. Keep pushing at your strategy for holes as the market and organization evolve.

- Execution: The focus and discipline of execution can ebb and flow. All leaders must keep a disciplined focus on the cadence and process developed in their team: the focus of the leaders maintains the focus of the team. The KFFM live scoreboard is a way to keep all team members engaged as they can see how what they do every day affects the team score. This is a powerful place for any team truly moving to become high-performing! The team will continue to tweak as they learn, still moving forward as the team grows. The Growth Plan is visible and clear on the Open Playing Field. The active meeting cadence is utilizing the Open Playing Field to keep the focus on the plan every day.

- Cash: The team is getting more comfortable with the 36-month rolling forecast! The monthly meeting is keeping the team focused and prompting timely discussions. The leaders wonder how they ever survived without a detailed widget-based profit-and-loss rolling forecast incorporating a cash-flow statement.

- Coach Cascade: The leaders are excited about starting the regular 90-day coaching reviews with their team members based on the newly created Scorecards. They know how valuable this has been for themselves and are excited to bring the same 2-way discussion to their team members. They are looking forward to continuing their coaching-leader journey. The result of the huge focus on WDYR has developed positive habits in the team to always bring a recommended solution with two other options considered. This has saved time and increased learning for the whole team. The engagement level is high.

QUARTER 8:
BHAG, 3HAG, AND 1HAG ALIGNMENT

The big annual meeting is where you look to keep the momentum going, check in that you are confident in your strategy, develop a new 3HAG, and build your next annual plan in the context of the market in which you are playing.

Everyone is raring to go. Over the next two days, you move through the systems again. You recommit to your Core Purpose, values, and customer. You build your new 3HAG and evolve your Market Map. By echoing what you did the previous year, the steps become habits, and the habits lead to lasting practice and growth—and most of all to clarity about all parts of the business.

By the end of this fourth quarter meeting, the team leaves with a confirmed BHAG, a newly aligned 3HAG, and the most confidence they have ever had in their strategy. Team members have stopped asking questions, and instead, offer recommendations with options. There is strategic confidence throughout the company, not just in the leadership team. The team members are energized and proud of what they have accomplished. Every member of the team knows where they are headed and how they will get there, and everyone knows who is doing what, why, and when. There are cohesiveness and focus, and the enthusiasm continues to grow and grow and grow. The company's plan and metrics are connected to the team goal and all individual team members.

PREPARATION FOR THE MEETING

Have your leadership team—and yourself—prepare for the meeting like this:

1. Everyone should have read the book *Scaling Leadership* by Robert J. Anderson and William A. Adams and complete the Leadership Circle Assessment.

2. Complete the Quarterly Prep Survey and review the results before the meeting.

3. Complete the Five Dysfunctions team assessment.

4. Everyone should bring the status of the priorities and metrics they own up to date on the Open Playing Field so everyone can review them prior to the meeting—otherwise, you'll waste time statusing the plan in the meeting.

5. Everyone should complete the Metronomics Checklist Survey. For more information, go to *www.metronomicsthebook.com*.

6. Everyone should have read the *Turning the Flywheel* monograph by Jim Collins. The team has built the company's first Flywheel and is ready for review, discussion, and next steps.

The agenda follows the flow of all the other meetings, following all seven systems over the two days.

AGENDA

Compound Growth System	Day 1
Cohesive System	· Good News · Cohesive Question · Left and Right · 5 Dysfunctions Team Assessment
Human System	· Organizational Function Chart · KFFM—Review
Cultural System	· Core Purpose · Core Values · Hedgehog with Simon Sinek's Golden Circle · BHAG™: Confirm/Evolve
Strategy System	· 3HAG™: Evolve Out + 1 Year · Market Map—Evolve · Core Customer—Confirm · Attribution Framework—Re-do · Swimlanes—Re-do

The objective of this 2-day annual meeting is to evolve the current strategy to ensure that it is truly differentiated in the marketplace and aligned with the execution and cash plan. In this meeting, we will roll out a new 3HAG.

The meeting will follow the same flow as the other 2-day meetings, with the strategy being the focus on Day 1 and execution the focus on Day 2.

DAY 1: STRATEGY

COHESIVE SYSTEM

Kick off the meeting as usual, with Good News followed by some questions or icebreakers to further build team trust and get the meeting off to a fun, positive start.

Team Trust 2.0

We will check in on the Team Trust 2.0 initiative that the team committed to at the last meeting and discuss how well it worked or did not work and why. We will then decide what the next activity should be. The leadership team will commit to the next initiative together.

COACH CASCADE SYSTEM

Scaling Leadership

As each leader completed the Leadership Circle Assessment from the Scaling Leadership framework, we will review each leader's results together.

This assessment is a self-assessment, not an assessment from the team, but it provides great insight for each of the leaders as well as a positive discussion around their reactive tendencies and creative competencies.

Some leaders may be very uncomfortable sharing their results. This is why we have not done this sooner, so we could ensure that the cohesiveness of the team is at a level where we have can have an open and vulnerable discussion with the whole team.

The CEO will share their results first to show the way, and we will then review each leader's results one by one. At the end of the discussion, each leader will suggest what reactive tendency they will focus on over the next 90 days, with specific actions they will look to adjust. They will also ask the leadership team to support them in the new behavior they are looking to evolve.

It's very important to ask for support and feedback from the leadership team over the next 90 days. That's why we have been working so hard to learn to give each other peer-to-peer feedback.

For more information on Scaling Leadership and Metronomics, please go to *www.metronomicsthebook.com*.

What Do You Recommend?

Check in and review with leaders how the WDYR is going with their teams and instigate a discussion for leaders to provide examples from the last 90 days.

HUMAN SYSTEM

Organizational Function Chart

Review the Organizational Function Chart for any adjustments.

Key Function Flow Map

Fully review the KFFM Level 1 and Level 2.

Part of the homework from the last meeting was to read Jim Collins's *Turning the Flywheel* monograph and build your company's Flywheel.

Just a quick recap on what a Flywheel is. The concept came from the book Good to Great, where Collins found that the greatest companies did not become great in one fell swoop. There was no one defining thing. Instead, there was an organic process of relentless grit as the company focused on pushing in the direction of its "one big thing," bit by bit, step by step, with each push getting a little easier and easier, and thus creating momentum. A company's Flywheel articulates the architecture of the key components on which the company must focus push by push to create the energy needed to break through the inertia and reach enduring momentum.

A lot of people may wonder why this is coming up so late in the Metronomics regimen. The reason is simple. A Flywheel without a fully active KFFM is just a nice abstract view of the momentum your company either has or doesn't. Having an active and owned KFFM allows you to *impact* your Flywheel's momentum by adjusting it and aligning it to the KFFM.

The two are fully connected: the KFFM is the foundation of everything in your company, the grit you need, and the Flywheel is a great blueprint of how you create momentum through your operations in the marketplace. We have been creating momentum this whole time. Now, for the first time, we get to see the huge momentum we have created. It's another great view for creating confidence as we evolve.

When we drew our very first Flywheel in our business, we were excited. It showed how we thought we would take our marketplace by storm. We could see how we were going to catapult from component to component in the wheel, with the right-hand side of the wheel, 12 through 6, creating and generating the marketplace value, while the left-hand side, 6 through 12, captures the value to refuel the next revolution of the wheel.

What we could not see was how we were actually going to line this up to our day-to-day operation, the current design of our company, to ensure we could create the momentum we needed. The KFFM unlocked it for us. The relationship of the KFFM to the Flywheel and back again is key to creating sustained execution momentum as you grow toward your 3HAG.

Fully review the Flywheel you have created. Rate the components of the Flywheel—red, yellow, or green—according to their current status, and discuss the metrics of the components of the Flywheel.

Now look at the Flywheel and your KFFM and discuss the similarities and differences of the components, the functions, and the metrics. There should be full overlap between the Flywheel and the KFFM widgets metrics and between the current color status of the KFFM and the Flywheel. This view will give you and your team great clues as to what is creating momentum in your wheel and what is stalling it and how to unlock it in your company through the visibility of your KFFM. It's another very powerful view.

For more information, please go to *www.metronomicsthebook.com*.

A-Player Team Assessment

As usual, leaders assess their direct reports on the A-Player Team Assessment graph for everyone to review and discuss.

Team View

The Team View was introduced for review four quarters ago. It gives your team the context of how the company is designed, aligned to the KFFM. This view provides A-Players with a view of what positions they can take for their next step of growth! It also provides the leadership team with another view of how to design the company, both for now and for the future. At a recent client planning session, this discussion unlocked a huge design challenge for the growth of the company, but redesigning this view helped the team address the challenges in their KFFM. The KFFM, the Team View, and the Scorecards are tightly coupled, which is why we have taken a step-by-step progression through this key element of Metronomics.

Make sure you and your team have a good discussion at this stage and continue to keep this view up to date.

CULTURAL SYSTEM

Core Purpose

In the last 2-day annual planning session, we utilized Simon Sinek's Golden Circle to confirm the company's Core Purpose. If you feel at this point your Core Purpose is solid and locked in, move on to Core Values. If you feel it's not solid or you need to check, go back and work through the Golden Circle strategic picture.

Core Values

Review the Core Values. Check that they're good enough for now. If they are, have a discussion about how else the team can celebrate and bring alive the great core-value behavior of the team. One of my clients keeps track of the number of Core Values stories shared by team members of their peers as a weekly, monthly, and quarterly metric. As this number has risen, so has their team member Net Promotor Score.

BHAG

Review and check in on your BHAG. If your BHAG is clear and the leadership team is confident, one of the best next steps to take your BHAG to the next level is to "paint" the BHAG picture. The Painted Picture is a great way to collaborate with your team and create an image of what it will look like when you get there, to your BHAG. The process we use was adapted from Cameron Herold's book *Double Double.* I love doing this picture as everyone gets a great unified view of where they want to end up. The collaboration will be high, and the outcome is clear. To create your Painted Picture with your team, you can find a tool to create this strategic picture at *www.metronomics thebook.com.*

If the feedback you receive from the leadership team makes you feel that the BHAG could use some confirmation, follow the steps you took at last year's annual meeting to create Jim Collins's Hedgehog View, which will help confirm your BHAG and take it to the next level.

Don't be discouraged if you feel that the team is not as confident as you'd like. You and they have learned a lot over the last nine quarters, so they are getting more aware of and more critical about what "good enough" is. The team might want to dig in further, or you might feel you need to dig in further. This is never a waste of time.

Profit/X

With the BHAG review in mind, confirm your Profit/X with the team.

STRATEGY SYSTEM

3HAG

At this meeting, you'll create a new 3HAG, following the same steps as in last year's 2-day annual. Since we have been working with and forecasting the 36'er rolling every month, the team will have the 3HAG forecasted widgets and fiscal metrics ready to go. I love it when a team is in this place in their progression. Things just get easier.

You'll review and confirm the 3HAG statement or create a new one.

3HAG: *Market Map*

Review the Market Map and make any necessary updates based on how it's evolved.

3HAG: *Core Customer Analysis*

Review the Core Customer Analysis. Discuss and confirm the present Core Customer and the Core Customer predicted in 3 years' time.

3HAG: *Attribution Map*

I like the team to work through building a new Attribution Map *without* reviewing the last one. This ensures we are completely up to date with our knowledge on the current market and where we fit. It also ensures that we have a really good look at where we want our 3HAG line to be looking over the next 3 years.

3HAG: *Differentiators*

Having rebuilt our Attribution Map, take the time also to rebuild our 3 to 5 differentiators from the brainstorm step all the way through to displaying them in Michael Porter's Activity Fit Map view. Even if you feel they are solid, take the time to build them from the ground up. If the differentiators are the same as you currently have, it will build confidence in your team. If they are different, this will allow us to evolve our strategy as the market has evolved by reflecting them. Use the same process we utilized in the last 2-day annual to complete this step.

3HAG: *Swimlanes*

If you have new differentiators, create your Swimlanes as you did at the last 2-day annual meeting. If your differentiators remain the same, I would still recommend using blank Swimlanes to map out the 3 to 5 key milestones for each differentiator lane out over 12 quarters. That ensures that each differentiator will be in a good place by 3 years out. Go the extra mile here as this helps create the confidence we need in the strategy and our plan. This helps create momentum. This helps create clarity.

DAY 2: EXECUTION

AGENDA

Compound Growth System	Day 2
Execution System	• Status Review Annual Plan • Status Review QHAG • 1HAG • QHAG • Meeting: Check In • Team Assessment—ABC + Plan • Cascade 3 Key Messages
Cash System	• Review Next Year 12 Month • F/C Starting with Widgets out 36 month over month • Put Metrics into Rolling Metrics in Metronome Software
Coach Cascade System	• n/a

The second day of the 2-day annual is dedicated to the Execution and Cash Systems while of course keeping the accountable, cohesive behavior high. We kick off with personal Good News, reflections from the day before, and any wrap-up items from Day 1.

COHESIVE SYSTEM

Team Assessment

This will be the second time this team has completed the *Five Dysfunctions of a Team Assessment*, so we can compare the results to last year's. We'll have a great discussion on the work we've accomplished to become a more cohesive team and focus on the areas that might need further work.

In my experience, my clients are usually in a very cohesive state by this stage. They have formed, stormed, and are now in a norming stage for the team, meaning that most of this assessment is green, with perhaps one area being yellow. The yellow area represented is very close to borderline-green. It's not always the case, but it usually is. That means the team's cohesiveness is ready to take it into the third year of Metronomics and up to the next level of a high-performing team.

To learn more about the *Five Dysfunctions of a Team Assessment* and Metronomics, you can find the information at *www.metronomicsthebook.com.*

Status: 1HAG and Current QHAG

This review will be quick as long as the team has the status up to date before the meeting and the team has been reviewing and discussing it on a weekly basis.

New 1HAG

The second part of the morning should be spent with the team working through the usual questions to come up with a new 1HAG. The great news is that the forecast of widgets and fiscal metrics has been prepared and discussed every month rolling up to this meeting.

New QHAG

You'll spend the rest of the day agreeing on a new QHAG. Don't skip mapping out the 13-Week Sprint Lanes.

CASH SYSTEM

The leaders and finance team have created a 12-month widget-based forecast for the next fiscal year and the 24 months beyond, taking the forecast all the way out to your 3HAG. This process has gotten easier and easier for both the leaders who own functions and for the finance team. The cash forecast is well understood for the next 12 months as well as the subsequent two years.

As at all our meetings, we will do a meeting check-in with everyone and take note of the 3 Key Messages that need to be cascaded out to the rest of the organization in tomorrow's huddle.

As in the previous annual planning session, review the results of the Metronomics Survey and have a good discussion about them. Make a plan as

ROI OF A 36'ER FULLY IMPLEMENTED

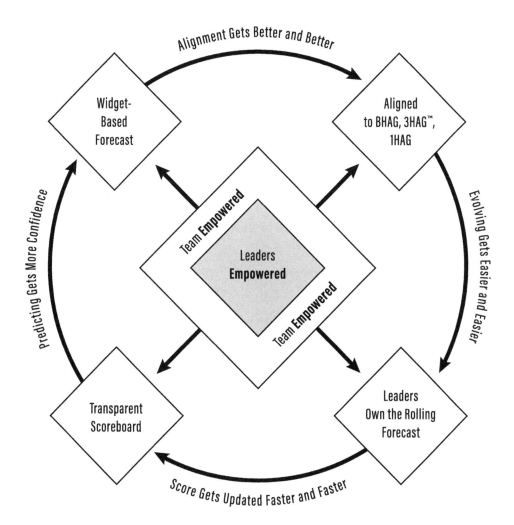

to what needs more focus or a different approach. As the team continues to become more self-aware during the process, they will assess themselves with more vigor.

One-Phrase Close

The day wraps up as always asking each of the leaders for 5 words or less to describe how they feel right now.

NEXT STEPS/HOMEWORK

- Update the Open Playing Field as necessary.

- Each leader should add to the Open Playing Field the annual Corporate Priorities, the quarterly Corporate Priorities including the 13-week subpriorities from the Sprint Lanes, and their own individual priorities.

- Add updated Market Map to the War Room.

- Add updated Core Customer to the War Room.

- Add Attribution Framework to the War Room.

- Add Differentiators to the War Room.

- Update the Swimlanes.

- Update the Rolling Metrics for the 36'er on the Open Playing Field.

- Continue to run all company meetings through the Open Playing Field.

- Review KFFM in weekly leadership team meeting.

- CEO leads the Quarterly Coaching Reviews with the leaders based on functional Scorecards.

- All leaders book out Quarterly Coaching Reviews every 90 days with their team members into the next year and beyond.

- Leaders make plans or take action on any C-Player team members.

YEAR 2: MOMENTUM—WORK ON THE BUSINESS, NOT IN THE BUSINESS

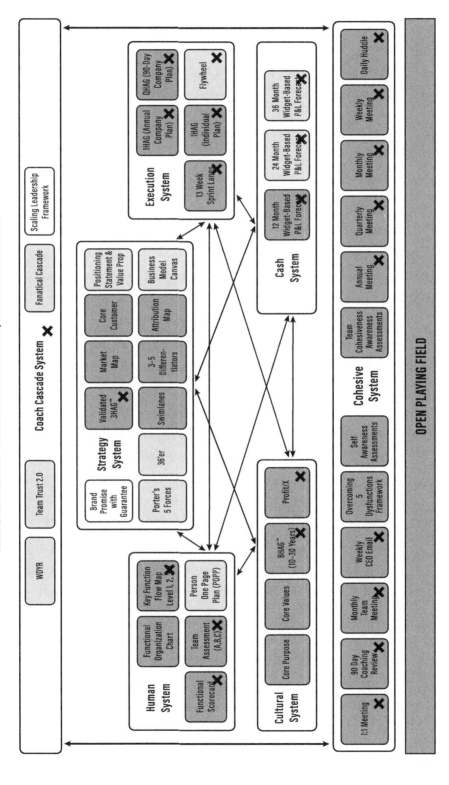

- All leaders cascade 3 Key Messages to their teams.

- Leaders read the book *Dare to Lead* by Brené Brown before the next quarterly meeting.

OUTCOMES

- Cohesive: This has been a great year for taking the team to the next level of cohesiveness. The *Five Dysfunctions of a Team Assessment* reflects this over the year, but more importantly, the team members recognize that their behavior has evolved through the depth of conversations they now have that couldn't have taken place previously, from their commitment to the team goal first, and from their focus on the decisions they make together. This is a fun team to be a part of. Cohesive behavior is the norm in the team, and everyone is committed to continuing to evolve.

- Human: The clarity of expectations has progressed to the next level, with all team members owning a Scorecard aligned to the company widgets. This is the ultimate connection to ensure the engagement of the whole team. The practice of leveraging the KFFM Level 1 and 2 as the company scoreboard is active and effective. The CEO and all leaders have completed the Coaching Reviews with all leaders and team members, both giving and receiving feedback. The Team View provides a new view of the organization, its expected growth, and how team members can grow and contribute to success.

- Cultural: The team is excited about its consistent behavior, the clarity of the Core Values, and the discipline with which it projects the Core Values. The engagement level is high, as is the level of fun they have working together.

- Strategy: New year, new 3HAG. This session continues to raise the level of confidence in the team strategy. Building a new Attribution Map and Differentiators from the ground up increases confidence through the analysis of the brutal facts of the market. The continued validation and evolution of strategy feel good. And everyone knows they must stay knowledgeable, as experts in their market. The highly cohesive team also plays a big role in confidence in strategy at this point, because the team knows that if an individual member disagrees with a decision, they will share and discuss their view.

- Execution: A new 1HAG has been created with the known process, and the team is feeling good about aligning this to the strategy, Swimlanes, and the plan for the year. The team members have their first view of the Flywheel with the KFFM and the action to keep them aligned. This was a great foundation for building the 1HAG and the QHAG. The team is feeling good about execution and ready to take it to the next level. They know everyone must keep a disciplined focus on the cadence and process the team has developed and not get complacent. The rhythm of the execution system helps keep all the other systems aligned.

- Cash: The 12-month widget-based forecast is ready to rock. The team members are continuing to improve their forecasting detail, which is improving their accuracy and their ability to achieve the plan and metrics. This is a common outcome after the great work the team has achieved thus far aligned to the KFFM Level 1 and Level 2. Ownership of the forecast by the team is strong, through the widgets connected to each individual team members.

- Coach Cascade: The leaders are feeling good about the Coaching Reviews, which focus on a team member's performance aligned to the function Scorecard they own. All team members are having a weekly 1:1 with their team leader. This is changing the discussions in the business. The commitment of the leaders to grow themselves as well as their team members is attractive and well known. The team members are excited about the next step in growing as leaders, evolving their reactive behaviors and replacing them with creative behaviors. The engagement continues to remain high.

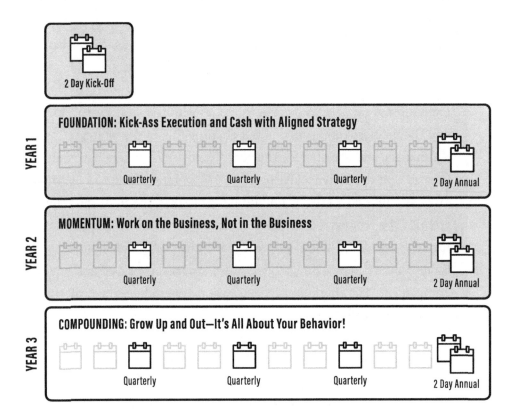

The team has now been executing Metronomics for nine quarters. They are more than fully bought into this system. They are so proud of their accomplishments and know there is more to accomplish as a team. The execution system is kick-ass and working. Their cash is forecasted and visible with the 36'er. Everyone knows the company widgets and understands that this is what each and every team member is striving for and committed to.

The widgets are for the team win. They're how we win the game together. Consistently.

The KFFM Level 1 and 2 is the foundation of execution and the company "real-time" scoreboard that every team owns and contributes to. The team is highly cohesive and connected to all the key elements to achieve their plan.

Remember, these elements are:

- Clear objective and goals (BHAG, 3HAG, 1HAG, QHAG)
- Aligned metrics (widgets)
- Continuous learning (quarter over quarter)
- Decision-making awareness (every day)
- Team rewards (celebrate); and
- Open Playing Field (Behavioral Team Accountability Platform).

A high-performing business team will be both highly cohesive and connected to these elements and vice versa! This is why we have carefully spent the time to progress the soft-edge systems aligned to the hard-edge systems. Both these systems must stay in sync.

The team is ready to move to the next year. This is where the leaders' cohesiveness will allow their individual vulnerability and team trust to take the whole team to the next level. The Coach Cascade System will be taken to a fanatical level and you will highly achieve the results you always wanted and more!! And you are thinking, "What more could there be...?"

CHAPTER 5

YEAR 3:
THE COMPOUNDING YEAR

"What are you doing home so early?"

Alex had decided to get out of the office. It wasn't a problem to leave early as by this third year, the whole system was cranking.

He told Lisa, "I've got something on my mind. Are you up for a run?"

"Sure. The girls are at Jan's for another couple of hours."

As they ran easily along the river path, Alex thought about that morning. At the start of the weekly meeting, Andrew, the VP of Sales, had quietly told the others that he and his wife had been trying to conceive but that the doctors had told them it wouldn't be possible. They were both devastated.

Everyone was shocked. There had been no sign in Andrew's performance at work. As ever, he was Mr. Reliability.

Alex at once suggested Andrew take time out, but he replied, "It helps us both to work as usual. I just wanted you all to be aware of what was going on."

As they sat in the kitchen drinking water after their run, Alex tried to explain to Lisa why he had found the conversation so striking. "Even this time last year, he probably would never have mentioned it. He's a pretty private guy. I don't think anyone's even met his wife."

"Maybe he just feels more comfortable sharing things now. He trusts the team more."

"Later in the meeting, Matt called me out in front of everyone because he didn't agree with a marketing suggestion I made. The others all agreed. They said it was the best way forward."

"Well, was it? You always said you wanted people to feel they could disagree."

"I know, I loved the discussion we had, and we agreed to take it in the direction that was suggested. I just can't help looking back to when I had to have all the ideas and everyone just agreed with me all the time. We are in such a good place now."

Alex thought about that the next morning as he drove to the office. Lee had promised that, in this third year, he'd notice even more cohesiveness among his leadership team. He guessed that was what he was seeing.

How would he describe it?

Not like friends, necessarily.

More like family. They might not particularly like one another—he knew for a fact that Matt and Jen didn't—but they worked together well, committed to the common team goal. Most importantly, they trusted one another individually and more importantly as a team. They were happy to be honest or to show their vulnerability when necessary.

As if she could read his mind, Lee brought the same topic up in their next monthly 1-on-1. She said, "You've all been working so hard on your cohesiveness and culture. You're ready for the leadership team to start cascading this behavior further throughout the company. That way *their* leaders will have more impact through continuing to coach their own teams. It's your leaders' behavior as they grow from reactive tendencies to creative competencies, shared with their teams, that will ensure that the results you have achieved continue to compound in every corner of the company and achieve longevity."

"Like we've done six of the seven systems and we need to focus on the Coach Cascade System?"

"Not exactly. We can't take our eye off the ball, as we need to keep the other six systems at the level we have them now. And in fact, we have been working on the seventh system anyway. It just means we have the whole team working with us on those systems, so now because of the level of cohesiveness of the leadership team and the whole team, we are ready to focus more on the Coach Cascade System. As we discussed at the beginning of this relationship, Metronomics is 99 percent team behavior. Over the last two years, we've been working hard on behavior in our repeatable, structured, and systemized way. You and your leadership team are in a great position to take this to the next level. Don't forget, it's taken over two years to get the team here."

"I know. But it feels so worth it."

"And remember, Alex: every year we continue to evolve Metronomics in your organization, you are becoming a better version of yourself, your leaders, too, and the whole company. I can't wait for our next quarter planning session to see the results the company will achieve."

Lee sent everyone a reminder to review their Leadership Circle Assessment or to redo the assessment if they were unhappy with the results.

In the past, Alex might have been anxious about asking the team to spend so much time analyzing themselves, but he knew they trusted Lee enough to follow her guidance. And that the more self-aware each individual leader was becoming, including Alex, the better it was for the whole team. He could see that this was the only way the team could "grow up."

At the meeting, Lee introduced the Coach Cascade System. "Over the last two years, we have been working together to grow from an Expert Leader to a Coach Leader. And this year we will take this to the next level. You have been coaching your teams. Now you will continue with the idea of coaching your teams to become Coach Leaders themselves. Think of it as preparing them to take your role. And they'll coach their teams to do their roles, and so on. Because an A-Player wants to be coached so they can grow into their next role."

"Not that we're about to replace any of you," interrupted Alex. Everyone laughed.

"It's hard to be a coach with low self-awareness," Lee said. "That's why for the last nine quarters, we have spent a lot of time getting to know ourselves and each other. The purpose of this Leadership Circle self-assessment is to really focus you on your behavior, so you understand the behavior that is positively received and the behavior that is negatively received. This assessment will make you all more aware of your own behavior and that of others. You need to be vulnerable to share with this leadership team and with your own team where you need to improve, and you have to commit openly to working on it. And be ready for your peers and your team to give you feedback at that moment."

"The CEO always goes first," she said. "Alex, you start."

Alex went through the Leadership Circle Assessment. Alex was more of a creative leader than a reactive leader. Everyone agreed with the result that he was more on the creative side rather than reactive, but it was a little tough to receive feedback on his reactive traits from the team.

They went around the table and learned a lot about each other's reactive tendencies and creative competencies. Alex knew how hard it was for leaders to talk through their reactive behaviors as their peers gave them examples, but he was impressed by the level of discussion so far. Still, he noticed that Jennifer, the COO, dropped out of her turn a couple of times. Finally, there was no one else left.

Jen said, "Listen, I rushed this. I need to do it again."

Lee said, "It'll be fine. Go ahead."

It was clear as Jen started that she didn't score the same as the others.

Alex could not care less. Jen wasn't his COO by luck. She was a hard worker. Tough on others and tough on herself. In this case, too tough.

Jen was in the bottom 10 percent in reactiveness in all categories. That's why she was reluctant to share, thought Alex.

She was particularly reactive in the Critical category. She tried to justify it by saying, "I just have really high standards."

Matt said, "But if you're so quick to criticize others, it'll make you reluctant to put forward ideas in case they get knocked back. That's no good. You understand the business as well as anyone except Alex, and we don't hear your opinions."

Lee put Jen on the spot. She made her identify her reactiveness to the others, commit to working on it, and asked how she might do that.

Alex said, "Why don't you start by keeping track of when you do it?"

Jen agreed. Lee suggested that in fact they all keep a tally of the times they noticed themselves engaging in the behavior they were trying to improve.

Alex would check in with them on their weekly 1-on-1s—and they'd check in on his as well with each leader.

For Alex, the improvement was almost instant. He couldn't avoid being aware of his behavior when he knew someone would pull him up on it later in the week. And he could tell that Jen was working really hard to become less critical, more creative.

Alex and the team knew that moving from reactive tendencies to creative competencies takes time, and they were committed to this part of the journey.

And then, suddenly, here it was. The 2-day annual meeting marking the twelfth quarter—and the milestone of reaching their very first 3HAG they'd gutted out at the very first Kick-Off. It was unbelievable that they had over-achieved the very first 3HAG they gutted out. They had thought it was a big goal when they wrote it down. But then slowly, quarter by quarter, it became more realistic, and they validated the path to achieving it all along the way. Now, everyone was absolutely blown away. Alex stood up front to congratulate the team and share the great news—and he could feel how ecstatic they all were.

Then Alex added *more* good news: the most recent team member Net Promoter Score (eNPS) OpenDoor used to measure the satisfaction and loy-alty of their teams. The score was off the chart: 83. It was incredible. The Coach Cascade focus this year was really having an impact in so many ways.

They ran through the usual annual planning agenda, working through the systems. They looked forward to a new 3HAG and 1HAG, and they did a great check-in on the BHAG now that they had stepped that much closer. Everything was working well and, where it wasn't, they dug in together to do the work to solve the problem.

Winding up at the end of the second day, Lee said, "So, you know the Metronomics system is well in place and you know you will never stop grow-ing with it."

Alex said, "I don't know how we ever tried to grow the company without it. We've got more time. We've got more ideas and more money to invest in the growth of the company. We could only dream of this 3 years ago. When we started out, I had no idea of what this system would bring—but I was willing to commit."

There were some murmurs of agreement.

Matt said, "What happens next?"

Lee said, "Now that you have the Metronomics regimen, the high-perform-ing business team system, in place and cranking, it's the leaders' responsibil-ity to keep it that way. We need to ensure the soft-edge systems of Culture, Cohesive, and Human stay aligned with the hard-edge business systems of Strategy, Execution, and Cash as you move forward. That probably sounds a bit boring after the last 3 years when you've been growing the company up, but believe me, it won't be. It won't be because things will evolve, and the sys-tem will evolve. People evolve, business evolves, the world evolves. But relax: OpenDoor is ready for anything because you have Metronomics in place. The system will allow you to take on any and all of the developments that might come your way."

They'd come such a long way together. Lucy, the CTO who'd replaced Daniel, was beaming. She'd already suggested to Alex that she might take a 2-month sabbatical, and he knew things would run fine in her absence. Jen was more relaxed and slower to jump on people's faults. As for Alex, he was fitter and trimmer than he had been since he started OpenDoor, exercising regularly, taking Lisa away on retreats, and checking out of the office when-ever one of the girls had something going on at school.

As a final clincher, when they were packing up, Andrew asked if he could speak quickly to the group. With a smile, he told them that he and his wife were about to adopt a baby boy. They were all thrilled.

Yes, Alex thought as he drove home to his family. That was what it was really all about—growing a high-performing business team together.

BEHAVIOR MATTERS

The third year of Metronomics is about compounding what you've already achieved, coupled with exponential behavioral improvements from the lead-ers and their team members.

Year 1 was about getting the Execution and Cash System implemented with clear accountability and clarity of expectations. We also got the company's

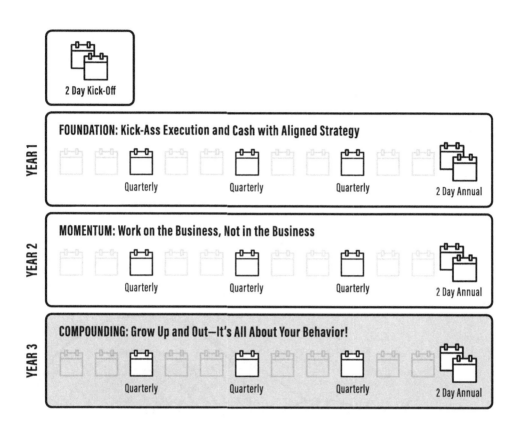

strategy mapped in visible pictures with clarity. Year 2 was about momentum, leveraging the Execution and Cash System while validating the company's strategy with confidence. You've got the right people in the right functional roles, doing the right, aligned functional things. And the leadership team has cascaded Metronomics throughout the company with great success.

Your strategy's success is visible and tangible, and the entire team is committed and passionate. Your leaders are coaching; the board and customers are impressed and enthusiastic. All of this is happening with the whole team enthusiastic and committed to the team goals while maintaining life balance.

Now it's time to take our behavior to the next level.

HUMAN BEINGS ARE THE KEY

Metronomics is based on humans and human nature. By this point, this is probably obvious. But to be clear, for the last two years, while it appeared that you've been focusing on execution and strategy, every time you turn the dial on each system you have also been turning up your focus on human team behavior and building a culturally strong cohesive team.

Team members drive everything.

That's why it has taken two years to get this far. Because evolving a person's behavior takes time. And evolving a team's behavior takes even longer with disciplined laser focus.

The key to Year 3 is the cascaded behavior of the CEO and the leadership team. That's why we've worked hard to get to this point. We wanted to get the leadership into the right place to be able to cascade out to the team.

THE REAL 10X SECRET

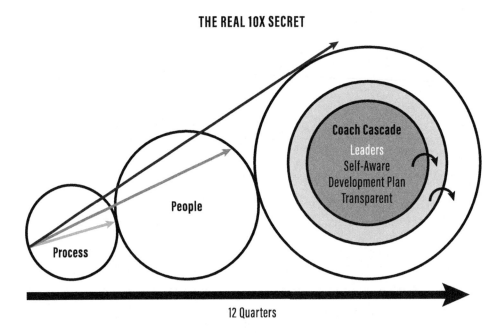

12 Quarters

The creative behavior of the CEO and leadership team is the REAL 10X secret of the Metronomics system. Each circle in the diagram represents a developing team. The first step (Process) represents building team cohesion while implementing a clear and simple business plan with metrics. The second step (People) represents growing team cohesion as the norm while connecting the clear team plan with metrics to all team members. The third step (Coach Cascade) represents taking the highly cohesive team coupled with the clarity of the connected plan and metrics to the next level of being known as a high-performing team, or in this case, a high-performing business team.

QUARTER BY QUARTER

Your team will be ready for the third year of Metronomics. They understand the alignment of their BHAG, 3HAG, and 1HAG. They have a confident strategy. Execution is cranking. The Open Playing Field is aligned, and the team is playing well together on it. Team members are fully involved in recommending solutions thanks to the clarity of the company plan and the direction we're heading. Leaders have time to coach their team members and are looking forward to learning more about how they can improve as coaches and train their team members to become coaches, too. The excitement that resonates around this third year comes from the success they've had in Years 1 and 2. The clarity of the process along with the path the company is on allows the team to be confident and remain cohesive as they look forward to this third year.

Like every other year, this year is structured around the quarterly meetings. And really it's around the 13 weeks in each quarter. 90 days.

- Y3, Q1: Team Trust 2.0
- Y3, Q2: The Coach Cascade
- Y3, Q3: Clearer and Clearer
- Y3, Q4: Results

Let's talk about each quarterly meeting.

QUARTER 9: TEAM TRUST 2.0

The team is excited to enter the third year of Metronomics. They're confident and relaxed with the process. They know how to prepare for each of these quarterly meetings with their teams, as well as what they need to do to be successful each time.

This first meeting of the year will focus on continuing the momentum of execution, homing in on further cascading the clarity of accountability and expectations out into the company. As with every quarter, we will always validate our strategy, and we'll take some time to discuss and put into practice the next level of leadership team behavior required to evolve and grow the company.

PREPARATION FOR THE MEETING

Have your leadership team—and yourself—prepare for the meeting like this:

1. Everyone should have read the book *Dare to Lead* by Brené Brown, which will confirm the importance of coaching team members through recognizing their potential and ideas, asking great questions, and leaning in with vulnerability when necessary.

2. Leaders ensure that the KFFM is up to date.

3. Leaders review the information on *www.metronomicsthebook.com* on Brand Promise with Guarantee and are ready to create the next strategic picture.

4. Everyone should bring the status of the priorities and metrics they own up to date on the Open Playing Field so everyone can review them prior to the meeting—otherwise, you'll waste time updating the plan in the meeting.

5. Complete the Quarterly Prep Survey and review the results prior to the meeting.

After reviewing the status of the whole plan, make notes, ask questions, and be ready to discuss in the context of building the next quarter's plan.

AGENDA

Compound Growth System	Day 1
Cohesive System	· Good News · Cohesive Question · Left and Right: Continue, Stop, Start · Leadership Circle Assessment
Human System	· Organizational Function Chart · KFFM · Team Assessment (A, B, C)
Cultural System	· Core Purpose · Core Values · BHAG: Confirm/Evolve
Strategy System	· 3HAG™: Confirm · Market Map—Review · Core Customer—Review · Brand Promise with Guarantee
Execution System	· Status Review Annual Plan / QHAG · Next QHAG · Meeting: Check In · Cascade 3 Key Messages
Cash System	· Widgets Act / F/C to P/L F/C · Book Monthly F/C Review Meeting
Coach Cascade System	· WDYR · Scaling Leadership Individual Leader Assessment Share with Leadership Team

It's your ninth quarterly meeting, so it goes without saying that you'll go through the familiar agenda, working through the seven systems of the Compound Growth System.

COHESIVE SYSTEM

Good News
Kick off with our usual positive start.

Cohesive Question
Personal get-to-know-you questions or icebreakers that continue to improve team trust.

TO THE RIGHT AND TO THE LEFT

One Thing to Continue

One Thing to Stop

One Thing to Start

Timeframe: 90 Days Past and Immediate Looking Forward

Left and Right
This time, there's a variation on this cohesive work that we call Left and Right: Continue, Stop, Start. We share feedback to the leaders on the left and right of us, as usual, but now we focus on 3 things: what should they continue doing, what should they stop doing, and what should they start doing.

A leadership team must be at a very high level of cohesiveness to do this level of Left and Right feedback with its peers. If you haven't done the *Five Dysfunctions of a Team Assessment* from the last chapter, don't try this yet. Continue with the regular Left and Right: Appreciation and Improvement as before until the cohesiveness of your team reaches the level that you are able to share this type of feedback.

For more information, please go to *www.metronomicsthebook.com*.

COACH CASCADE SYSTEM

Scaling Leadership

The team has read *Dare to Lead* by Brené Brown and *Scaling Leadership* by Anderson and Adams and has a better understanding of courageous leadership. The Leadership Circle framework in the assessment utilized in Scaling Leadership will be presented to the rest of the leadership team. You'll also have a fuller discussion about what each of them has learned over the last 90 days and what they will focus on for the next 90 days.

This discussion will be much easier than last time—and every time we return to it in this coming year and beyond it will get easier and easier.

The leaders will share the one behavior they look to improve on over the next 90 days with their team, as well as sharing their commitment to improvement and looking for their team's support in this behavioral modification. This is where leaders take vulnerability to the next level. By sharing with their team what each individual is working on, they will create the transparency required to develop leaders in the company.

What Do You Recommend?

Check in and review with leaders how the WDYR is going with their teams and instigate a discussion for leaders to provide examples from the last 90 days.

HUMAN SYSTEM

Organizational Function Chart

Review the Organizational Function Chart.

Key Function Flow Map

Fully review the KFFM Level 1 and Level 2 and the Flywheel.

A-Player Team Assessment

Review and discuss the A-Player Team Assessment graph and any action plans that are required.

Team View

Make sure you review the current Team View with the whole leadership team and continue to share at the Monthly Town Hall with the whole team.

CULTURAL SYSTEM

Core Purpose

A quick review to confirm that the Core Purpose is good enough for now.

Core Values

A quick review and confirmation that the Core Values are good enough for now.

BHAG

A quick review and confirmation that the BHAG is good enough for now.

Profit/X

A quick review and confirmation that the Profit/X is good enough for now.

STRATEGY SYSTEM

Coming out of the last 2-day annual planning session the team members are feeling quite good and confident around their differentiated strategy. They are looking forward to taking one of the advanced steps in the *3HAG WAY*, which is to focus on Brand Promise with Guarantee. In this meeting, we will focus on Brand Promise rather than the Guarantee—not quite yet. To prepare for this section, we will do, as we always have, the following:

3HAG

Quick review and confirmation that it is good enough for now.

3HAG: Market Map

Review the Market Map and make any necessary updates based on how it's evolved.

3HAG: Core Customer Analysis
Quick review of the Core Customer.

3HAG: Attribution Map
Quick review of the Attribution Map.

3HAG: Differentiators
Quick review of the Activity Fit Map.

3HAG: Brand Promise with Guarantee
Jim Collins described the power of what he called a "catalytic mechanism" on turning business goals into reality in an article for the *Harvard Business Review*, "Turning Goals into Results: The Power of a Catalytic Mechanism." The core of Jim's argument is that, if you make a promise that is important to the Core Customer, you should guarantee it with something that would benefit them—and hurt the company.

Yes, *hurt*.

It's not easy—but that doesn't mean it's not valuable. That's why we're going to work through the process to create a catalytic mechanism that is strongly connected to your strategy and founded upon your Core Customer and connected to your current cohesive, empowered team.

The catalytic mechanism has two parts: a Brand Promise and a Guarantee. In my experience, developing a great Brand Promise with Guarantee means you must be very clear on your Core Customers' prioritized needs. And you must have an empowered team who can make immediate decisions in favor of the Brand Promise with Guarantee.

The team will take the first step toward the Brand Promise with Guarantee by brainstorming the promises that could be made to serve the prioritized needs of your Core Customers (make sure your Core Customer Analysis is up to date for this meeting). After reviewing the top 3 prioritized needs of the Core Customer, the team will break into groups and brainstorm promises for each of those needs. The team then presents all the brainstormed ideas and focuses on one to 3 promises for each of the top 3 needs of the Core Customer.

BRAND PROMISE WITH GUARANTEE EXAMPLE

Each one of these guarantees serves the #1 Need of the Core Customer which is to "Make Money"

TOP 3 NEEDS OF CORE CUSTOMER	YOUR PROMISE	THE GUARANTEE
1. To Make Money	1.	1.
2. Easy Sale	2.	2.
3. No Support	3.	3.

1. Fit with Strategy   2. Fit with Execution   3. Test   4. Decide   5. Make it Known

At the end of the discussion, the team will agree to validate these promises softly over the next 90 days with their Core Customers and be ready next time to discuss further which promises resonated best with their Core Customers. For more information on how to create a Brand Promise with Guarantee please go to *www.metronomicsthebook.com*.

EXECUTION SYSTEM

The Execution System part of the day is well known and understood by your team and it will follow the same format as last quarter, including the Swimlane review. Do not skip the 13-Week Sprint Lane Map.

CASH SYSTEM

The 12-month widget-based forecast should be reviewed within the context of the 36-month rolling forecast, as usual. At this point, the leaders in the team have an in-depth understanding of this process, which in turn is improving the forecast at a detailed level, month over month and quarter over quarter.

CHECK-IN

As with every meeting, check in with the team about how the meeting cadence, agenda, and outcomes are progressing. This gives you as a team the opportunity to tweak anything that needs to be adjusted so everyone stays aligned with their teams.

Cascading Messages

As at all our meetings, we will do a check-in with everyone and take note of the 3 Key Messages that need to be cascaded to the rest of the organization in tomorrow's huddle.

One-Phrase Close

The day wraps up as always by asking each of the leaders for 5 words or less to describe how they feel right now.

NEXT STEPS/HOMEWORK

- Update the Open Playing Field as necessary.

- Each leader should add to the Open Playing Field the quarterly Corporate Priorities including the 13-week subpriorities from the Sprint Lanes developed with the team, and their own individual priorities.

- Add Strategic Pictures to the War Room.

- Investigate, test, and validate the Brand Promise—not the Guarantee—softly with Core Customers.

- Continue to run all company meetings through the Open Playing Field.

- Update the KFFM fully every week.

- All leaders should cascade 3 Key Messages to their teams.

- Team member Quarterly Coaching Reviews are completed based on functional Scorecards.

- Leaders make known and work on their creative competency. Team members are aware of each other's development and provide feedback as required at that moment.

- Everyone should read the book *Seeing Around Corners* by Rita McGrath.

OUTCOMES

- Cohesive: The whole team is excited for the year and committed to the plan. The leaders are eager to evolve their creative competencies and share this with their teams. They are all looking for support from the team, knowing they are playing in a safe environment.

- Human: The KFFM is alive and well. Depending on the size of the company, the teams will start working on a KFFM Level 3 to map the next level of subfunctions. The Quarterly Coaching Reviews are booked, and the team members and leaders are looking forward to this 2-way discussion. There is disciplined, conscious behavior to keep the A-Player team intact.

- Cultural: The team is proud of their clear, known culture. The company is getting known for its strong culture. The team embraces Good News at every meeting and has planned other events for the year that will complement and reward their strong culture.

- Strategy: With the confidence in strategy founded on the Core Customer, the team is eager to put in place a strong Brand Promise with Guarantee. They know this is the ultimate step in aligning strategy and execution and team behaviors while attracting the Core Customer. The team is eager to test out the top promises with the Core Customer.

- Execution: The team is feeling good about their results thus far and keen to execute the plan. They know everyone must keep a disciplined focus on the cadence and process developed for the team and not get complacent. Everyone needs to be vigilant about the plan and focused on the metrics.

- Cash: The leadership team is maintaining the cadence of the monthly forecast review meetings and is excited about the results they are getting.

- Coach Cascade: The leaders are excited about the next step in becoming more creative leaders, even though tough feedback has been given and received. This is getting easier, and the whole team is appreciative of and grateful to the leaders' commitment to grow themselves. The engagement continues to remain high.

QUARTER 10: COACH CASCADE

The second quarterly meeting of the year is here. We will be continuing to work on the leaders' behavior through the feedback from the Leadership Circle Assessment, as well as taking a deep dive into our strategy using Ian MacMillan and Rita McGrath's Consumption Chain Mapping Analysis. As always, it's very important to prepare for these meetings with your team, as laid out in Best Practice from Chapter 8 in *The Metronome Effect*. (You can also find this information at *www.metronomicsthebook.com*.)

PREPARATION FOR THE MEETING

1. Everyone should have finished reading *Seeing Around Corners* by Rita McGrath.

2. Leaders ensure that the KFFM is up to date.

3. Leaders review the information on the *metronomicsthebook.com* site on Rita McGrath's Consumption Chain Mapping and are ready to create the next strategic picture.

4. Everyone should bring the status of the priorities and metrics they own up to date on the Open Playing Field so everyone can review them prior to the meeting—otherwise, you'll waste time updating the plan in the meeting.

5. Complete the Quarterly Prep Survey and review the responses prior to the start of the meeting.

Again, you move through the system flow of the Compound Growth System. The process is more than familiar by now, and the team understands it and is enthusiastic about the growth they are seeing.

This meeting will continue developing the Coach Cascade System. It's the way invaluable experience flows out through the company. It's how you strengthen Metronomics. It's how you continue to build on the foundation of the company and grow people into a high-performing business team. It's also how you grow autonomy, freeing the leadership team to spend more time "growing up" with more coaches.

The data show that 15 percent of the corporate leadership teams that operate in a creative way like this are consistently knocking it out of the park. They have the company they want, the growth they want, they listen to their entire team, and they both invest in their team and inherently experience autonomy.

It takes time to grow team behavior, but it is *so* worth it as this is what will set you free to grow into the company you want to be.

AGENDA

Compound Growth System	Day 1
Cohesive System	· Good News · Cohesive Question · Left and Right: Continue, Stop, Start · Leadership Circle Assessment
Human System	· Organizational Function Chart · KFFM Level I and II Review · Team Assessment (A, B, C)
Cultural System	· Core Purpose · Core Values · BHAG: Confirm/Evolve
Strategy System	· 3HAG™: Confirm · Market Map—Review · Core Customer—Review · Consumption Chain Mapping Analysis
Execution System	· Status Review Annual Plan / QHAG · Next QHAG · Meeting: Check In · Cascade 3 Key Messages
Cash System	· Widgets Act / F/C to P/L F/C
Coach Cascade System	· Scaling Leadership Assessment Review incorporate into Quarterly Coaching Review and 1:1s

A small but important caveat: don't expect to reach the end. The end of what? The end of a high-performing business team? The end of growing? The funny thing is that there's no one champagne moment when it's all worth it. There are so many along the way it's hard to count. So, celebrate all of them, every milestone achieved all along the growth way! This is key.

COHESIVE SYSTEM

Start the meeting with Good News and then your personal get-to-know-you questions or icebreakers.

Left and Right

As last time, we share feedback to the leaders on the left and right of us: what should they continue doing, what should they stop doing, and what should they start doing.

COACH CASCADE SYSTEM

Scaling Leadership

The leadership team is well prepared for the discussion around each of their assessments. They have shared the key behavior they are working on with their teams and have received great feedback, which they share with the other leaders.

The next step is to discuss having each of the leaders' teams assess their leader in the next 90 days. This will give a great view of what the leader perceives as their reactive tendencies and creative competencies compared to how they are perceived by their team. Leaders can be uncomfortable taking this step.

It's not for the faint at heart—but it suits leaders who can be courageous and vulnerable with their team and their peers.

To end this section, leaders confirm the behavior they will work on for the next 90 days with all the other leaders. The Scaling Leadership Assessment will be incorporated into their 90 -day review with the CEO as well as in

1-on-1s with their team members. Now we're getting into very transparent behavior and feedback.

What Do You Recommend?

Check in and review with leaders how the WDYR is going with their teams and instigate a discussion for leaders to provide examples from the last 90 days.

HUMAN SYSTEM

Organizational Function Chart

Review the Organizational Function Chart for any adjustments.

Key Function Flow Map

Fully review the KFFM Level 1 and Level 2 and the Flywheel.

A-Player Team Assessment

Leaders assess their direct reports on the A-Player Team Assessment graph for everyone to review and discuss.

Team View

Review the current Team View with the whole leadership team, and continue to share at the Monthly Town Hall with the whole team.

CULTURAL SYSTEM

Core Purpose

Quickly review and confirm that the Core Purpose is good enough for now.

Core Values

Quickly check and confirm that the Core Values are good enough for now.

BHAG

A quick review and confirmation that it is good enough for now.

Profit/X
A quick review and confirmation that it is good enough for now.

STRATEGY SYSTEM

To prepare for this section we will do the following:

3HAG
A quick review and confirmation that the 3HAG is good enough for now.

3HAG: Market Map
Review the Market Map and make any necessary updates based on how it's evolved.

3HAG: Core Customer Analysis
Do a quick review of the Core Customer and update as necessary.

3HAG: Brand Promise with Guarantee
The team continues to work with the marketplace and their Core Customer to validate the Brand Promises that were brainstormed at the last meeting. This feedback will be ready for the next quarterly meeting.

3HAG: Consumption Chain Mapping
The team has prepared to work through a Consumption Chain Mapping Analysis by answering questions around their Core Customers' entire experience of the company. This provides a new and different view to validate our current strategy and to build confidence we are heading in the right direction.

I love working with clients on this view because the areas of strategy about which they may not be sure are either validated or not. In addition, this view forces the client to take action quickly to align their strategy with execution.

The first step is for the CEO and leadership team to map out the Core Customer Consumption Chain. The second step is to review this mapping

CONSUMPTION CHAIN ANALYSIS MAPPING
Rita McGrath + Ian MacMillan

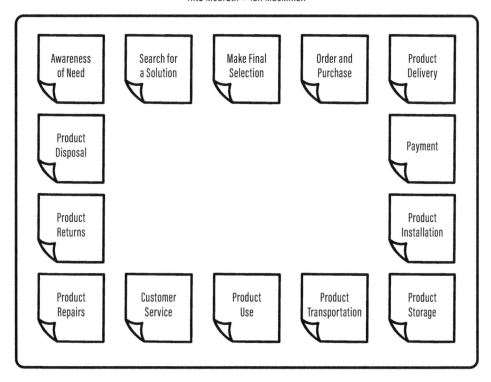

- **Awareness:** How do people become aware of their need for your product or service?
- **Search:** How do people find your current (or upgraded) offerings?
- **Selection:** How do your customers make their final selection?
- **Order and Purchase:** How do consumers order and purchase your product or service?
- **Delivery:** How is your product or service delivered? What happens when your product or service is delivered?
- **Payment/Financing/Receipt:** How is your product or service paid for?
- **Installation:** How is your product installed?
- **Storage:** Is your product stored?
- **Transportation:** Is your product moved from one place to another?
- **Use:** How are your customers really using your product?
- **Service:** What do consumers need help with when they use your product?
- **Repairs:** How is your product repaired or serviced?
- **Returns:** Can your product be returned or exchanged?
- **Final Disposal:** What happens when your product is disposed of or no longer used?

and analyze your Core Customers' experience with your company. As we know, the Core Customer is the foundation of our strategy. This analysis will highlight areas of your strategy and execution in serving the Core Customer that need more adjustment and focus. When I did this recently with a client, this view absolutely confirmed the specific area that was slowing down their momentum with the customer, aligned to their Flywheel and their KFFM. It was great to see this validated. The different view drove the plan of action required for the client to solve the problem.

Never stop looking for ways to validate your strategy and how it serves your Core Customer.

For more information about Consumption Chain Mapping and Metronomics, visit *www.metronomicsthebook.com.*

EXECUTION SYSTEM

Everyone understands the execution system part of the day, which follows the same format as last quarter, including the Swimlane review.

CASH SYSTEM

The 12-month widget-based forecast should be reviewed as usual within the context of the 36-month rolling forecast. By now, the leaders in the team have an in-depth understanding of this process, which in turn is improving the forecast at a detailed level month over month and quarter over quarter. The focus remains on the cash forecast goals and how to achieve them.

This part of the meeting will close out as always with checking in on the Leaders and Metronomics regimen and ensuring 3 Key Messages are captured and cascaded out after the meeting.

The day wraps up as always asking each of the leaders for 5 words or less to describe how they feel right now.

NEXT STEPS/HOMEWORK

- Update the Open Playing Field as necessary.

- Each leader should add to the Open Playing Field the quarterly Corporate Priorities, including the 13-week subpriorities from the Sprint Lanes developed with the team, and their own individual priorities.

- Add Strategic Pictures to the War Room.

- Investigate, test, and validate the Brand Promise.

- Continue to run all company meetings through the Open Playing Field.

- KFFM is active and is reviewed each week.

- All leaders cascade 3 Key Messages from the meeting to their teams.

- Team member Quarterly Coaching Reviews are completed based on functional Scorecards.

- Leaders have incorporated their Leadership Assessment into their 1-on-1s with the CEO and their team members. This assessment is also incorporated into their Quarterly Coaching Review with the CEO.

- Leaders make plans or take action on any C-Player team members.

- Leaders make known and work on their creative competency.

- Leaders and their team members complete the Leadership Circle Assessment for team leaders.

- Leaders should read *How Will You Measure Your Life?* By Clayton M. Christensen before the next quarterly meeting.

OUTCOMES

- Cohesive: Discipline remains focused on keeping the cohesiveness of the leadership and the whole team high. The leaders are remaining diligent to keep the cohesive rhythm high as the teams grow and evolve.

- Human: The KFFM is an active scoreboard in the company, and everyone refers to it every day. The coaching reviews are fully in place, with all team members looking forward to these coaching sessions. There is clarity of growth opportunities and expectations for all team members.

- Cultural: Culture remains strong and active every day.

- Strategy: Strategic confidence is high, and the team is learning a lot from validating the Brand Promise with the Core Customer.

- Execution: Focusing on the plan every day is working well. The team remains active on the playing field and is staying aligned to the clear plan and widgets.

- Cash: The leadership team is keeping the cadence of the Monthly Widget-Based Forecast Review meetings and is excited about their results thus far.

- Coach Cascade: The leaders are nervous and excited for the feedback from the "360" Leadership Circle Assessment from their team members. They want to grow the next best version of themselves as leaders and look forward to cascading this out to their team. The engagement remains high.

QUARTER 11: CLEARER AND CLEARER

The leadership team is excited about the feedback they're getting from their teams on improving their behavior, even though their teams were initially uncomfortable calling out their leaders. As the quarter evolved over the last 90 days, however, the team members got more comfortable. By now, they might even be having a little fun addressing and supporting their leader's evolving behavior.

PREPARATION FOR THE MEETING

Have your leadership team—and yourself—prepare for the meeting like this:

1. Having read *How Will you Measure Your Life?* by Clayton M. Christensen, this will align with all that has been implemented thus far and will give good confidence to the leaders.

2. Leaders ensure the KFFM is up to date.

3. Leaders re-review the information provided on the www. metronomicsthebook.com site on Brand Promise with Guarantee and are ready to create the next strategic picture.

4. All leaders ensure their priorities and the metrics they own are up to date on the Open Playing Field so everyone can review them before the meeting and avoid wasting time.

5. Complete the Quarterly Prep Survey and review the response prior to the start of the meeting.

6. After reviewing the status of the whole plan, make notes, ask questions, and be ready to discuss in the context of building the next quarter's plan.

By now, everyone is familiar with the format of the meeting: homework, review of systems, and data. More than ever seemed possible, execution is looking after itself as the teams take accountability for their own widgets. The Compound Growth System is humming along, showing results.

At this meeting, the need for, and the value of, the Coach Cascade System will continue to become clearer.

You might wonder why we haven't done this earlier. The reason is that we needed to do all the foundational work over the last years to get to a point where we can focus on leadership behavior with a strong cohesive team in order to roll out the Coach Cascade System. Without the strong foundation, the Coach Cascade System would not work.

KNOW YOURSELF

The overarching theme of this meeting is looking at your own behaviors. What in your behavior causes issues for your growth, your team's growth, and your business's growth?

You will again take the assessment results and wrestle with the brutal facts that arise from them. You will learn how weaknesses can kill strengths.

But there are positives. You will learn how to cancel out your negative behaviors. You will stop being reactive and instead focus your energy on working and evolving your behavior. Everyone has committed to the idea of moving from being reactive to being creative—now we just have to do the work. Given the human nature of individuals and teams, this process will take commitment, focus, and time.

AGENDA

Compound Growth System	Day 1
Cohesive System	• Good News • Cohesive Question • Left and Right: Continue, Stop, Start • Leadership Circle Assessment
Human System	• Organizational Function Chart • KFFM • Team Assessment (A, B, C)
Cultural System	• Core Purpose • Core Values • BHAG: Confirm/Evolve
Strategy System	• 3HAG™: Confirm • Market Map—Review • Core Customer—Review • Brand Promise with Guarantee validation
Execution System	• Status Review Annual Plan / QHAG • Next QHAG • Meeting: Check In • Cascade 3 Key Messages
Cash System	• Widgets Act / F/C to P/L F/C
Coach Cascade System	• Scaling Leadership Assessment to the Next Group of Leaders

COHESIVE SYSTEM

Start the meeting in the normal way, with Good News, get-to-know-you questions, and the Left and Right: Stop, Continue, Start (do this as you did it last time). And take time to reflect on *How Will you Measure Your Life?* by Clayton M. Christensen, which the leadership team read to prepare for this meeting.

COACH CASCADE SYSTEM

Scaling Leadership

At this meeting, each leader will have the results of their assessment, including their team's feedback. Each leader reviews this assessment, and particularly the differences in their own self-assessment and how their team members assessed them. This is a great discussion and time of learning.

Each of the leaders comes prepared to discuss the next behavioral evolution they will take on their journey to becoming a creative leader. They will share this with the leadership team and will also have a follow-up meeting with their own team to discuss their results.

Again, it takes a courageous leader to be able to have this kind of transparent conversation with their team. But conversations like this will take the company's behavior, cohesiveness, and culture to the next level. This truly unlocks a team's growth.

What Do You Recommend?

Check in and review with leaders how the WDYR is going with their teams, and instigate a discussion for leaders to provide examples from the last 90 days.

HUMAN SYSTEM

Organizational Function Chart

Review the Organizational Function Chart for any adjustments.

Key Function Flow Map

Fully review the KFFM Levels 1 and 2 and the Flywheel.

A-Player Team Assessment

Leaders assess their direct reports on the A-Player Team Assessment graph for everyone to review and discuss.

Team View

Review the Team View with the leadership team and note any adjustments required. Continue to share this at the Monthly Town Hall meeting with the whole team.

CULTURAL SYSTEM

Core Purpose

Quickly review and confirm that the Core Purpose is good enough for now.

Core Values

Quickly check and confirm that the Core Values are good enough for now.

BHAG

A quick review and confirmation that it is good enough for now.

Profit/X

A quick review and confirmation that it is good enough for now.

STRATEGY SYSTEM

To prepare for this section we will do the following:

3HAG

A quick review and confirmation that the 3HAG is good enough for now.

3HAG: Market Map

Review the Market Map and make any necessary updates based on how it's evolved.

3HAG: Core Customer Analysis

Do a quick review of the Core Customer and update as necessary.

3HAG: Brand Promise with Guarantee

This time, the team will be prepared to discuss the promises that were validated at the last meeting and lock in on one promise for each of the top 3 prioritized needs. They'll break into groups to brainstorm which guarantee for each of those promises best relates to the number one need of the Core Customer. The team will come back and share their brainstormed guarantees, settling on one for each of the 3 brand promises.

BRAND PROMISE WITH GUARANTEE EXAMPLE

Each one of these guarantees serves the #1 Need of the Core Customer which is to "Make Money"

TOP 3 NEEDS OF CORE CUSTOMER	YOUR PROMISE	THE GUARANTEE
1. To Make Money	1. Every new subscriber will produce a 10% gross margin	1. Or we will make up the difference to ensure the GM is maintained.
2. Easy Sale	2. Every sale is one click or less	2. Or we will pay 12 months subscriber fees in full and upfront.
3. No Support	3. A subscriber will never call you for support	3. Or we will pay for the next 12 months of that subscriber's fees in full

1. Fit with Strategy   2. Fit with Execution   3. Test   4. Decide   5. Make it Known

The action item coming out of this meeting is for the leaders to validate the Brand Promise with *Guarantee*. Once the leaders validate the guarantee, they need to decide which brand promise to make known.

Once they make known the brand promise, they are enabling a lot of hard work to ensure that the brand promise fits with the strategy and attracts the

Core Customer who buys at a profit. They are also ensuring that the team is empowered to execute on the Brand Promise with Guarantee.

The Brand Promise with Guarantee is advanced further, as this is where strategy and execution meet, coupled with the team's empowered behavior.

EXECUTION SYSTEM

The execution system part of the day is well known and understood by your team, and it follows the same format as before.

CASH SYSTEM

The 12-month widget-based forecast should be reviewed within the context of the 36-month rolling forecast.

End the meeting with a check-in with all leaders and ensure the 3 Key Messages are captured so they can be cascaded after the meeting.

The day wraps up by asking each of the leaders for 5 words or less to describe how they feel right now.

NEXT STEPS/HOMEWORK

- Update the Open Playing Field as necessary.

- Each leader should add to the Open Playing Field the quarterly Corporate Priorities including the 13-week subpriorities from the Sprint Lanes developed with the team, and their own individual priorities.

- Leaders make plans or take action on any C-Player team members.

- Add Strategic Pictures to the War Room.

- Test and validate the Brand Promise with Guarantee.

- Continue to run all company meetings through the Open Playing Field.

- The KFFM is active and is reviewed each week.

- All leaders cascade 3 Key Messages from the meeting to their teams.

- Team member Quarterly Coaching Reviews are completed based on functional Scorecards.

- Leaders have incorporated their Leadership Assessment into their 1-on-1s with the CEO and their team members. This assessment is also incorporated into their Quarterly Coaching Review with the CEO.

- Scaling Leadership continues to be cascaded throughout the company, with the leaders receiving active feedback from their teams.

- Leaders should read *Beyond Entrepreneurship 2.0* by Jim Collins again before the next quarterly meeting.

OUTCOMES

- Cohesive: With the leaders sharing the results of the "360" Leadership Circle Assessment with their teams and the company, the level of cohesiveness continues to rise. Most team members have never been on a team where the leaders are so open and vulnerable about their own growth paths. Disciplined focus remains on keeping the cohesiveness of the leadership and the whole team at a high daily level. The leaders are diligent about keeping the cohesive rhythm high as the teams grow and evolve into high-performing business teams.

- Human: The KFFM is an active scoreboard of the widgets in the company, and everyone refers to it every day to make decisions as circumstances evolve. The Coaching Reviews are fully in place, with all team members looking forward to these coaching sessions. There is clarity about growth opportunities and expectations for all team members.

- Cultural: Culture continues to remain strong and active every day.

- Strategy: Strategic confidence is high, and the team is learning a lot from validating the Brand Promise with Guarantee with the Core Customer. This process is simplifying what really matters to the Core Customer and how the team can deliver it.

- Execution: Focusing on the plan every day is working well. The team remains active on the playing field and is staying aligned to the clear plan and widgets.

- Cash: The leadership team is keeping the cadence of the monthly forecast review meetings and is excited about the results.

- Coach Cascade: The leaders are eager to discuss the results of the "360" Leadership Circle Assessment with their teams and to explain what they will be working on specifically to grow. They are actively coaching their team members in their meetings, including the 1-on-1s and the quarterly Coaching Reviews. The engagement continues to remain high.

QUARTER 12: RESULTS

You made it! 12 quarters! 3 years! Finally, you arrive at your very first gutted-out 3HAG!

Whoohoohoo!

The team can't believe how fast the time has gone. Never a dull moment!

The focus on implementing Metronomics has absolutely consumed their focus and achieved their team results. The team is excited to move into this full 2-day planning session for their next fiscal year.

PREPARATION FOR THE MEETING

Have your leadership team—and yourself—prepare for the meeting like this:

1. Having read *Beyond Entrepreneurship 2.0* by Jim Collins for a second time, be prepared to share the key impact and reflections you gathered; they will definitely be different from the first time you read it.

2. Complete the Prep Survey and review the survey response prior to the start of the meeting.

3. Complete the Five Dysfunctions of a Team Assessment.

AGENDA

Compound Growth System	Day 1
Cohesive System	· Good News · Cohesive Question · Left and Right: Continue, Stop, Start · 5 Dysfunctions Team Assessment
Human System	· Organizational Function Chart · KFFM—Review
Cultural System	· Core Purpose · Core Values · Hedgehog with Simon Sinek's Golden Circle · BHAG: Confirm/Evolve
Strategy System	· 3HAG™: Evolve Out + 1 Year · Market Map—Evolve · Core Customer—Confirm · Attribution Framework—Re-do · Swimlanes—Re-do · Brand Promise—Confirm · Secret Sauce

4. Ensure that the information on the Open Playing Field is up to date, so you don't waste time in the meeting.

5. Complete the Metronomics Checklist Survey.

The agenda follows the flow of all the other meetings through the systems.

The objective of this 2-day annual meeting is to keep the momentum of execution going, to validate strategy, and to celebrate the achievement of our very first gutted-out 3HAG. Of course, we will also confirm our BHAG and roll out a new 3HAG while validating strategy and aligning our 1HAG and QHAG.

DAY 1: STRATEGY

COHESIVE SYSTEM

Good News
Start the meeting in a positive way.

Cohesive Question
The usual personal get-to-know-you questions and icebreakers.

Scaling Leadership
Check in with each leader to review progress and set next steps.

What Do You Recommend?
Check in and review with leaders how the WDYR is going with their teams and instigate a discussion for leaders to provide examples from the last 90 days.

HUMAN SYSTEM

Organizational Function Chart
Review the Organizational Function Chart for any adjustments.

Key Function Flow Map
Fully review the KFFM Level 1 and Level 2 and the Flywheel. If necessary, take time to review and update the Flywheel.

A-Player Team Assessment
Leaders assess their direct reports on the A-Player Team Assessment graph for everyone to review and discuss.

Team View
Fully review the Team View to ensure it aligns with the KFFM and the Organizational Function Chart. Remember that you're not just reviewing the current status but also looking out to ensure that you are planning your future functional design with the 3HAG and team in mind.

CULTURAL SYSTEM

Core Purpose
In the last 2-day annual planning session, we utilized Simon Sinek's Golden Circle to confirm the company's Core Purpose. If you feel your Core Purpose is solid and locked in, move on to Core Values. Otherwise, work through the Golden Circle strategic picture again.

Core Values
Review and check in on the Core Values.

BHAG
Review and check in on the BHAG. If the BHAG is clear and the leadership team is confident, move on. If not, use Jim Collins's Hedgehog Concept to increase confidence in it or evolve it. If you are confident, create your Painted Picture as described in the last annual meeting. If you have already created a picture, review it and have a good discussion of what else it should include.

You can find more information at *www.metronomicsthebook.com.*

Profit/X

Review and confirm Profit/X. The "X" in the Profit per X will be connected to a widget in the current KFFM or a future one and will align to the 3HAG and/ or the 1HAG. The great news about this connection is that it ensures the plan is aligned all along the growth path and with the team and team members. The KFFM and widgets are the things that flow through your company that are owned and controlled by team members. This is the ultimate connection between a cohesive team and a high-performing team, and it's not easy to make. The high-performing business team is cohesive but also has direct connectivity through ownership of and control over the widgets, or nonfiscal metrics.

STRATEGY SYSTEM

3HAG

You'll create a new 3HAG at this meeting by following the same steps as you did in last year's 2-day annual. And the team will review and confirm the 3HAG statement or create a new one.

3HAG: Market Map

Review the Market Map and make any necessary updates based on how it's evolved.

3HAG: Core Customer Analysis

Discuss and confirm Core Customers.

3HAG: Attribution Map

Build a new Attribution Map without consulting the previous one, so that you have the most up-to-date view of the current market and where you fit. This also ensures we have a really good look at where we want our 3HAG line to be over the next 3 years.

3HAG: Differentiators

Since we rebuilt our Attribution Map, take the time to rebuild your differentiators. Even if you feel they're solid, take the time to build them from the ground up, either confirming our differentiators or building new ones. Use the process we utilized in the last 2-day annual to complete this step.

3HAG: Swimlanes

As we did last year, use Swimlanes to ensure that each differentiator gets in place by 3 years out. This helps create the confidence we need in the strategy and our plan, which helps create momentum.

3HAG: Brand Promise with Guarantee

Review and confirm the Brand Promise with Guarantee aligned to the Core Customer validation and the strategy. Create a plan to make the Brand Promise with Guarantee well known in the marketplace.

3HAG: Secret Sauce

If you have time, work with the leadership team to discuss the idea of a Secret Sauce, which is known as Step X in *3HAG WAY*.

The Secret Sauce is a problem the company solves better than anyone else—usually a problem no one else in the market wants to solve. It gives you a competitive advantage over the marketplace.

Lots of venture-backed companies start this way: they solve a problem then raise money on that advantage. My first company definitely fell into that bracket. My second company also had Secret Sauce from the very beginning.

Not all companies' Secret Sauce is obvious. And most Secret Sauces expire with time, as the market catches up. That means we should always be looking for the next competitive advantage, keeping our Secret Sauce fresh and valuable.

Most companies have no idea *how* to discover their Secret Sauce.

Whether or not you have time in this meeting for a detailed investigation, ensure you at least introduce the idea of the Secret Sauce. It's important for your strategy, for your understanding of the external marketplace, and for the understanding of your organization's internal analysis.

A Secret Sauce can be found externally in the marketplace—but it's just as likely to be found internally in your organization. For more information on how to discover your Secret Sauce, go to *www.metronomicsthebook.com*.

SECRET SAUCE

External	HOW TO SOLVE? VALIDATE			X ADVANTAGE
Integrate more than one message type	Important	Not solved in the market today.	We can solve.	10x
Resellers want to sell more than one type of messaging.	Important	Not solved in the market today.	We can solve.	2x
Resellers want to setup subscribers in less than 1 hour.	Important	Not solved in the market today.	We can solve.	5x
Internal	**HOW TO SOLVE? VALIDATE**			**X ADVANTAGE**
Reduce setup time of new subscribers to less than 30 minutes.	Important	Has not been solved.	Would save X time and X $$ and increase NPS	5x
Increase number of subscriber sign ups.	Important	Not solved in the market today.	This is solveable and must be aligned with above.	2x
Map any incoming message to an outgoing message type.	Important	Huge problem in the market.	We can solve.	10x

One-Phrase Close

The day wraps up as always, asking each of the leaders for 5 words or less to describe how they feel right now.

DAY 2: EXECUTION

AGENDA

Compound Growth System	Day 2
Execution System	• Status Review Annual Plan • Status Review QHAG • 1HAG • QHAG • Meeting: Check In • Team Assessment—ABC + Plan • Cascade 3 Key Messages
Cash System	• Review Next Year 12 Month • F/C Starting with Widgets out 36 month over month • Put Metrics into Rolling Metrics in Metronome Software
Coach Cascade System	• Scaling Leadership Check In

The second day of the 2-day annual is dedicated to the Execution and Cash Systems. We will kick off this day with Personal Good News, reflections from the day before, and any wrap-up items from Day 1.

COHESIVE SYSTEM

Team Assessment

This is the third time the team has completed the Five Dysfunctions of a Team Assessment. We can compare this year's outcomes to those of the past two years and have a great discussion on the work we've accomplished to become a more cohesive team, as well as identifying areas that might need further work.

Status: 1HAG and Current QHAG

The review will be quick, as long as the team has the status up to date before the meeting and the team has been reviewing and discussing it on a weekly basis.

New Annual Plan (1HAG)

Finish off the rest of the morning with the team agreeing to a new 1HAG. Use the same questions you've used before and the process from the last annual planning meeting:

New Quarterly Plan (QHAG)

Now set a new QHAG with the team, again working through the same questions you used last time, including the 13-Week Sprint Lanes. Don't skip this step.

CASH SYSTEM

The leaders and finance team have created the next 12-month widget-based forecast for the next fiscal year and the following 24 months, out to their 3HAG. This process has gotten easier for both the leaders who own functions and the finance team owning the detailed widget-based model. The cash forecast is well understood for the next 12 months as well as the subsequent two years.

CHECK-IN

As with every meeting, check in with the team how the cadence, agenda, and outcomes of these meetings are progressing. This gives you as a team the opportunity to tweak anything that needs to be adjusted so that everyone stays aligned with their teams.

As in the previous annual planning session, review the results of the Metronomics Survey results and have a good discussion about them. Make a plan as to what needs more focus or a different approach. As the team continues to become more self-aware during the process, they will assess themselves with more vigor.

CASCADING MESSAGES

The leaders discuss and agree on the 3 Key Messages that need to be cascaded out to the rest of the organization in tomorrow's huddle.

One-Phrase Close
The day wraps up as always, asking each of the leaders for 5 words or less to describe how they feel right now.

NEXT STEPS/HOMEWORK

- Update the Open Playing Field as necessary.

- Each leader should add to the Open Playing Field the annual Corporate Priorities, the quarterly Corporate Priorities including the 13-week subpriorities from the Sprint Lanes developed with the team, and their own individual priorities.

- Add the updated Market Map to the War Room.

- Add the updated Core Customer to the War Room.

- Add the updated Attribution Framework to the War Room.

- Add updated Differentiators to the War Room.

- Update, if needed, Differentiators on the Open Playing Field.

- Update the Swimlanes on the Open Playing Field.

- Update the Rolling Metrics with the 36'er on the Open Playing Field.

- Continue to run all company meetings through the Open Playing Field.

- Review KFFM in Weekly Leadership Team Meeting.

- Leaders make plans or take action on any C-Player team members.

- All leaders cascade 3 Key Messages from the meeting to their teams.

- Leaders begin and continue their analysis of the company's Secret Sauce.

- Scaling Leadership continues to be cascaded throughout the company, with the leaders receiving active feedback from their teams.

OUTCOMES

- Cohesive: Wow! This has been quite a year! The Scaling Leadership framework implementation has taken the cohesiveness of the team to a whole new level. The vulnerability shown by the leaders and throughout the team is far beyond expectations. Team trust, healthy team conflict, team commitment, team accountability, and the focus on team results have definitely made this a highly cohesive business team.

- Human: Clarity of expectations and accountability for every team member is clear. Team members know what to do every day, why they do it, and how it is measured through their widgets that are connected to whole business team results. Team members are eager to own and drive for team results while being coached to grow to their full potential. The KFFM is an active scoreboard

YEAR 3: COMPOUND—GROW UP AND OUT—IT'S ALL ABOUT BEHAVIOR!

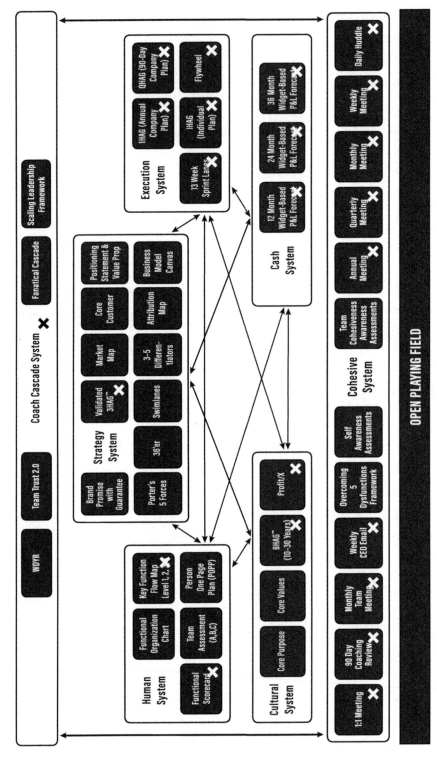

of the widgets in the company, connected to the plan and to the cohesive team.

- Cultural: Culture continues to remain strong, active, and known by all team members every day, with the belief in the BHAG high and the Profit/X connected through the widgets in the company owned by the whole team.

- Strategy: Strategic confidence is high as the differentiated strategy has been made simple and clear to align and execute. The widgets are aligned to each team member daily.

- Execution: All team members understand the plan and the forecasted widgets, and know what to do every day. They know what a successful day looks like for the whole company as well as for themselves.

- Cash: The leadership team forecasts cash first and then widgets to grow the company each and every day, week, month, and year all the way to the 3HAG and aligned to the BHAG.

- Coach Cascade: The leaders and the team are committed to growing into the best version of themselves as leaders and committed to growing their team members into the best version of themselves to achieve the best version of the whole team.

You have a fully connected, alive, and winning Metronomics system! The team has now been executing Metronomics for 13 quarters. Whoohoohoo!

The system is ingrained in the company, but leaders know they need to stay disciplined as a team to ensure it remains active, valuable, and in place. The system is founded upon the core business principles Jim Collins identifies as disciplined people, disciplined thought, disciplined action—and what

I call disciplined behavior. In a simpler way, the system is founded on building and balancing a highly cohesive team directly connected to the clear and simple strategy, execution, and cash plan systems for the business. Together, they enable a company to sustain disciplined endurance and win consistently.

Let's talk about what we should do next.

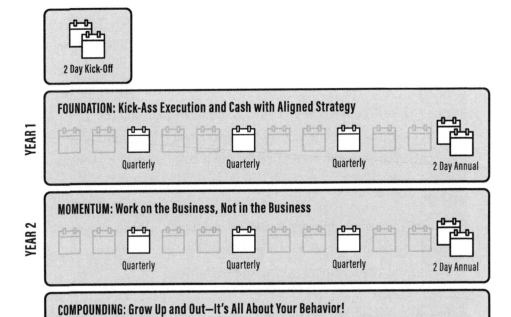

QUARTER BY QUARTER, SYSTEM BY SYSTEM

CHAPTER 6

TRUST THE SYSTEM

Ten years is a long time. In business, it can be an eternity.

Some executives burn out in less than that time because they eat, sleep, and breathe the business. It's more than their livelihood—it's their *life*.

For Alex, those days were a distant memory. It was 9:30 a.m., and he was checking their Open Playing Field platform in his office while he waited for the leadership meeting scheduled for 10:00 a.m. After that, he wanted to check in with some of his leaders before he had lunch with Delia, a friend from his old YPO group who was making shifts in her family manufacturing company but finding it difficult to evolve the culture after 3 generations of the business.

All the widgets and team members on the Open Playing Field aligned. It was second nature for everyone at OpenDoor now, owning their daily metrics (widgets) and being active on the Open Playing Field every day. Everything was there: Core Purpose, BHAG, 3HAG, 1HAG, QHAG, all the widgets and priorities that aligned to their long term, near term, and short term. Everything was super clear. Everyone knew what was expected of them. The system itself cranked away without their having to think much about it, and they had time to work on strategy and growing the team.

Since they had achieved their very first gutted-out 3HAG, so much had evolved. There'd been a challenge from a new team member to counteract. There'd been some political instability around the globe, which threw the currency markets out of whack. Jen had moved on to a smaller company, while Andrew and his young family had relocated. Alex had promoted one of Jen's team leaders and made an external hire to replace Andrew.

They shifted a couple of dials on strategy, the new folks slotted right in, and the execution kept cranking because the whole team was involved.

The system was strong and ready for whatever the future brought. It would roll on with the disciplined team in place. It could even survive without the CEO for a while—or any leader, for that matter.

Alex and Lisa had been discussing taking the girls to Europe over the summer. With everything running smoothly, the company could spare him.

At the annual meeting, Lee pointed out that they were two-thirds of the way to their original BHAG. Alex could hardly believe it.

Six years ago, she had pushed the team to be as courageous as they dared in setting their first BHAG. Alex remembered how uncomfortable he had been with the very first gutted-out BHAG. He had certainly never dreamed that what they came up with would become a reality.

But now, the Compound Growth System had not only brought their original gutted-out BHAG within reach but they would be likely to achieve it within the next 3 years. That just showed the power of writing down your long- and near-term goals and driving for them. Their evolved BHAG was definitely hairy and audacious, in the words of Jim Collins, and the team was excited to drive through their current 3HAG.

At lunchtime, Alex waited in the restaurant for Delia. She arrived late, full of apologies, and at once excused herself and stepped outside to make a call. Alex could see her through the window, gesturing as she talked on her cell.

"Sorry," she apologized as she sat down. "My COO needed help solving a problem." She ordered a black coffee. It was noon, but her eyes were heavy, and she looked worn.

Alex recognized the look. She was almost ready to throw in the towel and call it quits.

She said, "We're all so frazzled trying to inject some new life into the business. I know we can evolve, but we're so busy rushing around that it's just not happening. We can't get any traction."

Alex felt like he was looking in the mirror at his own reflection from over a decade earlier at OpenDoor. Was this the kind of face his daughters saw when he walked through the door at night? Was it the face his wife had to look into every day? How was it possible that he was able to pull himself out of it?

Delia was a Desperate CEO who was committed to her goals. She needed to get unstuck.

Over lunch, Alex told her about Metronomics. He explained how it had helped him grow himself, his team, and his company and ultimately to live the life he wanted. And how it could help her. "You'll be able to have lunch without firefighting calls from the office," he promised.

By the time he got home that evening, Delia had emailed to say that she'd booked an appointment with Lee.

And in the next 3 years and beyond, whenever they had lunch, she was a completely different person: relaxed, happy, confident—and able to turn off her phone.

As for Alex, OpenDoor was 13 years into Metronomics now. They had reached so many 3HAGs they lost count, and when they came up with an evolved BHAG for the next 10-plus years, he could feel the commitment of the whole team.

Metronomics was more second nature now. It was who they were: a high-performing business team. A glance at the Open Playing Field revealed what widgets to alter and what dials to nudge to make the whole system easier and faster. The strategy kept being tweaked as internal and external circumstances evolved—but the system could cope.

There were a couple of relatively new faces at the leadership meetings alongside the few that had been around for the whole journey, but the company kept growing, even through a market downturn.

That was the benefit of a Compound Growth System. It got them through because they were able to make better, faster decisions together as they needed to.

When competitors went out of business, OpenDoor bought them—but only if Alex was satisfied they would be able to commit to the Metronomics system.

He was used to the leadership teams in those new companies being skeptical. It reminded him of Daniel and Alison, back in the early days.

"We know it worked for you, but are you sure it'll work for us?" the former competitors would ask. Alex wanted to say straight out, "It will if you're human and are committed to grow." But he refrained.

Instead, he responded, "Of course. It will work for anyone who's willing and has the desire to grow. Let me line you up with a Metronomics coach, and we'll get started. You're going to love the journey."

Not every new leadership team got to meet with Lee, who was booked out a year or two ahead. She had her work with OpenDoor and with Delia's company, which was changing rapidly. She had other clients too. But she could also recommend other Metronomics coaches she assured Alex were just as good as they all followed the same Metronomics System.

Alex was a huge fan of Lee and relied on her uncanny ability to ask the right questions at the right time to get him and his team to see what they needed to see and act upon. Whenever they discussed her schedule, he said, "I hope you're not going to abandon OpenDoor. You're part of our team for continuing to grow the company into the future!"

"No way! I love working with you and your team. Remember, while you've been growing, I've been growing with you."

"Like the Coach Cascade," said Alex.

They both laughed, but Alex wasn't *completely* joking. At the back of his mind was a small worry that Lee might move on.

On their next monthly 1-on-1—he figured out they had had well over one hundred such meetings in the last 13 years—he brought the question up more directly. He was about to take some time out of the office to help Lisa start looking at colleges around the country for their older daughter.

"I've been meaning to ask you," he said. "When does Metronomics ever stop?"

She laughed. And her response was exactly what he already knew: "How could it stop now? What else is there? What would you graduate to? Do high-performing teams ever stop? Even if you wanted to, it's ingrained in who you are and in every member of your team. You will never stop. You will continue to hone your high-performing business team system. That's Metronomics!"

TRUST THE SYSTEM TO GET RESULTS

Metronomics works.

Trust it.

It works because it's founded upon the best practice of how people want to perform well as a team, make a plan together as a team—and win as a team.

Metronomics is founded upon the best practice of how to progressively develop a highly cohesive team and sustain it while building a business. It also includes the best practice on how to develop a unique and valuable position in your marketplace, through clearly and simply stating a differentiating strategic execution and cash plan. And it builds a high-performing business team—over time.

Time is a key factor. That's why in the previous chapters we walked quarter by quarter through the steps of how to build a highly cohesive team while creating a great business plan and aligning it with the team. We've looked at the seven systems carefully in order so that we know when and *how* they should be leveraged for any team.

Over time, these steps produce a high-performing business team.

When I was a young CEO, my coaches told me again and again that only 1 percent of the effort of growing a company is planning. The other 99 percent of the effort goes into aligning the team with the plan.

I didn't really understand what they meant.

It's only today, after over 25 years of building high-performing business teams, that I get it.

It's so clear to me now, but it's still so hard to explain and implement in a snap—which is why Metronomics exists.

It's a progressive regimen created for CEOs and their leadership teams struggling with the same thing: alignment.

Most leadership teams do not even realize that alignment is the problem. They usually think there is something wrong with the plan or the team. But

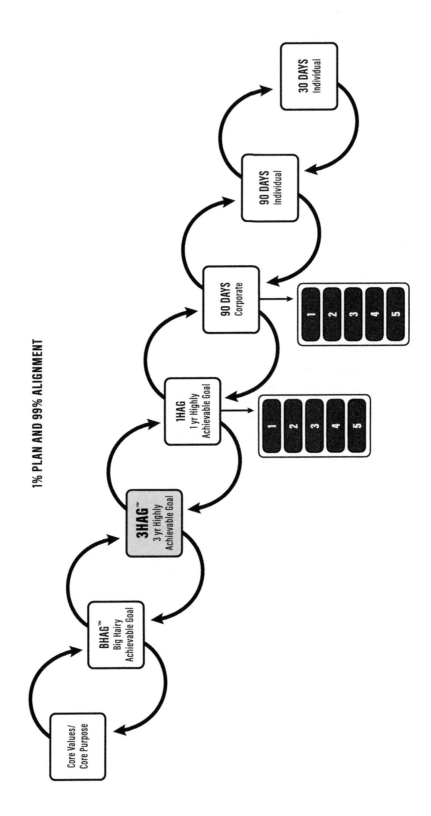

1% PLAN AND 99% ALIGNMENT

even if you have the best plan to grow your business, you'll never achieve it if you don't instill the team behavior required to achieve team alignment to the plan.

It all starts with you as CEO and with your own behavior.

That's what struck me. When my coaches talked about alignment, they were really talking about behavior.

Growing up a company is 1 percent plan and 99 percent behavior: 1 percent of the effort goes to build the plan, and 99 percent effort goes to building a highly cohesive business team that is deeply connected to the plan through the things the team controls: the widgets.

It's easy to *tell* a team what a plan is. It's much harder to get them to *own* that plan. In order for them to own the plan, they have to collaborate and build the plan together. In order to collaborate to build and achieve the plan together, they must be a highly cohesive team. That's the only way they'll really get there.

That's well known. What's less well known is how to do it.

How do leaders get the team aligned to the plan? That is what Metronomics explains. It's all about the "how."

Metronomics takes what we know about growing a cohesive team and connects it with the team's plan. It shows you how to create and build a cohesive business team quarter over quarter, while also implementing a connected strategic, execution, and cash plan and system. It's all about how to keep building a highly cohesive business team and building a simple and clear strategic execution cash plan at the same time.

TEAM DYNAMICS

The most successful teams are united by a common goal. Bruce Tuckman, a psychology researcher who studied team dynamics, identified four clear stages of team development: forming, storming, norming, and performing. In order to develop a high-performing team, leaders must keep team members focused and motivated through the process, particularly the challenges of the storming and norming stages.

1% PLAN + 99% HIGHLY COHESIVE TEAM = 100% HIGH PERFORMING BUSINESS TEAM

Metronomics is set up in a way for your team to successfully navigate each stage of team development.

- Forming. At the beginning of Metronomics, the forming stage, the team has great expectations and is excited about the journey. We focus on relationships, clarify our purpose, and clearly establish our team values.

- Storming. The storming stage is difficult, as there can be stumbling, conflict, and positioning as the team clarifies its strategy, plans, and goals. At this stage, team leadership must be unwavering. The CEO must show their commitment to Metronomics by their own example, as well as by addressing the feedback and concerns of the team through clarifying the purpose and goals.

- Norming. Once the team moves through the storming stage and into the norming stage, it is ready for open communication and clarity of function. Trust is high and momentum is picking up, and it's now that the team achieves cohesiveness as their norm. This becomes evident in team trust, healthy team conflict through open and easy discussions, and the beginning of team commitment and team accountability. Now, everyone realizes that they are all working toward team results.

- Performing. From the norming stage, the team moves to performing. By now, the team is highly cohesive and well connected, and accountable to the team results before their own individual results. And as the team members get clearer and more confident in the performing stage, they move from performing to highly performing.

When I first read Tuckman's work, I was almost disappointed. It was so simple. The stages of development were so obvious. I could look back and map the stages to teams I have been a part of or coached and could now see easily why some became high performing and others did not.

METRONOMICS YEAR-OVER-YEAR ALIGNED TO TEAM DEVELOPMENT

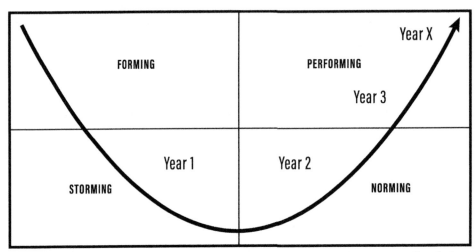

Bruce Truckman

What I found most impactful was that the progression of the four stages was not a straight line. The forming and storming stages are when the team is most challenged, when the team is most stuck to grow and to gain momentum.

We need to be aware that the forming and storming stages of developing a high-performing business team will challenge us as leaders. We need to set a strong example and guide the motivation and commitment of the team.

What I find great about this graph is that it clearly overlays the experience my teams and I have had with Metronomics.

Metronomics is designed to help the CEO+Leadership team get through forming and storming so they can reach the norming stage with speed, before moving on confidently to performing and high performing.

The most interesting thing is that, as a team goes through the forming and storming stages with Metronomics, their business results don't follow the same downward path. The business results start to head in the right direction before team development catches up. That's one reason so many teams get

fooled during the forming and storming stages. They believe they can continue their business growth without truly developing the team into the highly
cohesive state needed for the norming stage.

It's a deception. Don't be fooled. Trust the system. The reason we've
shared this 3-year progression is to show you to lead your team through all
four stages of team building while growing your company.

At this point, you might feel that the system looks like a whole lot of effort
laid out over 13 quarters and beyond. You're wondering whether it's worth it
to commit and invest. What I'd ask you in response is this: Is there another
way? Can you achieve your plan without developing a highly cohesive business team connected to the plan?

STRAIGHT A'S

The key to team building is making sure the leadership team members are
100 percent A-Players. We've seen it in the story of Alex, working through the
system at OpenDoor, and I've worked through it many times myself both as a
CEO and as a CEO+Leadership team coach.

A-Players fit with the culture, are consistent, high-performing team members, and want to grow themselves and with the team.

It's obvious, I know, and I'm not the first person to say it. But it's easier said than done. The behavior of the leadership team is the hinge that
ensures the system gets in place and endures. The bar of an A-Player slowly
rises as the system is implemented, so the CEO needs to ensure that the
leadership team (and ultimately the whole team) is growing up with the
organization.

Process. People. Behavior. In that order.

When the bus is barreling down a highway and we're trying to keep it out of
the ditches, we need to start by overlaying the execution process with a cash
process before we can even think about focusing on getting the right people
on the bus in the right seats doing the right things.

But process will only take company growth so far. People will take the
company a lot farther, combining the process with the right people with clear

expectations and ownership. With a 100 percent A-Player leadership team with the willingness and desire to grow through transparent vulnerability, a company will knock it right out of the park.

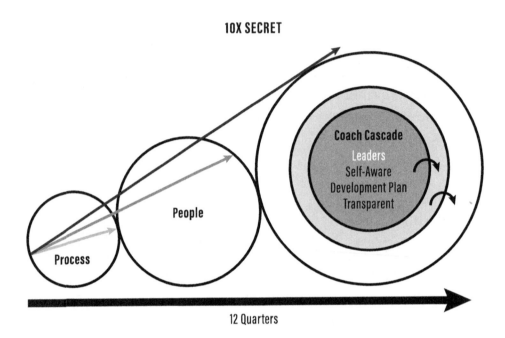

With the right processes and the right people in place, you can work on your own behavior and that of the rest of the team. (See the case study of one of my clients, AML Oceanographic, who has more than eight years of experience with Metronomics and the solid consistent team and business growth results at *www.metronomicsthebook.com*.)

CREATIVITY IS KEY

A highly creative leader is incredibly effective. A highly reactive leader is at the bottom of the effectiveness scale—and there's data to prove it.

Around this point, let me share a controversial opinion.

Some of the best-known business leaders are or were *too* reactive.

In my opinion, Steve Jobs, Bill Gates in his early days at Microsoft, Elon Musk, and Larry Ellison: all reactive.

They're celebrated as business icons. They got outstanding results. But if you take a closer look at the cultures of their organizations, in my opinion, they were *highly* reactive—and that culture came from leadership.

I sometimes wonder how much more they could have achieved in a shorter period of time if they were more creative sooner. (And over time, a lot of these leaders grew into more creative versions of leaders and their company cultures evolved too.)

I see myself in a similar way, from growing up as a CEO in my twenties and thirties, to my forties and now my fifties. I was so reactive as a young CEO, and each year grew into a more creative leader year over year. Each year a better version of a leader. Today, as a CEO+Leadership team coach and CEO, I am more creative—but there is so much further to go in growing into the best version of my creative self.

Reactive leaders have an ineffective interpersonal interaction style. Their teams are not held accountable and they're often poor listeners. They're self-centric and lack emotional control—like me in my twenties.

A creative leader has strong people skills. Creative leaders are visionaries, team builders, personal, and approachable. They lead by example, have a passionate drive, are good listeners, and develop their people through empowerment.

Leaders need that ability, willingness, and desire to grow up the people in their company. What do you do as a leader or coach to grow them up? You have to focus on the "soft edge" of the business: the Cultural, Human, and Cohesive Systems.

A high-growth company sees a turnover in the leadership team approximately every 3 years. The leaders must grow at the same pace as the business.

Most leadership teams operate at the 75 percent reactive stage. Only 15 percent get to the creative stage, where they listen and grant autonomy and empowerment to their team members.

Those 15 percent outperform reactive organizations every time.

The more self-aware you become as a leader, the more effective you become, which leads to getting the team to work with you to achieve consistently. You'll see far less turnover throughout your organization because people will love being a part of a team that is self-aware, vulnerable, and receptive to feedback at any level and from any level.

According to Anderson and Adams in *Scaling Leadership*, the integral leadership stage is where leaders understand and leverage their teams. The leaders get the big picture, and they're intuitive about the complexities of what it takes to grow their leaders at the same rate that the organization grows.

When that happens, companies get into a very desirable cycle. As the organization grows, and the leaders grow at the same rate, the organization grows quickly, and so do the leaders—and so on. The good news is that every leader can grow into a creative leader.

KEEPING IT HUMAN

Whether you're about to start Metronomics or you're six or nine years in, remember one thing.

It's not a traditional hard-edge-only business development system. It isn't some piece of software that gives you a checklist of what to do or that only improves the results or actions of a single leader or a tiny team.

It's a *human nature* system. And a high-performing *human business* system. And a highly cohesive *human trust* system.

It's built on the idea that a company achieves prolonged success by coaching its greatest assets—its people—as a team so that they all have the best qualities of its greatest leader. It has startup or restart actions associated with its early years, but once they've been created, it simply evolves as the leaders guide it.

Metronomics is designed to endure. It evolves your strategy and shows year-over-year progress, predictability in the future, and cohesive team strength. And your team will love the system because it is a progression that is patient with them and grows with them. The team has time to learn and adapt.

The system will carry on for as long as you need—or want. And the best part? It gets more powerful each year. Each year builds on the last, and so on. Not only that. It generates more enthusiasm and commitment with each passing year. Every year, your team and your company will continue to grow into the best version of themselves: the best version of a high-performing business team.

The system will point you in the right direction, right your ship, and set you out on your way, helping you to attain those highly achievable goals you've always desired.

"GROW UP," QUARTER OVER QUARTER

SECRET SAUCE

Metronomics is based on the secret sauce of your team: human nature. Let me tell you how it works.

We started at the very first Kick-Off Meeting when we gutted out the Baseline Growth Plan. That's really significant because once everyone collaborates on a gutted-out plan, human nature takes over. We don't want to be wrong. That drives the team to take action to validate, validate, validate the gutted-out plan and make it correct. That is the key to the Kick-Off. The team's need to be right is just human nature.

The core is the team and its individual members. From the Kick-Off, Metronomics provides the way to start building a highly cohesive team. The high-performing business team is only enabled when the highly cohesive team is truly connected through all team members, all owning an individual widget that is aligned to the company widgets.

The path is visible. Individuals understand the goals. They own them. They work with the team to achieve them. The more cohesive and connected a team is, the more achievable their results.

The Metronomics regimen provides CEO+Leadership teams with a conscious, disciplined awareness of building a cohesive team every day, week, month, quarter, and year by year. It tightly weaves the soft-edge systems with the hard-edge systems to ensure that the team not only creates a truly differentiated strategic execution plan but also implements the systems to know it will last.

Each team member knows what is expected of them today, tomorrow, and so on. They can measure it and connect it to the company widgets and priorities, the team priorities, and to other team members.

Each step is aligned to ensure that the team's cohesive behavior evolves quarter over quarter, along with the strategic execution plan and systems.

That's what every CEO wants to know: how to align the behavior of the team to the plan.

It's about the connection of each and every component of Metronomics.

Every member on your team will own a functional Scorecard that is connected to and founded on your Key Function Flow Map (KFFM) through the

1% PLAN + 99% HIGHLY COHESIVE TEAM = 100% HIGH PERFORMING BUSINESS TEAM

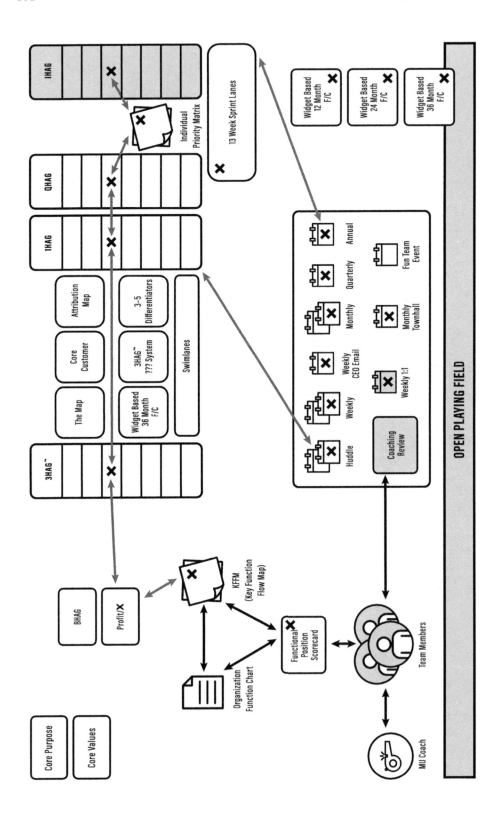

widgets that flow through your organization. (A last reminder: widgets are the things that flow through your organization that the team can control. The KFFM is how the company makes money!)

The X in your Profit/X will align to the company's widget identified in the KFFM. The Profit/X will align to the widgets identified in your 3HAG. The widgets in your 1HAG, your annual plan, will align with the widgets in your 3HAG. Your widgets in your QHAG, the 90 -day corporate plan, will align to your 1HAG. The widgets in your QHAG align with your 1HAG. The widgets in the 13-Week Sprint Lanes align to your QHAG week over week. And these align to individual team members and to the daily widget score.

Everything aligns, or, in other words, is connected through the widgets.

The widgets align throughout the whole plan—but they're also clearly owned by the team and its members, daily, weekly, monthly, quarterly, annually, 3HAG, BHAG. Through the team members' cohesiveness (trust, conflict, commitment, accountability, results), they collaborated on the plan and the widgets—which is why they will now own making sure it happens together.

The whole team plays on an Open Playing Field with the score visible every day.

You've set up meetings on a disciplined cadence: from the huddle, to the weekly, to the weekly CEO email, to the monthly, to the quarterly, to the annual, to the monthly Town Hall, to your weekly 1-on-1s, to your 90-day Coaching Reviews. Why?

Those meetings keep your team focused on the winning score in the game by looking at the actual-vs-forecast widgets it owns. And the meetings also create and sustain a highly cohesive business team. Meetings are at the core of developing a highly cohesive team that is focused on and committed to achieving the plan. That is why the cadence of the meetings must be set like a metronome. It gives the beat to the rhythm.

To go back to the sports parallel I've used before: the widgets are the score. In order to win, the team must achieve the widgets forecasted in the plan. To win, you have to focus on the score. And the team must discuss day in and day out how they're going to win the game together. To play the game in real

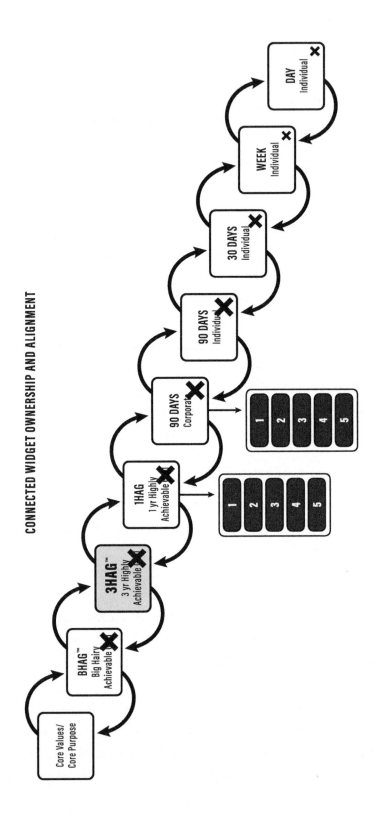

CONNECTED WIDGET OWNERSHIP AND ALIGNMENT

time, they need to measure their widgets daily. That will lead to better, faster decisions on the Open Playing Field.

In Metronomics, widgets are cascaded through the organization through the aligned KFFM. Think KFFM Level 1, 2, 3...and so on.

The whole team owns a cascaded widget, or metric, with the company widgets being broken down and shared through the functional leaders and then broken out further into the functional teams. This cascade takes time, and the understanding of the company widgets and the team's behavior need to stay aligned. Your team will progress and grow with the system. And with each step, each progression, the connected widget will cascade further out into the organization.

WIDGET CASCADE

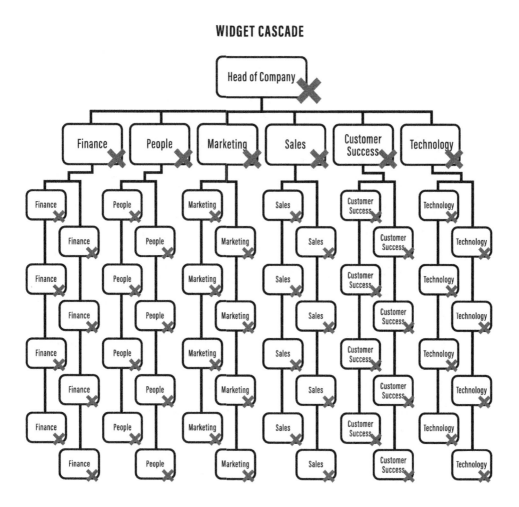

You're probably wondering why I didn't just say this back at the start of the book.

Because so many great thought leaders have told us this same thing—but have not been able to show us how to achieve it. I wanted to show you. I wanted you to see that you could implement this system step by step with your team while growing your company.

I wanted to show you *how*. I wanted you to see that this is a system you can implement for the duration of your company. I wanted you to see that this is a system for life. This is a high-performing business team system that you can implement quarter over quarter with your team, no matter where you are now.

It sounds clichéd, I know. But this is the system that allowed me to grow up my companies. And when I started learning this system with my leaders, and we started implementing it step by step just as I've outlined, I started getting my life back. As the team grew more cohesive, collaborated on the plan, and owned it both as a team and individually, the more confidence we all had in our own performance. The more we grew into a high-performing business team together, the more time we got back in our lives.

I was five years into building my first company, and 15 to 24 months into learning this system when I got married.

It may sound strange, but I probably wouldn't have ever gotten married if we hadn't implemented this system. Because up until that point, I was married to my first company.

But I did live in Whistler, British Columbia (and still do, and I never forgot that I lived here for a reason: I lived here to build a great company with a great team and have a great life).

Shortly after I got married we had our first son, then our second son, and then our daughter: 3 children in less than 3 years. I was in hypergrowth with my first company and my family.

There is no way I could have built a family without my husband—and without Metronomics. And I feel I would have missed out on so much if I were not able to do both.

This is a system that allows you to grow up the company you want and live your life.

YEAR X: KEEP IT GOLDEN—IT'S ALL ABOUT DISCIPLINE

The secret sauce in the progression of Metronomics is that, quarter over quarter, the team's cohesive behavior is tightly connected to the simple clarity of the plan through the widgets.

CHAPTER 7

METRONOMICS: GREAT COMPANY *AND* GREAT LIFE

The purpose of Metronomics is to ensure that no leader is as desperate as I was to "grow up" their company.

And not just to grow up a company and reach their business goals, but to have time for life.

Looking back over the last 25 years, one of the things I am most grateful for is the opportunity I had to develop this high-performing business team system with the team at my first company. It was born purely out of our desperation and our deep commitment to win. And our refusal to give up all the other things we love in life.

The teams I have been so humbled to work alongside have always been committed to the team goal, to working together, and to having a great life outside of the business.

We think this is only human.

I've written this book to show CEOs, leaders, and business teams how they can achieve their goals *and* have a great life outside of the business. I want to help any leaders who are stuck get unstuck by implementing what we know is true: a highly cohesive business team connected to a simple and clear strategic execution cash plan will allow you to achieve your goals every time.

I wanted to show you *how*.

METRONOMICS: HOW

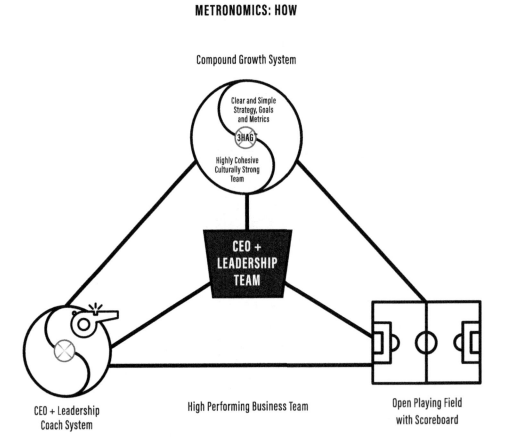

The Metronomics regimen is founded on four elements:

- *CEO+Leadership Team.* The CEO and leadership team must have the willingness and desire to evolve their own behavior as a team to achieve their team goals.

- *Compound Growth System.* This is a repeatable, structured system that cascades through the whole company team the seven systems: Cohesive, Human, Culture, Strategy, Execution, Cash, and the Coach Cascade.

- *Open Playing Field.* This is a place for the team to play together, to see one another on the field, to communicate, and to ask for and offer help. It lets you know the score and whether the team is winning or losing so you can make better, faster decisions together for the win.

- *CEO+Leadership Team Coach.* The coach is the blind-spot remover. They are an expert at the system and diagnosing the game while the team is on the field. By watching the game, the coach can unlock blind spots and move the team forward to win with ease, speed, and confidence—every time.

CEO+LEADERSHIP TEAM

It takes a humble and fiercely committed CEO to implement Metronomics with their leadership team. As we've seen often throughout this book, the progression, evolution, and growth of the CEO and their leadership team is key to the system's success.

The courage the CEO needs to start the journey makes many people feel uncomfortable. But a Desperate CEO knows that the thought of failing is even more uncomfortable—and unacceptable.

And so the journey begins.

COMPOUND GROWTH SYSTEM

The repeatable, structured system is for the whole company, not just the leadership team.

If you only implement it at the leadership team level, you will definitely get results—but it won't be at the same level of compounding, enduring growth as if you take it out to the whole team.

The Compound Growth System comprises seven systems that exist in every business, whether the team is aware of them or not, and provides balance as you develop and grow a high-performing team to win the game—or the business. It breaks the process down into practical, efficient, and progressive steps, each building on the next. It clearly identifies the systems that create a highly cohesive team and the systems that align the team to a differentiated strategic plan to be executed. The result is a consistent, confident, high-performing business team that achieves its goals consistently and with confidence.

Let's return to the house diagram we used in Chapter 1 to represent the seven systems, which are divided into the hard-edge systems (Human, Execution, and Cash) and the soft-edge systems (Cultural, Cohesive, Human, and Coach Cascade). Most CEOs talk most about and focus on the hard-edge systems. The soft-edge systems are often passed over. The soft-edge systems are where the true compounding effect of growth gets ignited.

COMPOUND GROWTH SYSTEM

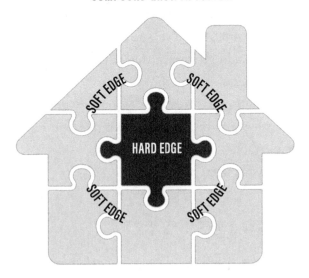

In our diagram, the load-bearing structure of the house is built on the soft-edge systems, while the hard-edge systems make up the core. It's the exact opposite of what you would expect.

COMPOUND GROWTH SYSTEM

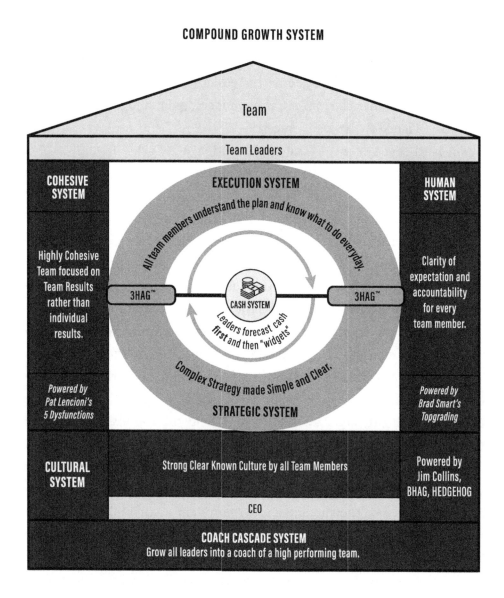

The soft-edge systems that give the structure its foundations and strength represent a highly cohesive team with the ability to achieve the plan, with the CEO both as the ultimate foundation of the system and also at the top of the house with the team leaders. Together, they ensure the Cultural System, the Cohesive System, and the Human System are alive and remain in place. If any one of these systems is missing, the team's ability to become a high-performing team will suffer, putting their ability to achieve the plan at great risk. The stronger the foundation and frame of the house, the easier it will be to execute and achieve the strategy, with a greater return to an organization's value. The stronger the soft-edge systems, the easier it is to make even a complex strategy clear so that all team members understand it and know what to do every day, aligned to the cash forecast.

The hard-edge systems—Strategy, Execution, and Cash—are only as good as the soft-edge systems. We can develop the greatest strategy, execution plan, and widget-based fiscal forecast only to miss our goals every month, every quarter, and every year *unless* the soft-edge systems are in place.

If we can achieve a great balance between the soft-edge systems and the hard-edge systems, that's when we will have a high-performing business team who is highly cohesive and committed, aligned to their plan, and achieving their goals. The awareness of keeping the systems in balance is what unlocks the growth of the team—from creating the foundation to accelerating the momentum to consistently maintaining the compounding effect each year.

The Compound Growth System is founded upon the principles of the top business thought leaders of our time—people like Jim Collins, Michael Porter, Brad Smart, and Patrick Lencioni—and the top execution system thought leaders: Verne Harnish, Gino Wickman, and Jack Stack. The principles and lessons of each of their specific expertise are built into the system. We learned and developed the whole system from all of their ideas and those of many others too. They're inherent in the system, so they all work together.

All of these thought leaders have great research, tools, and business principles, but the individual who most influenced Metronomics is Jim Collins. His commitment to entrepreneurs, research, and learning is why so many of us have read his books over and over.

I started reading Jim Collins's latest book, *Beyond Entrepreneurship 2.0*, the day it came out. I'd not read *Beyond Entrepreneurship*, so I was excited and curious. I was looking for new principles that could be shared within Metronomics, which has grown up over the same timeframe as Jim has been researching and writing his books.

Beyond Entrepreneurship 2.0 reminded me of the solid principles behind all of Jim's work and building a high-performing business team that endures.

Jim's work is founded upon every company having a Vision, Strategy, and Tactics.

So is Metronomics.

To be frank, however, we initially struggled to create a repeatable, structured system that was practical enough and progressive enough to grow with a company. We were struggling to figure out *how* to combine building a cohesive team with alignment to the plan. That's why we started using the principles of top thought leaders like Jim to evolve the system over the last 25 years. The business thought leaders brought the technical expertise to the strategy, execution, and cash systems, while funnily enough, studying the best coaches in the world, who consistently won, and the work of Pat Lencioni, influenced how we built a highly cohesive team. We've never stopped learning and plugging their principles, research, and tools into the system. These thought leaders knew the "what"—for which they have my greatest respect—but we were looking for the "how." How to do all these great ideas that made sense while growing a company.

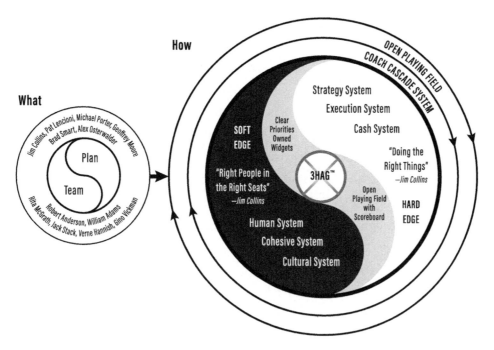

High Performing Business Team

As I said earlier, one of the best things about this system is that it's not this *or* that; it's always *and*. The Compound Growth System is the path to building a high-performing business team where you can utilize any or all of the thought leaders' tools, research, and principles by plugging them into the system.

We searched for a system that incorporated them all—and couldn't find one. So we started implementing what we learned from thought leaders month by month. We made many missteps, but we never wavered from our commitment to finding a practical, progressive, repeatable, and structured system for the whole company to grow into a high-performing business team.

We were convinced that there must be a way to grow with ease, speed, and confidence.

There *had* to be a way.

As you know, we found it! We found the Compound Growth System.

This repeatable, structured system is founded upon the work of great thought leaders and will only get stronger as more thought leaders share their work.

The system allows us to continue learning and growing, as the world around us learns and grows too. It allows you to "crowd brain" your company. It allows you to commit to a system that will grow as the world evolves.

OPEN PLAYING FIELD

When we were growing up our first company—our first taste of the sport of business—we were searching for a playing field. This might sound ridiculous, but it was something of a surprise that there is no playing field in business where you can see how everyone plays, where you can see everyone, communicate to everyone, offer help if required, or ask for help if you need it.

One of the toughest things for us in those early years was not being able to see the whole game being played.

How can you know if you're winning?

The One Page Strategic Plan, a key tool of *Mastering the Rockefeller Habits*, was the closest thing we had to a playing field. I remember it being a great view—but it was not real-time, and it took a whole lot of work to keep it up to date and the team aligned. We kept our One Page Growth Plan in Word, so if we made an adjustment, we had to share it with all four hundred people on the team. Whenever we updated the plan or something evolved, everyone had to re-input their information and print the plan out again.

It brings a smile to my face even describing it because we've come so far.

The one thing that hasn't evolved is that the team needs an Open Playing Field.

The great news is there are ways to create a playing field that is far easier to maintain and update than Word or Excel, such as our Metronome software platform or other virtual platforms that have been created. It's a virtual Open Playing Field that ensures the same behavior your team would experience on a soccer field. Just as they play together to win the game on the field, they play together in the game of business on the virtual Open Playing Field.

The Open Playing Field, like any playing field, only comes alive if there is a real-time score that tracks whether the team is winning or losing. The more visible, real-time, and alive the score is, the more the team uses the Open Playing Field.

The Compound Growth System and the Open Playing Field work together with each progression of Metronomics, implementing the system and feeding the next quarter of play. The Open Playing Field is tightly tied to both the Compound Growth System and the team, growing the company together, and they're all tied to the CEO+Leadership team coach.

CEO+LEADERSHIP TEAM COACH

I had a coach every year growing my businesses.

My coach was the blind-spot remover. They asked me questions in a way that got us to see things that I would not have seen on my own—that's why I'm so grateful to all of my coaches in business (and my sports coaches too).

Metronomics can be implemented without a coach. It will just take the team longer to win and risk more capital. I always thought of my coaches as an investment in the greatest risk of my life: building a company to win at the business Olympics. So as a young CEO—and for all the years I was in business—I had a CEO+Leadership team coach.

I grew up as an athlete with a coach, so I thought it would be normal while growing a business. In fact, I discovered that, in the late 1990s, coaches for business weren't really a thing. Consultants, but not coaches.

I was so fortunate to find some great CEO coaches. They were experts who had had success growing their own businesses and had retired. They were great blind-spot removers.

The funny thing is I asked each one of them over the years what system they used. They pointed me to all the great business thought leaders of our time—but never to a system.

All the coaches I hired were CEO coaches. Over time, I challenged my CEO coach to come and work with me *and* my leadership team. Getting coached by myself was a good thing, but getting coached with my team was a *great* thing!

My coaches found this impactful too. Now they weren't just getting me to see what I couldn't see; they could guide my team to see things that we couldn't see together. This saved me time, too, because I didn't have to look out on behalf of my team. Because I wasn't having to teach them, and we could learn together.

This had a huge impact on our success.

Looking back, the one thing I wish is that my coaches had known about Metronomics.

In my first company, it would have saved us two-thirds of our time. And when I work with other CEOs now, they look back at how long they spent trying to figure this out and realize they have wasted so much time and money and missed so many market opportunities.

The blind-spot remover is key to implementing Metronomics with ease, speed, and confidence. They save you time and money. The amount you will invest in a CEO+Leadership team coach is only a fraction of the amount you will risk without one.

Metronomics is a strong, progressive high-performing business team system because at its core is the CEO and leadership team, with the whole company and team connected to each and every component: the Compound Growth System, the Open Playing Field, and the CEO+Leadership team coach.

If you think about that, that's exactly what you cheer for in the greatest sports teams that keep winning, over and over again. They win because they have a strong, progressive high-performing team system founded upon a highly cohesive team that is connected to their team goals—and the winning score.

RESULTS

METRONOMICS: EASE, SPEED, AND CONFIDENCE

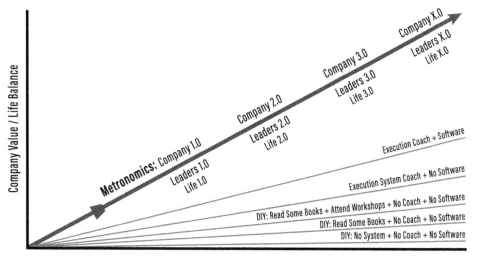

The results we've gotten from Metronomics have been consistent across my own companies, the companies I coach, and the companies with which other Metronomics coaches work. Those companies, and the companies I lead, are increasing their value over a shorter time and having invested fewer dollars. And, of course, their leaders' life balance has improved immensely too.

I couldn't mention my second company much in my previous books because of an extensive nondisclosure agreement. But I can tell you that we customer-funded it, meaning we did not use investment dollars to start it.

In that company, we applied Metronomics before we even opened the doors. We innovated a business model that generated revenue in the first month and then funded our growth beyond that. That was all thanks to Metronomics. It saved us time. It saved us equity dilution. It exponentially grew our company value over 12 quarters, when we exited on the 3HAG, achieving the top 3 mid-market valuations on Wall Street that year. We had the life we wanted while achieving this high growth.

It is a great validation of the system. (One of my clients, Milo's Tea, a 70-plus-year-old family-built business, just entered their fourth year using the Metronomics system, having more than doubled their top line in less than 3 years utilizing the system. You will find great similarities of what was described in the Year 1–3 progression captured in this case study. You can find this case study at *www.metronomicsthebook.com*.)

The progression of the four components of Metronomics reflects and incorporates all the experiential innovation done directly through my hands-on learning with my team, my clients, the Metronomics coaches, and their clients for more than 25 years around how to build a high-performing business team. It lines up how to build a highly cohesive, culturally strong team with a clear and simple strategic execution cash plan connected through the widgets and glued through the 3HAG to align your BHAG with your 1HAG and QHAG and the team.

WHAT I WANT FOR YOU...

The name "Metronomics" is derived from the words *metronome* and *economics*. The "metronome" represents the CEO, humble and fiercely committed to implementing this rhythmical regimen by setting the speed of the progression through the consistent cadence of a metronome. The CEO is the metronome that determines how fast the regimen progresses. "Economics" represents the relationship of time and investment in relation to company value and life balance.

A third powerful word is implied in this etymology: "metrics." Metrics represent the widgets that provide the powerful connection between the highly cohesive team system and the clear and simple business system to create a highly cohesive business team system.

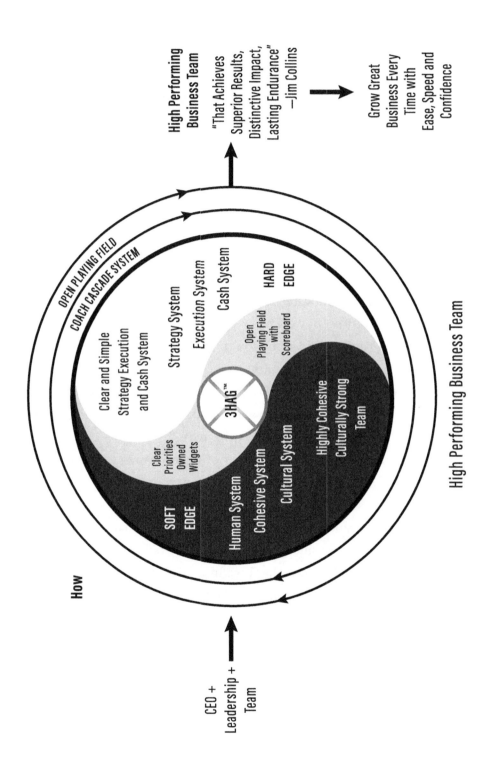

High Performing Business Team

Metronome, economics, metrics: this is Metronomics!

When my leadership team and I started creating Metronomics over 25 years ago, we experienced great success. We didn't know if it would work for everyone. Then, after we sold both our companies less than six years apart, I got a call from a CEO colleague to coach their company on the system. Lo and behold, they got the same results as we had.

At this point, some coaches asked if they could use the system, so I sent them all the materials I used. They got the same fantastic results with their clients. More and more coaches asked to be certified in the system so they could get the same consistent results.

Now, I'm confident that the system gets the same results every time. I ran the iterative innovation loop on the system with my leadership team for 15 years; I coached and innovated it for another 10 years; I've had coaches using it since 2016. It just keeps working.

The system works, and I want you to have it. I want you to implement it. And to experience the same results.

There are many stories out there that underline the system's effectiveness. The results have been consistent, and the feedback has been fantastic—and that's what continues to fuel my "re-priorment."

My purpose is to ensure you will never be as desperate as I was to grow up a company. It's to ensure that you can grow your company, your business team, with ease, speed, and confidence.

The more I share Metronomics, the more I realize that the success of our first business, of the business that bought our first business, of my second business, and of the business that bought my second business—the success of *all* those companies was founded on Metronomics. And the more I realized that, the more I wanted to ensure this system was written down, clarified, and available for you.

This book is all about *you*. This *system* is all about you. It's only you who can decide that this is the system that you want to commit to so you can achieve your goals and the life you want. This system has had an immeasurable impact on my life. Its impact on my clients has been just as momentous. Coaches around the world and their clients have experienced the impact too.

My life's goal is to ensure that anyone who wants to commit can use this system to make an impact and reach their goals. That's why this book is a practical prescriptive progression—because it needs to be. It shows you and your team how. That's why we gave out the secret sauce. Because I *know* this book, the Metronomics regimen, will help CEOs, leadership, and their teams grow up into the high-performing business team they have always dreamed of and that wins every time.

It will make an impact on your life, on your team's lives, on the communities they live in...and far, far beyond.

My wish for you is a Great Company and a Great Life!

All you have to do to get started is:

Commit!

Gut it out!

Enjoy the ride!

READING LIST

Jim Collins and Bill Lazier. *Beyond Entrepreneurship 2.0: Turning Your Business into an Enduring Great Company*. Portfolio, 2020.

Patrick Lencioni. *The Five Dysfunctions of a Team: A Leadership Fable*. Jossey-Bass, 2002.

Bradford D. Smart. *Topgrading*. Portfolio, 2012.

Verne Harnish. *Mastering the Rockefeller Habits: What You Must Do to Increase the Value of Your Growing Firm*. Gazelles, Inc., 2002.

Robert J. Anderson and William A Adams. *Scaling Leadership: Building Organizational Capability and Capacity to Create Outcomes that Matter Most*. Wiley, 2019.

Patrick Lencioni. *Overcoming the Five Dysfunctions of a Team: A Field Guide for Leaders, Managers, and Facilitators*. Jossey-Bass, 2005.

Jim Collins. *Good to Great: Why Some Companies Make the Leap and Others Don't*. HarperBusiness, 2001.

Shannon Byrne Susko. *3HAG WAY: The Strategic Execution System that Ensures Your Strategy is not a Wild-Ass-Guess!*. Ceozen Consulting Inc, 2018.

Morten T. Hansen. *Great at Work: The Hidden Habits of Top Performers*. Simon & Schuster, 2019.

Shannon Byrne Susko. *The Metronome Effect: The Journey to Predictable Profit*. Advantage Media Group, 2014.

Patrick Lencioni. *The Four Obsessions of an Extraordinary Executive: A Leadership Fable*. Jossey-Bass, 2000.

Simon Sinek. *Start with Why: How Great Leaders Inspire Everyone to Take Action*. Portfolio, 2011.

Stephen M. R. Covey. *The Speed of Trust: The One Thing that Changes Everything*. FranklinCovey, 2008.

Geoffrey A. Moore. *Crossing the Chasm: Marketing and Selling Disruptive Products to Mainstream Customers*. Harper Business, 2014.

Alexander Osterwalder and Yves Pigneur. *Business Model Generation: A Handbook for Visionaries, Game Changers, and Challengers*. John Wiley and Sons, 2010.

Patrick Lencioni. *The Ideal Team Player: How to Recognize and Cultivate the 3 Essential Virtues*. Jossey-Bass, 2016.

Jim Collins. *Turning the Flywheel: A Monograph to Accompany Good to Great*. Harper Business, 2019.

Cameron Herold. *Double Double: How to Double Your Revenue and Profit in 3 Years or Less*. Greenleaf Book Group, 2011.

Brené Brown. *Dare to Lead: Brave Work. Tough Conversations. Whole Hearts*. Random House, 2018.

Jim Collins. *Turning Goals into Results: The Power of Catalytic Mechanisms*. Harvard Business Review Press, 2017.

Rita McGrath. *Seeing Around Corners: How to Spot Inflection Points in Business Before They Happen*. Houghton Mifflin Harcourt, 2019.

Clayton M. Christensen. *How Will You Measure Your Life?* Harvard Business Review Press, 2017.

ACKNOWLEDGMENTS

I find writing a document longer than two pages a hard thing to do. Writing a book is even harder. I love pictures, diagrams, infographics, and one-page documents. A book is a very different beast. Many people use the quote, "it takes a village"; well, in my world, it has taken *many* villages to put this book out into the world. It was a fantastic journey, and I am so grateful to everyone who took the time to support me along the way.

Thank you to all the Metronome United Coaches around the world. Your support, questions, feedback, and commitment to learning and growing with me are why this book exists. I am extremely grateful and appreciate each and every one of you: Keith Millar, Tom Reich, Ian Judson, Cleo Maheux, Bill Napolitano, Donald Haché, Robert Monson, Max Kozlovsky, Damian Byrne, Jerry Fons, David Butlein, Sean Evans, David Chavez, Mike Mirau, Jeff Dorman, Keith Upkes, Beth Fisher, Mark Miller, Ethan Martin, Ron Huntington, Elizabeth Crook, Michael Langhout, David Baney, Cheryl Biron, Paul Cronin, Mike Goldman, Lisa Foulger, Douglas Diamond, Bill Flynn, Vivek Thomas, Ged Roberts, Brad Giles, Stephanie Cote Mongrain, Tim Wiley, Ken Lewis, Howard Shore, Bruce Eckfeldt, Jon Iveson, Pamela Carrington Rotto, Paulin Laberge, Dominic Monkhouse, Dale Meador, Corwin Smith, Jeff Redmon, Ted Sarvata, Anita Cabell, Aquiles Nunez, Zahir Ladhani, Ann Ralston, Gary Ralston, Matt Kuttler, Mark Green, , Robert Fish, Juan S.Folch, Sid Panjwani,

Wayne Ferrari, Jennifer Berkowitz, Paul O'Kelly, Glen Dall, John Ninkovich, Darren Gardener, Ashley Kline, Peter Boolkah, Steve Moss, Warren Sager, Scott Pollock, Srikanth Seshadri, Doug Wick, Mick Winker, Nicholas Reade, Shelley Voyer, Jauna Werner, James Akin-Smith, Adrian Pickstock, Hugh Gyton, Mo Rousso, Matt Blanton, and Carl Saunders.

Thank you to my all my clients past and present. Thank you to my CEO+Leadership Team Roundtable (BULLDOGS) members from the last seven years. You have been key in validating that Metronomics works for all companies and providing me with the confidence to share it with the world.

I would like to thank the Metronome team: Benoit Bourget, Mara Glouberman, Shannon Perry, Keith Upkes, Artur Holish, Yuan Xu, Hilco Wijbenga, Hannah Putnam, and Leigha Henderson for their incredible insight, feedback, and expertise throughout this process, and for always being available to support me when needed—no matter what day or time.

I would like to thank the team at Scribe, especially Meghan McCracken, Maggie Rains, John van der Woude, JeVon McCormick, and the rest of the team, for enabling me to publish this book.

Thanks to all the thought leaders mentioned throughout this book. Their research, tools, and wisdom challenged me to unite their great work with my practical experience, to create and evolve this prescriptive, progressive growth system for all coaches, teams, and companies to use every day.

Finally, I want to thank my husband, Sko (Chris Susko), and my 3 children, Cain, Matthew, and Embyr-Lee, who supported and encouraged me all along the way. You are forever my inspiration to continue my growth journey! I love you to the mountains and back and beyond!

I beg forgiveness of all those who have been with me and supported me over the years whose names I have failed to mention. Thank you!

ABOUT THE AUTHOR

Shannon Byrne Susko has spent over 25 years building, iterating, and innovating what we now know as Metronomics, a system utilized by hundreds of coaches and thousands of companies of all sizes around the world. After using the system as a CEO for decades, coaching the system to thousands of leaders, and training coaches how to coach it themselves, Shannon has spent the last two years writing this book, which for the first time makes Metronomics accessible to everyone looking for the "silver bullet" that will grow up their company. Shannon is also the author of two bestselling business books, *3HAG WAY* (2018) and *The Metronome Effect* (2014), and she is the founder and CEO of Metronome United, a community of more than 80 coaches worldwide who use the system every day to create lasting impact for their clients, teams, and communities.